CLASSICAL PRESENCES

General Editors

LORNA HARDWICK JAMES I. PORTER

CLASSICAL PRESENCES

Attempts to receive the texts, images, and material culture of ancient Greece and Rome inevitably run the risk of appropriating the past in order to authenticate the present. Exploring the ways in which the classical past has been mapped over the centuries allows us to trace the avowal and disavowal of values and identities, old and new. Classical Presences brings the latest scholarship to bear on the contexts, theory, and practice of such use, and abuse, of the classical past.

Myths of the Underworld in Contemporary Culture

The Backward Gaze

Judith Fletcher

OXFORD
UNIVERSITY PRESS

OXFORD
UNIVERSITY PRESS

Great Clarendon Street, Oxford, OX2 6DP,
United Kingdom

Oxford University Press is a department of the University of Oxford.
It furthers the University's objective of excellence in research, scholarship,
and education by publishing worldwide. Oxford is a registered trade mark of
Oxford University Press in the UK and in certain other countries

First Edition published in 2019

Impression: 1

Published in the United States of America by Oxford University Press
198 Madison Avenue, New York, NY 10016, United States of America

British Library Cataloguing in Publication Data
Data available

Library of Congress Control Number: 2018966634

ISBN 978–0–19–876709–1

Printed and bound by
CPI Group (UK) Ltd, Croydon, CR0 4YY

For Nick, Emma, and Oscar

Acknowledgments

I am thankful to all who helped me bring this book above ground. These include my colleagues at Wilfrid Laurier University, Jane Campbell, for her thoughtful and generous advice on A.S. Byatt's poetics, and Ed Jewinski for steering me to John Barth's *Lost in the Funhouse*. I am also beholden to David Lipovitch (for advice on things Near Eastern), and fellow members of the Inspir(d) Historians writing group (David Smith, Amy Milne-Smith, and Dana Weiner) for their close readings of Chapter 1. My book would have been much delayed and greatly diminished were it not for my stalwart student research assistants, Kathleen Vahey, Kyleigh Poultney, and Jenna Lee, who helped me to organize unwieldy quantities of material. Any remaining errors or infelicities are, I confess, entirely my own.

My thoughts about underworld themes in contemporary culture were enhanced when I gave a series of lectures for the Classical Association of Canada Atlantic Provinces tour in 2012. I am indebted for the hospitality and engaged audiences that I encountered at all seven host universities, but especially to Kathryn Simonsen (Memorial University), and Alison Barclay (Saint Mary's University). Thanks are also due to Lisa Trentin, her students, and colleagues at the University of Toronto Mississauga, who providentially steered me towards a deeper investigation of Neil Gaiman's work. My understanding of ancient eschatology was enriched by participating in a conference on "Imagining the Afterlife in the Ancient World," at Newman University in Birmingham in 2016. I am grateful to Juliette Harrisson for organizing a stimulating few days of talks, and to audiences and participants for valuable suggestions on my paper on Ann Patchett's *State of Wonder*, which became part of Chapter 4.

My gratitude extends to Wilfrid Laurier University for teaching relief in order to complete this manuscript, to Georgina Leighton of Oxford University Press for editorial advice, to Christine Ranft for her expert copy-editing and Priyanka Swansi for overseeing production, to the Classical Presences series editors, and to the anonymous readers of the manuscript at various stages. And I fondly acknowledge the resources of the beautiful library of the American Academy in Rome between 2013 and 2017. Thanks also to Daralyn Ward, who made life easier for me, and to my husband Rick Nixon for support, tolerance, and encouragement.

I have revisited and reworked previously published material for this book. Preliminary ideas for part of Chapter 2 appeared in 2002 as "Lost in the underworld: John Barth reads the *Odyssey*," *Classical and Modern Literature: A Quarterly* 23: 65–76. My thoughts on A.S. Byatt in Chapter 3 are developments of my 1999 "*The Odyssey* rewoven: A.S. Byatt's *Angels and Insects*," *Classical and Modern Literature: A Quarterly* 19: 217–31. And my 2006 "Signifying Circe in Toni Morrison's *Song of Solomon*," *Classical World* 99: 405–18 is an embryonic version of some of ideas in Chapter 4.

Contents

List of Figures

Whilst every effort has been made to secure permissions, we may have failed in a few cases to trace the copyright holders. We apologize for any apparent negligence. Should the copyright holders wish to contact us after publication, we would be happy to include an acknowledgement in subsequent reprints.

Introduction

What happens to us after death is a tale that only our dying can tell, although this discouraging truism hardly prevents the living from imagining the hereafter. The oldest stories in our narrative tradition are those in which a mortal or divine being descends to and returns from the land of the dead, a place where heroism is defined, insight obtained, and identities transformed. This book is a study of nine contemporary authors who draw on a fantasy that has intrigued storytellers, their audiences, and readers for over four thousand years—and that is only according to written records.[1] Ancient Near Eastern myths of the descent of the goddess Inanna to the realm of her sister Ereshkigal, queen of the netherworld, survive as a 415 line Sumerian poem in cuneiform (*c.*1900–1600 BCE), although scholars estimate that the story had been circulating for at least 1000 years before this inscription.[2] During her downward journey Inanna is gradually stripped of her clothing and power at the seven gates of Hell, then sentenced to death, and suspended from a hook. Ereshkigal's judges decree that Inanna can ascend if she finds another living soul to take her place; she selects her husband Dumuzi, who is enjoying life without her too cheerfully, but whose devoted sister agrees to share his sentence for half the year. *The Descent of Inanna* is among the first in a long line of underworld stories

[1] Zaleski (1987: 12–13) speculates that cave paintings from the Upper Paleolithic period might depict some form of a shamanistic, otherworldly journey.

[2] Kramer discusses dating the Inanna poems (Wolkstein and Kramer 1983: xii–xiv); for further discussion, see Laneri 2002: 9–51. In the Akkadian version, *The Descent of Ishtar*, the entrapment or death of Ishtar, goddess of fertility and sexuality, results in harmful effects in the human realm, which might recall Demeter's response to Persephone's abduction. It was not only goddesses who descended to the netherworld in Near Eastern myth, but also gods such as the Canaanite Baal. Lease (1926: 602–6) offers thumbnail sketches of different versions of descent stories from ancient Near Eastern and Egyptian sources up to early modern European literature.

that feature tests of endurance, substitutions and cycles, and a return to the realm of the living. In it we detect Ur-versions of the Greek myth of Aphrodite and Adonis, Persephone's cycle between Hades and the upper world, or the story of Alcestis who died as a substitute for her husband Admetus, and then came back to life. From the perspective of ancient peoples of the Mediterranean basin, including the Akkadian, Ugaritic, Hittite, Hebrew, and Greek cultures, the soul went downward after death.[3] Thus a visitor to the land of the dead, like Inanna, undertakes a catabasis (from the Greek *katabainein*, to go down), a descent to the underworld, but then performs the supernatural feat of ascending back to the terrestrial realm (an anabasis).[4]

Not every attempt to return from the netherworld is successful, needless to say, and not every underworld tale involves an actual visit to the land of the dead. The twelfth tablet of the Akkadian *Epic of Gilgamesh* (also told separately as *Gilgamesh, Enkidu and the Netherworld*) relates how the semi-divine hero's closest friend, the mortal Enkidu, descends to Irkalla, and although he never returns, his ghost can transmit knowledge about the great beyond to Gilgamesh through a portal linking the two worlds. This dialogue with the dead, or *evocatio*, is precursor to Odysseus' conversations with the parade of shades at the mouth of Hades in *Odyssey* 11. In their interviews with ghosts, Gilgamesh and Odysseus enact the appealing fantasy of gaining knowledge about the afterlife without actually dying. The topic was a popular one. A fragmentary Hittite text (*c.*thirteenth century BCE), entitled *The Voyage of the Immortal Human Soul* describes topographical details of the underworld, such as meadows, a common feature of Greco-Roman Hades, and the dreary diet served to the dead, elements that recur in Greek gold leaf tablets over 1000 years later.[5] Knowledge of the layout of

[3] West 1997: 152. That death is considered to be a descent is evident from passages in the Hebrew Bible, for example: "The Lord kills and brings to life; he brings down to Sheol and raises up" (1*Sa*. 2.6).

[4] Bernabé (2015: 17) offers this definition of the catabasis: "a tale of the journey to the subterranean world of the dead led by an extraordinary character while alive who has a determined purpose and is keen on returning." Since I include the descent of the goddess Persephone in this book, this is an improvement on Clark (1978: 3): "a *catabasis* can be defined as a Journey of the Dead made by a living person in the flesh who returns to our world to tell the tale."

[5] See Watkins (1995: 284–90) for text, translation and analysis. He also observes some similarities with Orphic gold leaf texts.

the underworld apparently provided some assurance that one could achieve a comfortable afterlife, but stories of visits to a subterranean kingdom also related to the here and now by advising the living on how to behave. A seventh-century BCE cuneiform text known as the *Underworld Vision of an Assyrian Crown Prince* is distinguished by its human protagonist, one of the first of many mortals in literature to take a tour of the netherworld, during which he sees the ghost of his father, and a host of fearful beings including a grim ferryman with the head of a bird. The prince, Kummay, obtains life-changing instruction and an apocalyptic prophecy from Nergal, king of the dead, before he awakens in terror.[6] The text is the prototype of a story repeated in Jewish and Christian accounts of tours of Hell, such as the apocryphal *Book of Enoch*, as well as literary versions in Vergil's *Aeneid* 6, Dante's *Inferno*, and indeed several of the contemporary versions discussed in this book. Of special interest is the conceptual overlap between dreams and the land of the dead, a connection that we shall see repeated throughout this volume.

Over a period of several millennia, ancient Mediterranean cultures, including those of Greece and Rome, exchanged stories that responded to human curiosity about the afterlife, although these tales often had more oblique purposes. The *Underworld Vision of an Assyrian Crown Prince* served the political objectives of King Assurbanipal, just as its literary descendant, *Aeneid* 6, enhanced the imperialistic agenda of the first Roman emperor, Augustus. Stories of a descent, by far the most common type of underworld narrative, often supported Greek and Roman mystery religions, thereby functioning as "an ideological guarantee" to legitimate rituals and other cultic practices that helped individuals prepare for life after death.[7] Some scholars believe that Vergil's detailed description of Aeneas' tour of the underworld reflects the experience of an initiate of the Eleusinian Mysteries, thus appealing to Augustus who had undergone the popular ritual that honored the goddess Demeter and her daughter.[8] Every telling of the myth of a journey to the land of the dead has a unique resonance within its specific social

[6] Sanders (2009: 157–61) provides a summary of the text and a comparison with Jewish and Christian apocalyptic Tours of Hell, or visionary texts such as *Ezekiel* 40–8, (which was composed in Babylon *c.*sixth century BCE), or *The Book of Enoch* (*c.*300 BCE). See Almond (2016: 14–18) on the Jewish underworld in *The Book of Enoch*.

[7] Bernabé 2015: 31. [8] Bremmer 2014: 181.

context, and although we suspect influences that go back very far indeed, we are also missing large chunks of data that would help chart the shifting meanings of the infernal voyage. In any event, the story of Inanna's descent meant something very different to its audience than that of Aeneas meant to the Romans.[9] While underworld stories have served various purposes throughout the ages—not the least of which was to entertain—they draw on an archive of shared features. Among the most important is the concept of a physical location inhabited by the dead. Hades, according to the speculative etymology of the Greeks, was "A-ides" or the "unseen place," difficult to access, but which certain exceptional individuals could enter temporarily through a portal such as a door, a hole in the ground, the jaws of a monster, or across a body of water.[10] Hades is governed by the god of the same name (also known as Aidoneus, Pluto, Dis, or Orcus); so too the Hebrew underworld Sheol can be personified as an insatiable being with "hands, womb, throat, and a mouth to swallow the dead."[11] The recurring figure of the infernal ferryman, who takes the traveler to the land of the dead, suggests a dynamic cultural exchange between Babylonian, Hittite, Assyrian, Canaanite, Phoenician, Greek, Egyptian, Etruscan, Roman, and other ancient Mediterranean societies.[12] This concept of a physical location, informed by the conviction that the dead must be *somewhere*, is pervasive, and also ripe for parody. In his *Cataplus* the Syrian poet Lucian

[9] Edmonds (2004: 14–15) justifiably warns against putting too much importance on cross-cultural influences when interpreting ancient underworld mythology, since an emphasis on the transmission of motifs still does not reveal what these elements of the myths meant to the Greeks.

[10] Mesopotamian myths tell of a "Great Door" to the underworld that can only be reached after travelling to the far West through barren lands and over a river with the help of a boatman (Bernabé 2015: 21). In Canaanite mythology, the god Baal descends into the Underworld through a "voracious mouth" (Clark 1978: 35).

[11] Almond (2016: 9). References to the insatiable appetite of Sheol include: "Therefore Sheol has enlarged its appetite and opened its mouth beyond measure, and the nobility of Jerusalem and her multitude go down, her throng and he who exults in her" (*Isa.* 5.14). See further Almond's discussion (2016: 12) of the translation of the Jewish underworld Sheol into Hades in the Greek Septuagint, the version of the Old Testament produced in Alexandria in the third century BCE for the Jewish population of Greek-speaking Egypt.

[12] Grinsell (1957) studies the Egyptian funerary texts of late Fifth Dynasty, *c.*2450 BCE, which describe the boatman who transports the dead king to the afterlife. Lincoln (1980: 41–59) identifies the cross-cultural figure of the ferryman of the dead. According to Horsfall (2013: 254), the first occurrence of Charon is in a surviving fragment of a Greek poem known as the *Minyas* (perhaps composed in the sixth century BCE); he also appears in fifth-century Greek vase paintings. Cf. Bremmer (2014: 184–5) and West (1997: 155).

(writing in Greek in the second century CE) played with the millennia-old idea of the underworld as a vast city by satirically representing Hades as a bureaucracy administered by the ferryman Charon and other infernal personnel who exhibit officious concern with paperwork and accounting.[13] Throughout literary history poets built on this inherited sense of place: physical features of the Vergilian underworld reappear in Dante's *Inferno*, Milton's *Paradise Lost*, and Spenser's *Faerie Queene*. In the latter (1.i.37–44) the conniving sorcerer, Archimago, dispatches a spirit to the underworld (the House of Morpheus) to bring back a false dream; his entrance through embellished double gates recalls that of Aeneas at the beginning of his trip to Dis, while the quest itself reminds the learned reader that Aeneas left the underworld through the gate of false dreams (*Aen.* 6.893–8). Of course, these fine poets emulate their classical predecessors in much more intellectual ways. Philip Hardie observes that for both Vergil and Spenser, "the mythological underworld is a vivid setting for issues of cosmic, psychological, theological, and moral order and disorder."[14] A less elevated composition, the English satirist Maurice Atkins' *Cataplus* (1672), adheres to the structure of *Aeneid* 6, but alludes to Lucian's ironic critique when he shapes Aeneas' descent as a commentary on the English civil war, all in a jocular tone peppered with colloquialisms.[15]

As cultural critic Linda Hutcheon argues in *A Theory of Adaptation*, there are really no new stories, and this book is, among other things, an illustration of that assertion. The following chapters offer a study of the adaptation of underworld mythology in a selection of contemporary cultural products created in the past half-century. All of them preserve the literary footprints of their Greco-Roman predecessors, most obviously in how they borrow and develop the well-established physical features of Hell, but also in their use of the underworld as place to examine psychosocial matters pertinent to our lives above ground. The temporal range extends from John Barth's postmodern tour de force, *Lost in the Funhouse*, published in 1968, to the enigmatic Italian author Elena Ferrante's highly acclaimed novels, most recently *The Story of the*

[13] *Cataplus* narrates the journey of a boatload of souls being ferried to the underworld. Nesselrath (2017: 42–50) discusses several of Lucian's works featuring satirically pragmatic treatments of the constitution and governance of Hades.

[14] Hardie 2010: 185.

[15] See further Power 2010: 191–2.

Lost Child (translated into English in 2015). Other specimens include Salman Rushdie's *The Ground Beneath Her Feet*, A.S. Byatt's *Angels and Insects*, Toni Morrison's *Song of Solomon*, Ann Patchett's *State of Wonder*, and Amy Bloom's *Away*. The prolific gothic energy of Neil Gaiman is represented by *The Sandman* comic series, and Henry Selick's filmic adaptation of his children's novel, *Coraline*. This mélange of different cultural registers, from Nobel and Booker prizewinners to popular and children's media, is comprised of adaptations of the ancient story pattern of the descent to the underworld (*catabasis*), or a conversation with ghosts (a *Nekyia* or *evocatio*). The same could be said of a very long list of novels, films, music, art, and videogames produced within the last fifty years; my book makes no claim to comprehensiveness. I have tried to incorporate a range of genres, including novels, short stories, comics, a cinematic adaptation, juvenile literature, and the occasional reference to poetry and music, in order to illustrate not only the ubiquity of the motif in our contemporary culture, but also to identify how the fantasy of a visit to the underworld locates specific concerns of a historical moment within an ever-evolving and complex tradition. The selections share several common elements, which studied collectively bring to light the rich possibilities of the underworld theme in the context of three intersecting discourses—postmodernism, feminism, and postcolonialism—represented by cultural products that cite and adapt the literary canon while ironically undercutting it. This disruptive impulse can be symbolized by boundaries crossed or transgressed in some fashion. The stories that we are about to encounter involve versions of the archetypal passage between life and death, and then back again. Although these border-crossings are often physical and even geopolitical, many of our heroic protagonists are positioned along divisions between social groups (including gender, class, and age), or even straddle different genres (epic poetry and rock music, for example). Consequently allusions to ancient prototypes in which a divinity or mortal crosses between the realms of the living and the dead, the ultimate transgression of boundaries, and then returns to quotidian reality, infuse such crossings, actual or symbolic, with connotations that speak to contemporary sensibilities in ways that take into account the experience of women, children, refugees, and other social groups not traditionally valorized by the European canon. Such citations of classical underworld stories position these works of fiction, and thus the lived realities of their audiences, within a continuum that stretches back to the deepest antiquity, but they also question the canonical status of the source texts within the societies that transmit and preserve those myths.

These citations, playfully ironic, defiantly critical, or even respectfully complicit, are possible because the culturally resonant trope of the catabasis has been such a definitive element of literature for millennia up to the present. In *The Secular Scripture: A Study of the Structure of Romance* Northrop Frye identified the descent as one of four major themes in Western literature, an observation that emphasizes the privileged place that this story pattern occupies in our cultural heritage.[16] From their position in the genealogy of underworld mythmakers, contemporary authors can draw on and critique a tradition that has been foundational to Western culture and literature for millennia. The fantasy has never died. Stories of a visit to Hell remained popular during the Middle Ages: for example, *The Visions of the Knight Tondal*, originally written in Latin by a twelfth-century Irish monk and translated into fifteen different languages including Icelandic, tells how Tondal falls unconscious at a banquet and is led by an angelic guide to witness the torments of Hell and pleasures of Heaven, another iteration of the tour of the underworld. The experience, as it does for Prince Kummay, Odysseus, and Aeneas, transforms him for the better. The influence of Vergil's description of the underworld is unmistakable in the poem, and Dante in turn was influenced by tale of Tondal (and of course its prototype, the *Aeneid*) when he wrote his *Divine Comedy*.

While the ancient tradition contributed to the prestige of Dante's *Inferno* or Milton's *Paradise Lost*, its very antiquity and familiarity expose its conventions to parody, critique, and subversion—that was true as early as Aristophanes' *Frogs*, and Lucian's *Cataplus*. That Milton's nephew, John Phillips, published his own travesty of *Aeneid* 6 in the seventeenth century testifies to the persistence of a subversive urge to deflate the canon.[17] Today an author such as Margaret Atwood can stand the tradition of the *Nekyia* on its head in her *Penelopiad* (2005) by channeling the ghost of Penelope to critique the patriarchal underpinnings of the *Odyssey*. Atwood's sly revision provides ample testimony that the ancient myth of the *descensus ad infernos* can be adapted in ways that

[16] Frye 1976: 95–226.

[17] There is a brief discussion of Phillips' poem in Power 2010: 92.

challenge how dominant ideologies shape literary history. This book is an inquiry into how and why a persistent fascination with life after death, and fantasies of accessing the world of the dead while we are still alive, work so powerfully with themes of cultural rebellion in postmodern authors, the social marginality and alterity addressed by feminist fiction, and the fragmentation of identity endured by the diasporic subject.

The endlessly adaptable underworld narrative can be identified in countless contemporary novels, poetry, films, the visual arts, children's and popular culture. For example, scholars have discerned elements of the descent myth in various American Westerns including *The Searchers* and the Coens' *True Grit*, although there is no overt signpost to link the films to ancient texts.[18] This book, however, focuses on work with explicit references to ancient descent myths. Writers such as Wendy Lesser in *The Life Below the Ground* (1988) and Rachel Falconer in Hell in Contemporary Literature: *Western Descent Narratives since 1945* (2005) have examined subterranean motifs in literature of the recent past in their creative and illuminating studies. And David L. Pike (*Passage through Hell: Modernist Descents, Medieval Underworlds*, 1997) makes the intriguing argument that Dante's medievalist descent narrative structures modernist works that often have very little to do with Hell. Michael Thurston has written an elegant analysis of how modernist poets such as Ezra Pound, and T.S. Eliot exploit a catabatic genealogy linking themselves with Odysseus, Aeneas, and Dante. Thurston (The *Underworld in Twentieth-Century Poetry*, 2009) offers an insightful analysis that locates these literary underworlds as sites of confrontation with the past, and crucibles of poetic innovation. As Thurston remarks, Pound's evocation of the Odyssean *Nekyia* at the beginning of *The Cantos* declares, "not his independence from the tradition but rather his interdependence."[19] By examining the descent theme in culture of the postmodern era (from the late 1960s until the present), I argue that an engagement with the descent tradition, so central to the self-fashioned identities of modernist literary celebrities, becomes a different, more subversive project.

[18] Holtsmark (2001) discusses the catabasis theme in cinema including Westerns; Clauss (1999) looks specifically at the theme in John Ford's *The Searchers* (1956); see also Fletcher (2014) for my analysis of the catabatic subtext of the Coen Brothers' *True Grit* (2010).

[19] Thurston 2009: 29.

While this book has profited from these contributions to the reception of underworld mythology in recent literary culture, I focus on material with explicit references to canonical underworld narratives, or to related ancient texts, rather than works that suggest less overt structural or psychological features. Thus, for example, Falconer quite persuasively identifies the descent motif in work such as Ann Michaels' *Fugitive Pieces* (1996), the fictional memoir of a Holocaust survivor whose psychological trauma reflects a Dantean descent into Hell. Holly Virginia Blackford detects a resonance with the myth of Persephone in children's literature such as E.B. White's *Charlotte's Web* (1952), despite the absence of any overt reference to the myth itself. Undoubtedly these readings are well suited for their authors' specific projects, but my selections share an explicit engagement with classical mythology. Some of these writers, such as Byatt, Morrison, and Ferrante, have publically acknowledged an education in Classical Studies; others, including Barth, Gaiman, and Rushdie, demonstrate such a sophisticated engagement with ancient literature that there can be little doubt they have read Homer, Vergil, and other classical authors with close attention. As the analyses of their novels will demonstrate, their interaction with these texts is a crucial element of their poetics.

Although there are many versions of the catabasis myth I focus on adaptations of the four best known ancient literary versions: the *Nekyia* of Homer's *Odyssey* 11, the myth of Orpheus and Eurydice from Vergil's *Fourth Georgic* and Ovid's *Metamorphoses*, the descent of Aeneas in Vergil's *Aeneid* 6, and the myth of Persephone in the anonymous *Homeric Hymn to Demeter* and Ovid's *Metamorphoses*. The works discussed in the following chapters signify their debt to at least one of these texts, and often cite more than one, with conspicuous clues. Some authors such as Rushdie are very explicit about their ancient source text, others more understated, but the signs, always discernible, are invitations to participate in a form of literary archaeology. In certain cases, for example Patchett's *State of Wonder*, the most overt allusion is to an adaptation of a classical predecessor (in this case Gluck's operatic version of the Orpheus tale), but digging deeper we inevitably reach an ancient substratum. And that realization leads us to understand why underworld myths are so enduring: Hades has taken on an archival quality as a repository for catabatic tales; the underworld is a literary space where narrative ghosts reside, waiting to be reanimated, but also existing among earlier versions of themselves. Thus an author who wants to cite and challenge an ancient cultural tradition will have no better recourse than to enter the realm of Hades, and access a cache of several millennia's worth of ghostly narrative layers: an intervention that automatically engages her or him in a self-reflexive enterprise that considers the relationship between author, reader, tradition, and text. In short, a trip to the underworld is often a story about storytelling.

The book is divided into four chapters and a short conclusion. The first chapter "Source Texts" is an overview of ancient Greek and Roman descent tales, which also serves as a synthesis of some of the important themes that they share with each other and with the adaptations treated in this book. The focus is on the Odyssean *Nekyia*; the stories of Heracles' descent, reenacted by the god Dionysus in Aristophanes' *Frogs*; the catabasis of Aeneas in Vergil's *Aeneid*; two Latin versions (by Vergil and Ovid) of Orpheus' trip to Hades to retrieve Eurydice; and finally the myth of Persephone in the *Homeric Hymn to Demeter*. Bear in mind that although these are the most widely disseminated descent stories from the ancient Mediterranean world, there were numerous other tales of the underworld, for example by the Roman playwright Seneca and the epic poet Statius, both writing in the first century CE. The contemporary adaptations that I have selected are for the most part based on the descents of Odysseus, Aeneas, Orpheus, and Persephone, but they occasionally evoke Platonic philosophy, and other significant treatments of the underworld, which will be considered at the appropriate time.

Chapter 2, "The Ghost of the Father: Spirits of the Postmodern," examines how John Barth's experimental novel, *Lost in the Funhouse*, and Neil Gaiman's *The Sandman* comic book series deploy two classical myths of the descent, that of Odysseus in the former and Orpheus in latter, set in tension with literature by James Joyce and John Milton. Both authors engage with the mythical story pattern as a metafictional device that pays homage to literary tradition while also critiquing their own literary forefathers. This chapter argues that the polemical stances of Barth and Gaiman epitomize postmodern literary practices by fragmenting and recombining their source texts, drawing attention to the existence of their own work as fiction, and by setting the heroic paradigm in culturally marginal contexts, or using media not conventionally associated with high culture.

Chapter 3, "Engendering the Haunted Text," acknowledges that Hades has come to represent an intertextual archive, but explores how two feminist, postmodern novelists, A.S. Byatt and Elena Ferrante, approach the tradition of the catabatic narrator by revising a patrilineal convention to include the female novelist. Byatt's *Angels and Insects* bears the imprint of Homer's *Odyssey* but in the form of postmodern fragments that incorporate some of the scientific, intellectual, and cultural modes of the Victorian period. Byatt's critical intervention is to rewrite the *Nekyia* as a children's fable in one novella and a séance in the other, both of which highlight the role of the female storyteller. Set between the analyses of Byatt's and Ferrante's novels is a discussion of Gaiman's children's novella, *Coraline*, as a filmic adaptation by Henry Selick. This analysis serves as an intermezzo, which develops the inquiry into why girls but not women can take trips to the underworld, and thinks about the role of the female creator, the horrifying beldam that Coraline encounters there. Thus prepared we advance to the work of Elena Ferrante to explore how she incorporates the chthonic female demon and the Persephone myth in the context of female authorship.

Chapter 4, "The Wanderer's Descent: The Underworlds of Diaspora," outlines how the story of a trip to the underworld can capture the experiences of diasporic populations, including refugees, enslaved peoples, exiles, and immigrants. A selection of four novels exemplifies the potential for the catabasis, the most dramatic border-crossing possible, to work as a metaphor for a transition between continents. The descendant of an ex-slave in Toni Morrison's *Song of Solomon* enters a cave that evokes the Odyssean *Nekyia*, and also symbolizes his family's past. In the remaining novels other migrant characters metaphorically reenact the infernal voyages of Orpheus, Aeneas, and Persephone. Postcolonial theory guides some of the interpretations of these appropriations, but, acknowledging the affinity between postmodern and postcolonial poetics, we can also recognize themes developed in the preceding sections. Thus Rushdie's *The Ground Beneath Her Feet* critiques the master narrative of the West by utilizing Saïd's concept of Orientalism, but also blends elite and mainstream culture with a revision of a canonical text that reinvents Orpheus as a rock star. High status literature again melds with mainstream culture, as it does for Neil Gaiman. Amy Bloom's *Away* makes parallels between the story of a Jewish refugee woman and the myth of Demeter and Persephone. Although the central character makes these connections herself, she does not access the myth through the original Greek and Latin texts, but by means of a popularized version of the story in Bullfinch's mythology. And while Ann Patchett's *State of Wonder* makes an explicit reference to the Orpheus story, it is through Gluck's opera, rather than classical versions. These citations of different points in the long history of underworld themed fiction convey a sense of a recursively layered tradition; each layer replicates the previous iteration of the tale, and yet adapts the myth to its historical context.

The book concludes with a brief epilogue that draws together some of the themes and ideas that recur throughout. The topic is a large one, and the following pages are not meant to be the final word on a myth that has seemingly infinite possibilities for adaptation in contemporary contexts.

1

Source Texts

ἀλλ' ἄλλην χρὴ πρῶτον ὁδὸν τελέσαι καὶ ἱκέσθαι
εἰς Ἀίδαο δόμους καὶ ἐπαινῆς Περσεφονείης

But first you must complete another journey and go
to the house of Hades and dread Persephone.

(*Odyssey* 10.490–1)[1]

Travel was an essential activity for ancient Mediterranean peoples whose economies flourished through trade and commerce, although getting from one distant point to another was seldom easy and often dangerous. Small wonder then that their most resonant narratives recount voyages of supreme difficulty and peril, the topic of this chapter. For the ancients these fantastic descents to the world of the dead mirrored occurrences of historical or quasi-historical figures going underground to achieve wisdom, consult or pronounce an oracle, or participate in a religious cult. Not limited to fiction, the notion of a catabasis was germane to the lived reality of ancient peoples for whom conceptual boundaries between myth and history were less distinct than they are for us. The fifth-century BCE historian Herodotus includes in his *Histories* (4.93–6) a brief reference to the legendary Thracian sage Zalmoxis, who preached a doctrine of the soul's immortality, and then descended to an underground chamber where he lived for three years. After his return he became the focus of a religion practiced by the Getae, a tribe in what is now Romania.[2] Zalmoxis has been associated with the sixth-century BCE

[1] All translations from Greek and Latin are my own, using the most recent Oxford Classical Texts, unless otherwise stated.

[2] Eliade and Trask (1972: 278–83) identify the descent of Zalmoxis as a metaphoric initiation. See Ustinova (2009: 100–4) for more recent discussion and bibliography.

philosopher Pythagoras, who also reputedly lived underground before returning, emaciated but lucid, to speak among the people of Croton, his community in southern Italy, about what he had seen in Hades.[3] Even if these stories embellish reality, there can be little doubt that subterranean rituals were a constitutive element of the cult of Demeter at Eleusis, as well as other mystery religions (so-called because they were only available to *mystai*, or "initiates") that required participants to descend into caves.[4] Evidence includes a scrap of magical papyrus, found in Egypt and dated to the third or early fourth century CE; it instructs the user to say, "I went down into the [underground] chamber of the Dactyls, and I saw the other things down below," as part of a charm against "fear of punishment," perhaps in the afterlife.[5] In all likelihood the man or woman who used the spell had undergone a ritual experience, probably initiation in a religious cult, which notionally provided him or her with some ability to ward off harm. It is but one fragmentary piece of data from the various mystery religions that proliferated among the Greeks and Romans. Some of these, including cults devoted to Orpheus, Dionysus, and Demeter and Persephone, are discussed in this chapter, but more arcane variants existed as well; they provided a sense of community, an emotional anchor in a precarious world, and the reassuring prospect of a blessed afterlife.[6] It is not hard to imagine that ordinary people of ancient Mediterranean societies connected literary traditions of a catabasis with their own religious activities. When mythical characters return from the land of the dead they are transformed in some way, just as real men and women experienced a change in status by descending underground: in both myth and ritual a catabasis was associated with coming of age, marriage, initiation into cults, and other social changes. This element of transformation is integral to stories of descent, both ancient and modern.

[3] Diogenes Laertes preserves the tales recorded by the late third-century BCE authors Hieronymus of Rhodes and Hermippus of Smyrna (8.21 & 41). Further discussion and bibliography can be found in Ustinova (2009: 186–91) and Bremmer (2014: 341–2), who concedes that it is impossible to disentangle fantasy from truth in these reports.

[4] See Stroumsa (1995: 141–4) for a brief survey.

[5] The charm is part of the collection of *Michigan Papyri* No. LXX. The translation and interpretation are from Betz (1980: 287–95).

[6] Further reading on mystery religions includes: Burkert 1987, Bowden 2010, and Bremmer 2014.

Covering a span of at least 800 years, the following survey outlines the most famous ancient descent stories to identify themes and characteristics that recur in contemporary versions of the visit to the great beyond. The materials are presented in the chronological order of their appearance in literary sources that treat myths of Odysseus, Heracles, Dionysus, Aeneas, and Orpheus. Because the story of Persephone is in many ways exceptional, the *Homeric Hymn to Demeter* (probably composed in the late archaic period of Greece, i.e. the early sixth century BCE) is treated last.

The Odyssean *Nekyia*

Have there always been stories of a visit to the other side of death? The myth's inscrutable origins suggest an "autochthonous knot," to borrow from Hugh Kenner, "a pattern persisting undeformable while many languages have flowed through it."[7] The first surviving Greek version occurs in Homer's *Odyssey* Book 11, known as the *Nekyia*, but a reference to his own previous descent and ascent by Heracles' ghost, whom Odysseus encounters among the dead, suggests that earlier tales had circulated in the Greek oral tradition.[8] At the core of such tales is the concept of the underworld as a geographical location cut off from the land of the living, which probably carried over from Mesopotamian beliefs into archaic Greek cosmologies.[9] Like several other ancient cultures, the Greeks imagined dying as a voyage to the West; thus the dead reside in the shadowy regions where the sun disappears.[10] Cross-cultural evidence suggests that Odysseus' visit to the underworld was modeled on Near Eastern antecedents, which infiltrated Greece by at least the ninth

[7] Kenner (1973: 148–9) is writing about the influence of the *Nekyia* on Pound's *Canto* I, discussed in the next chapter.

[8] Clark (1978: 51–3) is one of many scholars who speculate that there was a lost epic poem on the "Catabasis of Heracles" circulating before the composition of the *Odyssey* in the eighth century.

[9] Albinus (2000: 65) argues that while the underworld in the *Iliad* is "boundless", it has a more precise location in the *Odyssey*. Burgess (2016) discusses the localization of the Homeric underworld and its debt to Near Eastern sources. Tsagarakis (1999: 25) is less inclined to believe that a cosmology that included an underworld was influenced by Eastern literature, and suggests that it might have developed independently.

[10] West (1997: 153) provides examples from Babylonian and Hittite rituals and the Ugaritic Keret epic (*c.*1500–1200 BCE), which conceptualize a voyage to the land of dead as a movement toward the setting sun.

century BCE.[11] The poet whom we call Homer, probably composing in the mid-eighth century, had a wealth of material to adapt and develop, but what he chose to do with this well-established tradition represents a sophisticated intellectual accomplishment that grants intriguing insights into the archaic Greek worldview. Odysseus' visit to Hades exemplifies important notions of mortality, memory, and heroism. The position of the episode, at least in the written version that survives, is notable.[12] Not only is the *Nekyia* located at the midpoint of Odysseus' first-person account of his wanderings (the *Apologia*), but it sits practically in the middle of the entire poem.[13] Occupying this prominent position, and recounted at such length—the only adventure in the *Apologia* to take up an entire book of the *Odyssey*—his conversations with the dead stand out as a defining moment in the hero's journey, and it is given to Odysseus himself to tell.

The *Odyssey* narrates the attempts of Odysseus to return home after the Greek victory at Troy, while his wife Penelope and son Telemachus wait for him in Ithaca; his long-delayed homecoming in disguise as a beggar; his slaughter of Penelope's suitors and their supporters; and the reunion of husband and wife. The account of his adventures begins in Book 5, when he is finally released from the island of the nymph Calypso, and washed up on the shores of Scheria. This is the utopian kingdom of the Phaeacians, a fabulous sea-faring society, who will eventually take Odysseus home after his decade of war and another of wandering. It is here that he recounts his exploits including the escape from and blinding of the man-eating Cyclops, Polyphemus; a year with the sorceress Circe; and the gradual loss of all his companions, ships, and possessions.

[11] Burgess (1999: 171–210) makes robust arguments connecting Odysseus' experience in Hades with the adventures of Gilgamesh. Louden (2011: 197–221) argues that Odysseus' consultation with the dead conflates the catabasis motif with that of the visionary experience found for example in the Old Testament (e.g. *Samuel* 28), the *Epic of Gilgamesh*, *Aeneid* 6, and Plato's allegory of the cave in the *Republic*. For an excellent summary of the bibliography on possible influences on the *Nekyia*, see Tanaseanu-Döbler 2017: 12 n. 6.

[12] The bibliography on how Homer's text achieved its written form is extensive and ongoing. Milman Parry was the pioneer of the widely accepted theory of Homeric oral composition, based on the use of traditional formulae, although Shive (1987) and Powell (1991) have argued cogently that Homer had access to writing.

[13] There are 5586 lines before the *Nekyia*, and 6451 after it; in the *Apologia*, it is seventh in a series of thirteen stories.

Odysseus tells his rapt Phaeacian audience how he left Circe's island challenged with visiting Hades in order to continue his journey home. The prospect was horrifying, but he followed Circe's instructions, travelling with his unhappy crew on the river Ocean, which encircles the earth, until they reached the misty shores of the Cimmerians. Circe describes the landmarks including the infernal rivers (traditional features of underworld geography in later literature), the Pyriphlegethon and Cocytus, which merge into the Acheron (10.509–15). But descriptive details are sparse. Homer's near-contemporary Hesiod (*c.*700 BCE), another epic poet, provides more particulars about the layout and denizens of the underworld in his *Theogony*, an account of the origins and genealogies of the gods. "Murky Tartarus," as Hesiod describes the underworld (119), includes the terrifying children of Night, the captive Titans, the guard dog Cerberus, the goddess Styx, her cavernous house, and so on, all fenced in by an impregnable barrier (*Theogony* 721–819).[14] Homer, on the other hand, leaves it to his audience to imagine the topography and demography of Hades: his *Nekyia* is about interactions between the living visitor and the dead residents; the underworld is a place to observe, learn from, and then leave.

Once he arrives at his destination, and after completing the prescribed sacrifices and digging a pit, Odysseus separates from his companions to experience a unique and privileged access to the dead. As he sits on a rock, the *psychai* ("shades," or more literarily "breath-souls") swarm around him, drawn by the sacrificial blood that can revive their consciousness. The shade of his recently deceased companion Elpenor still hovers between the realms of the dead and living, and begs for burial. But the first to drink from the beaker is the shade of the Theban prophet, Tiresias, followed by Odysseus' mother Anticleia. He is then visited by a ghostly parade of famous queens and noble women, often referred to as the "Catalogue of Heroines."[15] At this point he interrupts his story with the suggestion to his

[14] Johnson (1999: 8–28) discusses the logic of Hesiod's representation of Tartarus, and Clay (2003: 14–15) explains the place of Tartarus in Hesiod's cosmology.

[15] Page (1955: 35–9) argues that the parade of queens was not part of the original *Odyssey*, but a later interpolation. In their commentary Heubeck and Hoekstra (1989: 90–1) accept the catalogue as part of the original poem; cf. Reinhardt (1996: 117). In her subtle analysis Doherty (1995: 82–136) considers the effect of the heroines' stories on the Phaeacian queen Arete, whose favor is essential to Odysseus' return home. Gazis (2018: 125–56) observes that the narrative of the parade emphasizes the perspectives and emotions

hosts that they call it a night, but they urge him to continue. The Intermezzo draws attention to his captivated audience, especially the Phaeacian queen Arete, and thus the frame tale self-consciously acknowledges that the underworld comes into existence through narrative.[16] In the following "Catalogue of Heroes," Odysseus relates conversations with the shades of two Iliadic comrades, Agamemnon and Achilles, who greet him with surprise and respect, and Ajax, who, still bearing a grudge from the Trojan War, turns away. In the distance Odysseus sees the fabled sinners, Sisyphus and his ilk, the mythic judges of the underworld, Minos and Rhadymanthus, and also the shade of Heracles, but then frightened by the prospect of an encounter with the Gorgon, he ends the visit.

Odysseus' encounter with Tiresias is a form of necromancy, a communication with the dead to predict the future, but there is more going on here. After the parade of heroines, Agamemnon is apparently the last shade who drinks the blood, yet Achilles seems able to recognize Odysseus without it; the shades of his other warrior comrades come forth to tell their stories, but there is no further mention of the beaker of blood. The simplest explanation is that the audience does not need repeated reminders that the same procedure brings consciousness to the spirits of his Achaean comrades. But the omission also helps to define Odysseus' sojourn among the dead as a catabasis, rather than only an *evocatio* (like that of Gilgamesh with Enkidu, mentioned in the Introduction). He no longer seems to be positioned at the entrance of Hades, but rather in the midst of the shades of his fellow warriors, and he can see the expansive landscape of the underworld beyond. Although Odysseus does not seem to be descending into Hades' realm when he first encounters the shades, the later vocabulary suggests a downward voyage. His mother, Anticleia, asks how he came "under the murky darkness" (ὑπὸ ζόφον ἠερόεντα, 11. 155); he replies that "necessity led me down (κατήγαγεν) to Hades" (11.164), two of several references to the descent of Odysseus.[17]

of the mythic queens, "full of personal longing and regret" (155), in addition to highlighting Odysseus' ability to see them.

[16] The Intermezzo allows Odysseus to gauge the effectiveness of his narration of the catalogue of heroines on Arete, whose approval is essential to his objective of returning home. Gazis (2018: 157–64) reviews the scholarship.

[17] Achilles also refers to Odysseus' voyage as to come "down" (κατελθέμεν, 11. 475), and Odysseus says to Penelope, "I went down into the house of Hades" (κατέβην δόμον Ἄϊδος εἴσω, 23. 252).

Considered in its entirety then, *Odyssey* 11 combines elements of necromancy with those of a catabasis.[18] The *Nekyia* can therefore be considered the first surviving literary example of a descent to the underworld in European literature, shaping subsequent accounts for thousands of years to come, including the postmodern fiction discussed in the next chapters. Yet in many ways it is unique among its kind.

Despite the supernatural nature of Odysseus' visit to the underworld, the fantastic elements found in other catabatic narratives are lacking. There is no grim ferryman to take the visitor over the Styx, no three-headed watchdog to placate, nor demons of any sort, although Odysseus does encounter hybrid monsters at other points in his wanderings. The emphasis is on his consultation with Tiresias, conversations with the shades of his mother and Iliadic comrades, and the stories of the heroines. The *Nekyia* is therefore less about the mythical grotesqueries of the underworld, and more about memory, knowledge, narrative, and personal interaction. Its length and central position in the poem invite close analysis in terms of these themes. George Alexander Gazis, in a book-length study of the "poetics of Hades," draws attention to a different kind of storytelling, focalized through the shades with more subjective and emotional color, which occurs in Hades.[19]

Scholars have noted other exceptional qualities in the *Nekyia*. Cedric Whitman, considering Book 11 in a larger context, observes that it exists as a "still-point" balanced on either side by corresponding adventures: the man-eating Cyclops mirrors the sea-monster Scylla, the dangerous allure of the Lotus eaters foreshadows the enticements of the Sirens, and the two seductive goddesses, Circe and Calypso, are essentially doublets.[20] Set in the midst of these fantastic adventures, yet also distinctly

[18] Clark (1978: 37–78) argues forcefully for understanding the *Nekyia* as a catabasis. For further discussion see Tsagarakis 1999: 12–16; Heubeck and Hoekstra 1989: 75–7. Dova (2012: 1–69) offers a nuanced discussion of the catabatic elements of *Odyssey* 11, and its relationship to the rest of the poem. The brief discussion in Felton (2007: 94–5) of the relationship between catabasis and necromancy in this context is a clear-sighted overview of the topic.

[19] Gazis (2018) analyzes each of the sections of Book 11 in these terms, and also notes a consistent emphasis on sight, particularly that of Odysseus, in the realm of the unseen (*A-idēs*).

[20] Whitman 1958: 288. Other scholars see different correspondences that balance the tales on either side of *Odyssey* 11. The important point is that they see the underworld episode as the center of the *Apologia*. For a good analysis of the symmetrical structure of the *Nekyia*, see de Jong (2001: 271–2).

different from them, the *Nekyia* is a pivotal point beyond time, in which Odysseus, poised between his past (the shades of his mother and comrades) and his future, learns that he will eventually return home. Furthermore, not only is his account of the underworld the longest narrative of Odysseus' adventures, it is also different in tone. Rejecting suggestions that *Odyssey* 11 is an interpolation by a different poet, Karl Reinhardt argues that this elegiac quality strengthens the counterbalance between life and death.[21] Like many literary treatments of the land of the dead, this one is chiefly about life, and offers explanations of its mysteries and advice about the future. The consultation with Tiresias is apt, writes Reinhardt, because the prophet has a special aptitude for understanding the nature of curses and wrath, a role that he assumes in tragedies such as Sophocles' *Oedipus Tyrannos*.[22] While this may be projecting a later tradition onto epic poetry, it is true that Tiresias helps Odysseus understand the cause of his nautical misadventures, specifically the anger of Poseidon for the blinding of his son the Cyclops, an important piece of knowledge that allows the hero to analyze other aspects of his travails.[23] Tiresias is singular among the dead; he alone has consciousness in Hades (his mind is still "in place," as Circe says, 10.493), in contrast to the other shades who must drink the blood to be cognizant. Blind while alive, he retains a supernatural kind of sight in Hades, and bears some similarities with the blind storyteller Demodocus, bard to the Phaeacian court. Both share "knowledge which is beyond the reach of ordinary human beings," as Barbara Graziosi observes.[24]

The interview with Tiresias is the purpose of Odysseus' visit: to consult about his *nostos* (homecoming) with the Theban prophet, who foresees the journey to come, what he will find at his destination, and finally his "soft" death far from the sea. Granted, Odysseus learns much more immediately useful information when he returns to Circe after his voyage, but the knowledge that he obtains in Hades enhances his ability to understand and analyze his adventures at sea. The Odyssean *Nekyia*

[21] Reinhardt 1996: 109–11.

[22] The Athenian tragedian, Aeschylus, staged Odysseus' necromantic consultation with Tiresias, which survives only as a fragment (fr. 273a Radt).

[23] Tsagarakis (1999: 45–55) notes the importance of the information about Poseidon's anger, and rightly points out that Odysseus never complains about the insufficiency of what he learns from Tiresias.

[24] Graziosi 2002: 142–3.

conforms to what Raymond Clark has described as the "wisdom tradition" of catabasis narratives, and even more broadly, to the idea that the earth itself holds knowledge to be obtained by descending into its depths.[25] Scholars have attempted to relate the *Nekyia* to Greek rituals that involve an individual making a sacrifice and then going down a pit (symbolic of the underworld) to hear an oracle, although speculation about any ritual practice known to Homer and his original audience has little literary or archaeological evidence to support it.[26] Nonetheless descending into a cave was one way of achieving knowledge according to later Greeks, including the philosopher Pythagoras mentioned above. In her study of the association between caves and knowledge in ancient Greek thought, Yulia Ustinova applies neuroscience and cognitive psychology to explain this phenomenon: when the seeker of wisdom experiences sensory deprivation in a cave or underground space the neurological effect is a sense of enlightenment. Whether we accept her methodology or not, it is abundantly clear that the ancients believed that going into a subterranean space was a means to access wisdom and prophecy, an idea that persists in the contemporary fiction that we are about to study.[27] Ancillary to this idea is the intermediary figure who can transmit knowledge contained under the earth, in Odysseus' case the prophet Tiresias. *The Underworld Vision of an Assyrian Crown Prince* (mentioned in the Introduction), roughly contemporary with the composition of the *Odyssey*, also features the wise person at the center of the underworld who dispenses advice, in this case to Prince Kummay. Aeneas' encounter with his father in *Aeneid* 6, which we explore below, owes something to the Homeric Nekyia and probably to other versions of

[25] In *Catabasis: Vergil and the Wisdom Tradition* (1979), Clark divides underworld myths into two categories: 1) "the fertility tradition" of Near Eastern myths in which a god or goddess descends to the underworld, but finds a substitute, for example Inanna who is replaced by Dumuzi; 2) "the wisdom-tradition" whose Near Eastern prototype is Gilgamesh's journey to Utnapishtim. This is the tradition that will inform Homer's *Nekyia*, and its literary descendant, Vergil's *Aeneid* 6, the focus of Clark's study.

[26] Ogden (2001) relates accounts of heroic descents to sites where necromancy was practiced, but concrete evidence for the association is sketchy at best, cf. Albinus (2000: 72–3). See further Clark (1978: 55–61) on possible references to actual ritual in the *Nekyia*.

[27] Ustinova (2009) exhaustively surveys oracles and mystery cults that took place in caves, such as the grottos of Nymphs, caves of Pan, oracular centers at Taenarum, Bura, and Athens, oracles of Orpheus on Lesbos. She uses historical examples of philosophers such as Epimenides of Crete (*c.*600 BCE), who spent time in a cave to achieve his powers.

the necromantic encounter. All of this is based on the fundamental assumption that communication is possible in the underworld, and that some kind of interpreter, prophet, or guide is available to impart knowledge.[28] The following chapters explore this element in John Barth's *Lost in the Funhouse*, A.S. Byatt's novella "Morpho Eugenia," and Ann Patchett's *State of Wonder*, all of which offer challenging variations of the wise man at the center of Hades. Along with the *Nekyia* and *Aeneid* 6, they belong to one subset of underworld stories in which a traveler will encounter a mentor and achieve knowledge and insight.

While the acquisition of wisdom is an integral part of the Odyssean *Nekyia*, it also defines the unique nature of Odysseus' heroic character. Individuals who have the power to visit and return from the underworld are remarkable, either of heroic or divine stature.[29] Framed by encounters with the shades of two distinctly different men, Odysseus' time in the underworld sets him apart from both: at the beginning there is the foolish drunk Elpenor, a patently unheroic figure, who falls headlong to his death from Circe's roof. Like Enkidu, who speaks to Gilgamesh from the other world, he provides a contrast between the superhuman hero and the all too fragile mortal life. The still unburied Elpenor seems to create an opening to the underworld, an important role fulfilled in *Aeneid* 6 by Palinurus the helmsman who fell overboard.[30] Toward the end of the episode is the shade of Achilles, whose trenchant remarks about life and death leave no doubt that Odysseus has the best of it because he is alive. As the champion fighter of the Achaeans, one who won ever-lasting fame with his death, Achilles represents the Iliadic concept of glory, or *kleos*, a contrast to a different kind of glory defined for Odysseus, one dependent

[28] Tanaseanu-Döbler (2017: 27–8) identifies the types of encounters throughout the ancient Greco-Roman tradition that include necromancy, journeys to the beyond, near-death experiences, rituals associated with mystery religions, dreams and visions. As she notes, "a particularly striking literary embodiment of this liminality between the dead and living is the figure of the witch or magician . . . cast as familiar with the realm of the dead conceived as a[n] underworld, as the ritual expert in communication with the dead, or the expert guide to their world." Since her interest is in late antiquity she uses Lucian and Apuleius as examples, but she traces the tradition back to the *Nekyia*.

[29] Lease (1926: 601) suggests that ancient heroes who make it to Hades and back, have some divine blood, either as a child or grandchild of a god.

[30] Dova (2012: 6) regards Elpenor as a "sacrifice in progress" meant to facilitate Odysseus' catabasis. A red figure Pelike by the Lycaon painter (MFA 111, 440 BCE) depicts the meeting between the two, with the figure of Hermes (not mentioned by Homer) off to the side.

on cunning and resilience rather than strength and violence.[31] And we should note that the omniscient Homeric narrator (rather than Odysseus himself) gives his audience a final glimpse of the underworld in the so-called "Second *Nekyia*" in the last book of the poem, when we follow the dead suitors of Penelope, vanquished by the returning hero, and led down by Hermes in his role as psychopomp ("soul guide") to Hades. Unlike their nemesis Odysseus, they will remain there.

Odysseus' encounter with the dead also epitomizes a theme that recurs in several later versions of the descent tale, that of transformation. Existing for an interval in a place defined by memory (because it is occupied by figures from the past), a place where time has stopped (as it must for the dead), and yet a place where he can learn of things to come, Odysseus is transformed by his exposure to this otherworldly distillation of past and future.[32] His subsequent adventures, although parallel to those before the *Nekyia*, reveal a much more deliberative approach to impending catastrophe, as Steven Scully has argued. It is worth quoting his analysis more fully:

> He [Odysseus, post-Hades] also appears to have gained over the course of his wanderings a form of spiritual growth. While he loses every appendage of his past—men, booty, ships—until finally he arrives naked at Scheria, he has been exposed to the limits of human existence: a vision of Hades, intoxication to the point of "forgetfulness", disorientation of identity through violations of civic conduct or sexual seduction, and he has gained a knowledge both of his own humanity and of the nature of man.[33]

The most discernible evidence of his transformation is Odysseus' narrative skill, an ability he did not seem to possess before he visited Hades, but which he displays among the Phaeacians, and during his extended reunion with his wife. His time, or non-time among the dead, was an exposure to a trove of tales, including that of his former commander-in-chief, Agamemnon, whose fate functions as a paradigmatic warning about wives and homecomings, and who continues to lament his own

[31] Graziosi and Haubold (2013: 135–8) note that for Odysseus survival is a form of *kleos*, but they also point out that the circumstances of Achilles' fame and those of Odysseus are significantly different.

[32] Tsagarakis (1999: 69) remarks on the function of memory in the *Nekyia* with a suggestion that "a latent 'collective memory' in Odysseus, essential to his survival and to the realization of his goal, comes to life."

[33] Scully 1987: 415.

ignominious death at the hands of his wife's lover.[34] There are also the mini-chronicles of the parade of ghostly heroines, many of which, like that of Epicaste (Oedipus' mother-wife Jocasta in later versions), are exquisite, compressed narrative capsules. Immersed in this chthonic archive Odysseus emerges as a storyteller. Strikingly he takes on this role in Hades when he narrates events from the war to the shade of Achilles. It is an identity that defines several characters who make a symbolic descent in the novels discussed in subsequent chapters. Indeed the subterranean seems to have a natural affinity with narrativity. For example, in her analysis of Kafka's 1931 short story "The Burrow," about a creature who has created a labyrinth of tunnels underground, Lesser interprets this network as a metaphor for literary creation.[35] Homer's *Odyssey* is the first surviving work of European fiction to relate a visit to the underworld with narrative ability, but the tradition continues to our own time, as the second and third chapters of this book demonstrate.

All in all then, the *Nekyia* episode characterizes Odysseus as an special kind of hero who holds the distinct advantage over the Achaeans of being alive and able to return to the story in progress—theirs have all ended—and recount it. He exemplifies Miguel Herrero de Jáuregui's assessment of the significance of the hero's descent:

> A catabasis draws an uncrossable line between those few heroes who are courageous, ingenious, and pious enough to accomplish it successfully and those who, no matter how strong in battle, are not fit for it (e.g., Peirithous, whose temerity was doomed to fail). It is the moment where the boundary between usual and special heroes is defined, where the hero becomes different.[36]

Both the real, tangible companions who wait for Odysseus outside the underworld and those insubstantial souls whom he meets within serve as foils to this remarkable mortal who can descend to the realm of the latter and return to that of the former.

[34] Agamemnon was slaughtered by his wife, Clytemnestra's, lover Aegisthus, when he returned home from Troy. Dova (2012: 8–18) examines the ghost of Agamemnon's reaction to his own death in detail. Gazis (2018: 175–8) remarks on how Agamemnon's personal version of the story emphasizes the emotional trauma.

[35] Lesser 1987: 193–6.

[36] Herrero de Jáuregui 2011: 62.

Heracles and Dionysus

Paradoxically, the land of the dead, where one might assume that nothing ever happens, is the locus of a rich tradition of adventure stories. Radcliffe Edmonds puts it this way:

> [T]he journey to the realm of the dead is not simply a conglomeration of *traditional* elements, but comprises a *tale*, and no story is interesting without conflict of some kind. Anomaly and crisis make interesting and tellable stories; normality and quotidian tedium do not. Only when the deceased experiences difficulty in the transition or when a living person crosses to the realm of the dead and then back again is there a story to be told.[37]

Homer's account of the underworld might suggest that his audiences had access to more exciting accounts of Hades, a place with a little less conversation and a little more action, which they remembered when they heard of Odysseus' descent. The catabasis of Heracles was probably treated in epic poetry circulating since the Dark Age (*c.*1100 to 800 BCE) and predating the *Odyssey*, since Homer refers to it twice.[38] Walter Burkert imagines a story of deep antiquity, perhaps reflecting some form of "shamanistic hunting magic."[39] Herrero de Jáuregui makes the persuasive argument that the final book of the *Iliad* follows the structure of a catabasis myth when the aged Trojan king Priam makes the trip across enemy lines to ransom the body of his son Hector from Achilles, in an act of supreme bravery.[40] If this analysis is correct, it suggests that descent stories were familiar enough for Homer's audiences to recognize the catabatic subtext in *Iliad* 24, and the most likely tale would have been that of Heracles. Although none of the contemporary narratives treated in this book deal with the Heraclean myth—with one minor exception—its substantial influence on ancient descent narratives makes it worthy of attention. The story, as preserved by the second-century BCE mythographer, Apollodorus, who had access to earlier versions now lost to us, is

[37] Edmonds 2004: 21(emphasis in the original): he develops this analysis into a pattern of catabatic tales comprised of obstacles and solutions.

[38] First in the *Iliad* (8.366–9), when Athena tells how she helped Heracles go to Hades to bring back the "hound," and again in the *Nekyia* (*Od.* 11.623–6) when Heracles' shade cites Hera and Eurystheus as the instigators of the quest.

[39] Burkert 1985: 209.

[40] Herrero de Jáuregui (2011: 37–68): led by Hermes, who acts a psychopomp in other descents, he makes a payment to Achilles, who resembles the king of the dead.

in many ways an archetypal catabasis featuring an extraordinary hero, typical landmarks of subterranean geographies, chthonic creatures and characters, and the familiar quest theme; it also links a visit to the underworld with initiation into a religious cult, a common association.[41]

Scholars speculate about the existence of an influential, but lost, epic poem, perhaps entitled "Heracles' Catabasis," apparently composed at some point in the sixth century BCE, but presumably indebted to that much older tradition known to Homer. It probably connected Heracles' quest to bring Cerberus above ground with his initiation in the Eleusinian Mystery cult, discussed below.[42] The heroic episode survives in truncated form thanks to Apollodorus (2.5.12), who recounts how Heracles descended at Taenarum in southern Greece (a common point of access to Hades' kingdom), drew his sword at the phantom Gorgon when she appeared, and captured Cerberus, whom he showed to Eurystheus (the king who set Heracles' challenges), and then sent back to his infernal master.[43] The Greek lyric poet Bacchylides composed his *Ode* 5 in 476 BCE to highlight Heracles' underworld encounter with the shade of Meleager, when our hero makes the fatal decision to marry his ghostly new friend's sister, Deianeira (who eventually causes his death), an incident probably indebted to the epic poem ("Heracles' Catabasis") as well.[44]

The extensive influence of the story of Heracles' visit to Hades on subsequent literature includes Aristophanes' *Frogs*, a comic drama first

[41] Dova (2012: 120 nn. 25 and 26) describes Heracles' catabasis as "archetypal" because it features all the elements of a successful descent according to her definition: the necessity of the labor involved, the help of a goddess, and the clarity of purpose (in contrast to the ambiguous purpose of Odysseus' descent).

[42] Clark (1978: 72–98) discusses Heracles' descent in the context of the Eleusinian Mysteries. Robertson (1980: 274–300) reviews evidence for the poem and speculates about its author. The fifth-century BCE Greek lyric poet Pindar also wrote a version of Heracles' catabasis which survives as papyrus fragments (Pind. fr. 346 Maehl. = OF 716). For further discussion and bibliography see Brown 1991: 49, n. 34. Apparently (according to Pollux *Onom.* 10.152) the Archaic Greek poet Steisichorus composed a *Cerberus*, of which only a fragment remains (fr. 206 Page), which may also refer to Heracles' catabasis.

[43] The tradition incorporated the unsuccessful catabasis of Perithous, king of the Lapiths, who accompanied Theseus, intending to abduct Persephone. Heracles was able to bring Theseus back to the light, but not Perithous, who, for his hubris, was tricked into sitting down, and remained trapped in Hades forever; his failure to return contrasts with the success of Heracles. Evidently the incident was treated in tragedy: a few fragments of *Perithous* possibly by Euripides survive. See Dover 1994: 54.

[44] The ode celebrated the Syracusan king Hieron's Olympic victory. Dova's (2012: 80–4) insightful analysis of Bacchylides' ode highlights its parallels with the Odyssean *Nekyia*.

performed in Athens (405 BCE); it is the longest surviving account of a catabasis in literature until the *Aeneid*, four centuries later. Dionysus, god of the theater, comedically reenacts the descent of Heracles in order to take the tragic poet, Euripides, (rather than Cerberus) out of Hades, although he changes his mind and leads the older tragedian, Aeschylus, back to Athens instead.[45] The comic depiction of his catabasis, while obviously referring to that of Heracles, is also informed by Dionysus' associations with the underworld in ancient myth and cult. In some accounts the god descends to bring back his mortal mother, Semele, from Hades to install her as a goddess on Olympus.[46] Relatedly, Dionysus was the figurehead of mystery cults that offered initiates knowledge of the afterlife, as attested by inscriptions on gold leaf tablets among grave goods. These tablets often include directions to help a soul find its path in the afterlife. In *Frogs*, however, Dionysus is ridiculously ignorant of details about Hades. After consulting with Heracles, who helpfully describes the subterrestrial landmarks (136–64), the god, clad in the hero's lion skin, makes his way across the Acheron, although Charon expects him to row as well.[47] When Dionysus and his slave Xanthias first arrive in Hades, they are hopelessly astray. Apparently the ancients had serious concerns about getting lost in what Plutarch (fr. 178) describes as the "frightening paths of darkness" in the world of the dead.[48] The idea persists in later catabatic tales. Dante finds himself "lost in a dark wood" (*Inf.* 1.2), for example, as he prepares to enter the underworld, and Barth's "Lost in the Funhouse" parodies the trope.

[45] Edmonds (2004: 120–58) reads many scenes in *Frogs* as adaptations of the myth of Heracles' descent. Aristophanes also parodied the catabasis in an earlier (lost) play, *Gerytades* (408), which has an embassy of poets descending to Hades.

[46] Extant accounts of Semele's ascent to Olympus are later than *Frogs* (e.g. *Anth. Pal.* 1.3, where she has the assistance of Hermes), but Santamaría Álvarez (2014: 217–40) offers a plausible hypothesis (based on iconography) that dates a version of the story to the last third of the sixth century BCE, when it served as an *aition* to explain the origin of mystery cults associated with Delphi and Lerna. He notes similarities with the early versions of the myth of Orpheus bringing his wife back from Hades. For a concise overview of (and source material for) Dionysus' relationship to mystery cults, which prepared initiates for the afterlife, see Cole (2007: 338–41).

[47] Edmonds (2004: 126–36) explains the jokes, which are based on conventional elements of the underworld journey: Heracles stressed the long and difficult journey over a great expanse of water, but Dionysus' crossing in Hades is over a shallow marshy lake; Charon is like a bored bus driver.

[48] As Edmonds (2004: 136–8) explains, the possibility of losing one's way is a common element of underworld narratives.

Aristophanes' comic duo are rescued from their dilemma by a ghostly chorus of Eleusinian initiates, whose membership in the religious community guaranteed an easy transition to life after death. The play features allusions to aspects of the Mysteries familiar to many audience members; for example, Xanthias' vision of the female demon Empousa may refer to a dramatic moment in the initiation of cult members.[49] The recurring female monster—Odysseus left Hades lest he encounter the Gorgon in *Odyssey* 11; Heracles drew his sword on her ghost, according to Apollodorus; Vergil's underworld is populated by Erinyes and other chthonic demons whom Aeneas also threatens with his sword—is a figure that we meet again in contemporary underworld landscapes, including those of Ferrante, Gaiman/Selick's *Coraline*, and Patchett's *State of Wonder*.

While the trip to Hades is the ultimate test in courage, Dionysus' reaction to the terrors of Hades is anything but heroic. His cowardice is obvious throughout the early part of the play: most tellingly he loses control of his bowels at the mere mention of gorgons (477), an example of the scatological humor that amused Aristophanes' audiences. As a parody of a catabasis *Frogs* subverts a well-established tradition in other ways. The idea of Hades as a vast city is humorously amplified with landmarks and characters of the Greek *polis*, for example a baker who demands payment of an overdue account.[50] Of course for a parody to work it must refer to a familiar tradition; Aristophanes' catabatic comedy reveals that the conventions of the *descensus ad infernos* were firmly in place by the late fifth century. And from the references to the Eleusinian Mysteries it is also evident that the descent myth was easily associated with initiation rituals. Ismene Lada-Richards has argued that Dionysus undergoes a coming-of-age rite in *Frogs*, and thus his adoption of the costume of Heracles conforms to some of the role-playing activities in ephebic rituals performed by young men of citizen status throughout ancient Greece. Edmonds, on the other hand, argues that attempts to fit the play into initiatory ritual paradigms are too rigid, although he does detect the motif of transformation, not of a particular character, but of Athens itself,

[49] Brown (1991: 41–50) has persuasively connected the reference to Empousa with the Eleusinian experience. See also Dover (1994: 208). On the recurrent image of the female bogey in the underworld, and her relevance to the *Aeneid* 6, see Clark 2009: 190–203.

[50] Santamaría Álvarez (2015).

teetering on the brink of disaster in 405, which Dionysus hopes to renew by bringing back a poet from the city-state's glorious past.[51]

Aristophanes' *Frogs* exhibits many standard elements of descent tales: a voyage across water, the traveler astray, an encounter with a fearsome female demon, the quest to bring back someone or something from the realm of the dead, and an association with real cultic practices. One of the most significant qualities of Aristophanes' version of Hades, at least for the purposes of this book, is that it exists as a literary space. This comic underworld is constructed from the intertextual bones of an earlier poem (the lost epic of Heracles' descent), but it is also a place where the ghosts of poets, Aeschylus and Euripides, compete against each other with citations of their own and each other's work. As the following chapters will demonstrate, contemporary authors continue the tradition of using the underworld as a symbol for the literature of the past, and also as a site of textual rivalry and contestation.

The Descent of Aeneas

Four hundred years later (30–19 BCE) Vergil would draw on and enhance these citational practices with a version of the underworld and descending hero whose essence can be discerned in literature centuries later including, most notably, Dante's *Inferno*.[52] His protagonist, the Trojan refugee Aeneas, after a year with the Carthaginian queen Dido, is ordered by Jupiter to leave his mistress and sail from North Africa with his followers. He arrives on the Italian peninsula at Cumae, north of what is now the city of Naples. The ghost of his father, Anchises, had previously instructed Aeneas to visit him for further consultation (5.737). *Aeneid* 6, which progresses toward that interview, is the most detailed depiction of Hades in surviving Greco-Roman literature; its intricate specificity and central position in the poem indicate its importance to the narrative as a whole. The catabasis is the transitional point of the entire epic, a division between its first and second halves: Aeneas enters the cave at Avernus, in

[51] Lada-Richards (1999); Edmonds (2004: 113–26).

[52] The topic of Vergil's influence is vast, but a good introduction to the topic is Burrow (1997: 79–90) who surveys Vergil's impact on poetry from Dante to Milton. MacDonald (1987) offers a sophisticated analysis of the themes of memory and history that link Vergil, Dante, and Milton.

the volcanic Phlegraean Fields, as a Trojan character defined by the Homeric tradition, and exits through the Gates of Ivory as the forefather of the Roman Empire. Nicholas Horsfall, in his splendid commentary on *Aeneid* 6, remarks on "the moral and emotional link" between Aeneas' catabasis and his future, when he, "will both live up to his Trojan ancestry . . . and set in motion . . . the Trojans' great destiny in Italy."[53] There is, needless to say, an ideological subtext here.

The *Aeneid* is a product of the cultural milieu fostered by Maecenas, a close friend of Augustus, and a wealthy patron of the arts in Rome: its sixth book, devoted exclusively to the hero's *descensus ad infernos*, culminates with the display of noble Romans yet to be born, and whose existence depends on Aeneas fulfilling his destiny of founding a colony in Italy. Still, to read Book 6 and indeed the entire poem, simply as propaganda to support Rome's first imperial dynasty is to miss its nuanced complexity. Rome must come into being, but at great emotional cost for *pius Aeneas*, as W.R. Johnson famously argues in *Darkness Visible: a Study of Vergil's Aeneid* (1976). The underworld encounters with the shades of his abandoned lover Dido, his Trojan companions, and finally his father, emphasize not only Aeneas' past, but also his sense of loss. His renunciation of his own emotional needs and acceptance of his father's vision of Rome's future glory define a new type of heroism that epitomizes the Roman virtue of *pietas*: devotion to family, the state, and the gods. Yet for all the pathos of his sacrifices, the political implications of the poem, and specifically *Aeneid* 6, are close to the surface; Aeneas must put his personal desires aside to fulfill a greater purpose. Vergil wrote the *Aeneid* as an "instrument of national aspiration and social criticism" for a learned, politically sensitive audience: Augustus himself.[54]

Like most of the poem, its sixth book is laced with allusions to earlier works, most obviously the *Odyssey*: the consultation with Anchises is

[53] Horsfall 2013: xiv. See also Williams' (1964: 48) excellent remarks on the relationship between *Aeneid 6* and the character development of Aeneas. Herrero de Jáuregui (2015: 342) remarks that: "We may say also of Aeneas that he changes identity along his journey, or rather, he discovers his deepest and truest identity. Anchises in fact had told him to go to Hades in order to get knowledge of his lineage (V, 737: *tum genus omne tuum et quae dentur moenia disces*). And after discovering not his ancestry, but his descent, his identity will change. In the first part of the voyage he meets all his Trojan past, and in the second all his Roman future."

[54] Clark 1978: 14.

indebted to Odysseus' interview with Tiresias; the unburied, but perhaps redundant, Palinurus recalls Elpenor, and so on.[55] The allusions to early works follow the literary methods of Callimachus, Apollonius of Rhodes, and other Alexandrian poets in their characteristic "imitation with variation," and also in their display of vast learning. Thus while the poet alludes to the *Nekyia*, he also changes it: for example, the monsters and horrors absent from the *Odyssey* are evident in all their grotesque variety. While Homer's Odysseus tells his audience very little about the topography of the underworld, Vergil provides a detailed description of the *domus Ditis* and its hinterlands, producing what Clark describes as "a magnificent composite literary integration" of multiple sources.[56] Most scholars agree with Eduard Norden that in addition to *Odyssey* 11 these include the lost sixth-century Greek epic treating the catabasis of Heracles, discussed above. Different readers have detected references to Eleusinian and Orphic mystery cults, both of which focused on the afterlife.[57]

The catabasis of Aeneas is steeped in a variety of different traditions; in a poem conspicuously indebted to earlier literature the catabasis stands out as exceptionally intertextual. Vergil was a master "poetic bricoleur or mosaicist," who incorporated a variegated mixture of literary and ritual predecessors in his version of Hades.[58] Deploying an eclectic collection of comparative material, Jan Bremmer demonstrates that Vergil's underworld is a rich pastiche of catabatic traditions that incorporates and goes beyond Greek texts. Recent discoveries of fragmentary papyri, especially Orphic texts, along with a cross-cultural archive of underworld narratives inspire Bremmer to speculate about the wide array of predecessors that Vergil draws upon for *Aeneid* 6, including perhaps the apocryphal Jewish *Book of Enoch*, which also features a tour of Hell. There is no

[55] Palinurus is "redundant" because Misenus has already has died "to ensure his commander's safe return from the Underworld" (Horsfall 2013: 278).

[56] It is possible that the catalogue of terrors, and poignant lists of untimely deaths and broken-hearted lovers might be derived from existing manuals. Horsfall (2013: 332, passim) speculates about the existence of such catalogues, for example in the list of women who died for love, but notes that the melancholy appearance of Dido, for example, is entirely the poet's own creation. Clark (1978: 13–14) notes that Vergil always transforms the material that he inherits. On the modes of Vergilian intertextuality see Farrell (1997: 222–38), who observes that we probably know more about Vergil's sources than those of any other ancient poet.

[57] Clark's 1978 study is devoted to the background to *Aeneid* 6; also see Norden (1903); Horsfall (2013: xvii–xxv) includes other sources.

[58] Bremmer 2014: 181.

orthodox or "fixed" version of the descent, and catabatic narratives have a tendency to borrow from and revise a tradition that was ancient, prolific, and variable. Vergil's mix and match treatment of the underworld is not unique. Fritz Graf and Sarah Iles Johnston identify the same approach in gold tablets that give instructions for the afterlife in Bacchic and Orphic mystery cults, and there are various other exponents of this intermingling of traditions in ancient texts that deal with the underworld and afterlife.[59]

It is not only ancient traditions that exhibit this phenomenon. Throughout this volume we will encounter recent specimens of the same tendency. Rushdie, for example, blends the Roman story of Orpheus with Parsi myths of the afterlife. The next chapter scrutinizes the underworld as represented in Neil Gaiman's comic book series, *The Sandman,* which features an eclectic assemblage of chthonic allusions that include Vergilian elements and Jewish legends woven through a version of Milton's Hell. Gaiman's fascination with the subterranean is also evident in his novel *American Gods* (2001), which features a catabasis exemplifying this chthonic decoupage. Its hero Shadow Moon, a modern day Baldur, travels across America, encountering different avatars of an international pantheon. The catabatic chapter, toward the end of the complex plot, is heavily based on Egyptian and Norse mythology, with a cameo appearance by the Hindu god Ganesh. The structure, however, is familiar: the reader can hardly be surprised—given Gaiman's predilections and the framework of the novel as a heroic journey—when Shadow makes his descent down a flight of stairs into another world where he learns the identity of his father. He carries a coin as a talisman that lights his way, and like many an underworld visitor he reaches a shore where a ferryman, here the Egyptian god Thoth who identifies himself as a psychopomp, conveys him across the water. A semi-divine hero makes a descent to an underworld formed from the fragments of different traditions that recombine in a unique and meaningful way, and in this space he sees his father. This synopsis is just as fitting for the descent of Aeneas.

The hero's guide through the underworld is the Cumaean Sibyl, a priestess who dwells in a vast cavern (*antrum immane*, 6.11), adorned

[59] Graf and Johnston (2007), cf. Edmonds (2004: 4) on how texts that treat the journey to the land of the dead exhibit bricolage with "elements from a pool of traditional motifs."

with gates decorated by the Cretan craftsman Daedalus.[60] The Sibyl foretells part of Aeneas' destiny, but she also functions as a mystagogue, as if she is leading an initiate through a ritual process.[61] She provides him with a talisman, the golden bough, that ensures passage through the different levels of the underworld, and which becomes a common element of descent narratives. The tour of Hell is extensive, beginning with "a lonely road though the shadows, dark in the night . . . through the empty halls of Dis and his insubstantial realm, like a journey through the woods under the emerging light of a half-seen moon" (6. 267–70).[62] Dante, among many others, used the idea of the dark woods (*selva oscura*, *Inf.* 1.2) through which the hero must travel; we see them again in Morrison's *Song of Solomon* and also in the Amazonian landscape of Patchett's *State of Wonder*. Commenting on the significance of these gloomy forests in Roman poetry Shane Butler reminds us that timber is "the very stuff of literary production" including the waxed wooden tablets upon which poets composed their work: "Enter the woods and you are in the poet's workshop."[63] His observation lends further meaning to the books that we are about to discuss, in which trees, the raw material of their production, are symbols of the literary tradition.

The vast chambers of Vergil's underworld, divided into six parts, reverberate with echoes of all the versions of Hades that have existed up to this point. Since our purpose is not to catalogue these esoteric references, but to identify Vergil's contributions to the tradition, some of these discussions are relegated to footnotes, which readers can consult if they want to pursue the topic.[64] While the Odyssean *Nekyia* is the most

[60] Bremmer (2014: 185) identifies the Sibyl, as a "travel guide," familiar from ancient Jewish religious texts, such as the *Book of Enoch*.

[61] Probable allusions to mystery religions are numerous; for example, arriving at a deep cave, Aeneas makes the requisite sacrifices to the infernal gods, heralded by eerie howls and shuddering ground; the Sibyl shouts *procul, o procul este, profani*, ("get away, away, o souls profane"). Horsfall (2013: 229) notes that the words allude to the beginning of the oldest Orphic theogony to signify the ritual details that follow. Other scholars have noted allusions to Eleusinian mysteries, although Clark (2009:199) sagely warns against reading *Aeneid* 6 as documentary evidence of the actual Eleusinian proceedings.

[62] Horsfall's translation. He observes that Aeneas and Sibyl do not descend yet ("as I seem to recall from Jules Verne"). At one point they are not in the underworld and then they are (2013: 229).

[63] Butler 2009: 64.

[64] In Tartarus, the deepest part of Hades, Bremmer detects echoes of Plato's eschatological texts (e.g. *Gorgias* 524a, *Phaedo* 108a; *Republic* 10.614cd). The complex structure of

obvious intertext, and there are also elements of Hesiod's Tartarus, it is clear that the concept of Hades had developed considerably over the previous 800 years, absorbing and adapting traditions as its contours become more distinct. A significant deviation from the Homeric template is the Elysian Fields. The underworld that Odysseus beholds is a dank, cheerless place with the paradisiacal Elysium in the far distance, but beyond the depths of Tartarus Vergil imagines in great detail a place of light and beauty where happy souls experience beatitude, and await reincarnation after drinking from the river Lethe to forget their former lives after a thousand years of purgation. As R.D. Williams observes: "Virgil comes nearest to a solution of the problem of human suffering with which the whole poem is so preoccupied, as he groped towards the conception of the life after death in which sin is purified away and virtue rewarded."[65]

Vergil's complex vision of the afterlife, regardless of its patriotic agenda, represents a learned amalgamation of eschatological beliefs, to be reworked by Dante and Milton, with a lasting effect on the Christian notion of Hell.[66] My interests lie more in how later authors have used the patterns of action that Vergil himself inherited from his predecessors—the passage across the river Styx, the guided tour of Hell, confrontations with hybrid monsters and a mentor, etc.—in ways that respond to the colonial and patriarchal ideology that the *Aeneid* takes for granted. This enterprise must acknowledge how recent receptions of the poem can challenge and subvert some of its basic precepts. For example, Benjamin Eldon Stevens demonstrates how Tolkien's *The Hobbit* (1937) upsets the theme of knowledge and prophecy exemplified by Aeneas' interview with

the Vergilian Hades may owe something to Pindar's *Olympian* 2, which pictures a tripartite afterlife in which the sinners are sentenced by a judge below the earth to endure terrible pains (57–60, 67): those who are good men spend a pleasant time with the gods (61–67) and those who have completed the cycle of reincarnation and have led a blameless life will join the heroes on the Isles of the Blessed (68–80) (Bremmer 2014: 191–202). A tripartite structure can also be noticed in the texts of the pre-Socratic philosopher Empedocles, who speaks about the place that the great sinners occupy (B 118–21 DK). In addition to Platonic influences, Williams (1964: 48–50) detects folktale elements and Pythagorean beliefs, such as those that influenced Cicero's "Dream of Scipio" (the sixth book of his *De Re Publica*) modeled on the myth of Er, a version of a near death experience in Plato's *Republic*.

[65] Williams 1964: 48; see Harrison (1978: 193–7) on the philosophical background to Vergil's concept of metempsychosis.

[66] See Braund (1997: 218) on how Vergil leverages his eschatology for patriotic purposes.

his father. While alluding to Vergil's epic poem, Tolkien constructs a subterranean world in which creatures such as Smaug and Gollum "disorder knowing and embody forgetting." Unlike Aeneas, who gains clarity from his interview with his father's shade, Tolkien's protagonist, the hobbit Bilbo, "encounters visions of his own potentially darker path in the forms of chthonic monsters to whom he is uncannily similar."[67] Stevens evaluates these distorted echoes of the Vergilian catabasis to comment on Tolkien's own conception of history, thus illustrating how a study of the influence of ancient concepts of the underworld is not simply a search for transmitters of the "classical tradition," but rather seeks to identify the transformation of source material in the process of "classical reception." Later in this volume I explore how the imperialistic agenda of the *Aeneid* is reconsidered in Ann Patchett's *State of Wonder*, a novel that addresses issues of dislocation and deracination set in the depths of the Amazonian rainforests, and which, rather than engaging in an unmediated transmission of the encounter with an underworld mentor, revises that ancient trope in a way that blends issues of gender and colonialism into its reception.

These adaptations have potency because Vergil's vision of the afterlife had such a profound influence on the Western tradition. Integrating diverse sources from earlier poetry, sacred texts, and philosophy he added significantly to the concept of a subterranean literary space that is constantly revising the meaning of the descent narrative. Now more well defined than ever, the topography and personnel of this carefully mapped out netherworld, infused with a particular ideological subtext, have cast long shadows on culture until the present day.

Orpheus and Eurydice

Greek and Roman poets associated the underworld with their literary heritage, but the figure of Orpheus suggests that language and music can actually give a hero access to the realm of the dead. Vergil's account of the mythical musician's descent, adapted a few decades later by the poet Ovid, is embedded in the Aristaeus epyllion (a "mini-epic") of his *Fourth Georgic* (316–527), a poem (*c*.29 BCE) ostensibly about agriculture, which

[67] Stevens 2016a: 122–4.

recounts how the farmer Aristaeus suffered a collapse of his bee hive, and descended to the watery depths to consult his mother the nymph Cyrene (a nod to Vergil's artistic influence, Callimachus of Cyrene). She sends him off to capture the sea-god Proteus for an explanation, whereby Aristaeus learns that his misfortune is related to the death of Eurydice, bitten by a poisonous snake when she escaped Aristaeus' attempt to rape her. Commentary on the literary allusions of the episode (and indeed of the *Georgics*) is vast, in proportion to its learned intertextuality.[68] Aristaeus' consultation with Proteus alludes to Menelaus' encounter with the same sea-god in the *Odyssey* (4. 235–592), while simultaneously evoking Tiresias in the *Nekyia*, since as a prophet, Proteus "knows all things" (*novit namque omnia vates*, *G.* 4. 392).[69] Proteus' account of Orpheus' descent at Taenarum provides a compact tour of Hell. It is with his song (*cantu*, 471), rather than a beaker of blood, that Orpheus attracts the ghosts and enchants the Furies and Cerberus, even causing the wheel of the sinner Ixion to cease. Yet he is seized by a strange madness (*dementia*, 488) just before the moment of reunion, and Eurydice fades away speaking her melancholy and only lines.

When Ovid composed his *Metamorphoses*, an epic poem about mythic transformations of gods and mortals, in the early first century CE, he elaborated and revised the Vergilian tale, excising the role of Aristaeus, and introducing his own variations. As Charles Segal sees it, Ovid makes *amor* rather than *furor*, love rather than madness, the focus of the episode, which results in a more romantic characterization of Orpheus. The contrast is evident in the climates of both underworlds. Vergil for example emphasizes the monstrosity of the Furies with their snakey locks, "grim and horrible, enforcers of the poet's stern order." Ovid's vision of Hades is "more yielding," and rather than describing their hideous appearance, he gives the Furies a sympathetic character as they

[68] Excellent examples include Farrell (1991) and Thomas (1999).

[69] Segal (1989: 73–5) suggests that Aristaeus' descent into the sea may allude to the *Nekyia* with Cyrene taking on the role of Circe. She "frames the quest to the wise old man; and in both cases the goddesses, rather than the wise old man himself, give the essential practical instructions for the immediate problem of survival." He also notes that Aristaeus' plunge into the ocean recalls the initiatory motif suggested by the dive of Theseus to his father Poseidon in Bacchylides *Ode* 17. See Konstan and Nieto (2011: 346) for the idea that Aristaeus is a doublet of Orpheus because he makes a catabasis.

weep at the poet's song.[70] Not every scholar is as sanguine about Ovid's Orpheus: W.S. Anderson dismisses him as a "melodramatic, egoistic poet of overblown rhetoric and shallow self-indulgent sentimentality."[71] John Heath notes that Orpheus makes a reference to the descent of Heracles when he appears before Dis (Hades) and his wife Proserpina (10.21–2), thereby inviting a comparison of the two heroes. While Heracles completes the task of bringing Cerberus to the light, Orpheus cannot bring his wife above ground and is thus "a failed Hercules."[72] Furthermore, as Heath notes, Orpheus does not even encounter Cerberus, which dilutes the danger and heroics of his catabasis even more.

It is a matter of subjective interpretation, and a careful weighing of Ovid's obvious sentimentality against his implicit cynicism, whether we understand his ending of the story to be satisfying or ironically saccharine. Ovid recounts that after Orpheus is murdered by the Bacchantes (angry because he has rejected the love of women for that of boys) and his shade descends to Hades (*umbra subit terras*), he is reunited with Eurydice, whom he can now look at as much as he desires (*Met.* 11. 61–6). However we regard this happy reconciliation in the underworld, we must keep in mind that it does not appear in any prior surviving source, and seems to be another Ovidian innovation, although one that might refer to an earlier version of the myth.[73] The Orpheus story is noteworthy for its variable conclusions. Orphic tales, both ancient and modern, tend to be flexible and open-ended narratives that acknowledge the different possible endings of the myth: Euripides and Plato knew a story in which husband and wife are reunited on earth; a Hellenistic poet seems to have influenced Vergil's rendition in which Orpheus ignores the interdiction not to look back; Ovid reunites the pair in Hades; the librettists of Baroque opera allow Orpheus a second chance, reuniting the lovers, or placing Orpheus in heaven.[74] The two surviving Latin renditions of Orpheus' disastrous curiosity have been the inspiration for countless

[70] Segal (1989: 61–2) goes on to say that Ovid transforms Vergil's "stern and unbending underworld into a fanciful realm that shares the emotional coloring and erotic sympathies of the rest of Ovid's world."

[71] Anderson 1982: 36. [72] Heath 1996: 363.

[73] Konstan and Nieto 2011: 346.

[74] Euripides *Alcestis* (357–62) indicates that Orpheus was successful, and this version of the myth seems to have been well established prior to Vergil's adaptation of the myth. Bowra (1952) surveys the evidence and concludes that Vergil may have adapted the tragic version from a recent Hellenistic predecessor.

operas, poems, films, novels, and other texts including those discussed in the following pages.[75] Gaiman, Rushdie, and Patchett each put their own stamp on the myth by splicing the story of love and loss with other underworld myths, another example of how the process of bricolage can shape the descent narrative. Since all these endings are possible, reception of the story is tinged with suspense: will Orpheus succeed in bringing Eurydice home; will he turn his head at the crucial moment and lose her forever; or will he be given a second chance to bring her back? My selected contemporary adaptations of the story exploit Orpheus' association with cultural production, intertextuality, and indeterminacy in ways that amplify and contest the surviving tradition(s).

The original readers of these two Latin accounts of Orpheus' failure to bring back Eurydice were aware that this mythical musician was the figurehead of a religion that believed in an immortal soul, offered instructions on how to achieve physical and spiritual purity, and gave useful directions for the afterlife.[76] Although detailed knowledge of the religion is not necessary for an appreciation of ancient or contemporary versions of Orpheus and Eurydice—Rushdie's obvious aquaintance with the tradition of asceticism in his Orphic novel notwithstanding—a quick overview of the cult adds texture to the myth and reaffirms the association of descent stories with initiation rites. Much of what is known about Orphic religion comes from ritual texts, including papyrus fragments, bone tablets (from Olbia, Italy), and lamellae, thin leaves of inscribed gold foil, buried with the deceased (perhaps strung around his or her neck), with instructions or directions on what to do or where to go once the soul had reached Hades. First discovered in the nineteenth century, these texts continue to be unearthed. For example one of the earliest discoveries, from an Italian tomb in Thurii proclaims: "Now I come, as a suppliant, to holy Phersephoneia, that she, gracious, may send me to the seats of the blessed." Another bears the instructions to

[75] Buller (1995: 61–2) traces the Baroque operatic happy endings back to the Renaissance drama of Polizian.

[76] The 1962 discovery of the fragmentary Derveni Papyrus, a commentary on an Orphic poem, along with funerary gold leaves from diverse parts of Greece (Macedonia to Crete), and other epigraphical material confirm that Orphism was an element of Greek religion and philosophy. Interpretation and reconstruction of the data is ongoing, including the important work on the topic by Bernabé (a three-volume edition of *Orphicorum Fragmenta* [2004–2007]). See further (Edmonds 2011a). Guthrie (1935) is still useful.

make "your way to the right, the sacred meadows and groves of Persepheia."[77] A body of Orphic Hymns, composed in the third century CE by devotees of the cult, gives further details about the religion. As these texts illustrate, the cult acknowledged the power of Persephone, who is an important figure in the Eleusinian mysteries. Further syncretism is obvious in how Orphism incorporated elements of Bacchic mystery cults (centering on the god Dionysus), which, according to Apollodorus (1.3.2), were established by Orpheus. All three cults feature a woman coming back from the land of the dead: Persephone, Semele (the mother of Dionysus), and the wife of Orpheus, who is not named in the earliest treatment of her story, but whose name when it appears, "Broad justice" (Eurydice), suggests that she might be a doublet of Persephone, an association that Rushdie's narrator, Rai, explores in *The Ground Beneath Her Feet.*

Scholars detect evidence of Orphic doctrine in the cult associated with Pythagoras, the Greek philosopher who espoused a doctrine of the transmigration of souls and descended underground himself; others argue that Orphic beliefs influenced Aristophanes' *Frogs* and *Aeneid* 6.[78] His impact on the culture of the ancient world was considerable, including an oracle that putatively housed his severed head in a cave on Lesbos, exemplifying a common conflation between poetry and prophecy.[79] All these expressions of belief, in mystery religions, ritual texts and oracles, were associated with Orpheus' descent to retrieve his wife from the kingdom of Hades, and that is the story that continues to shape culture up to the present.

The myth of Orpheus' trip to the underworld is distinct from other descent tales chiefly because, at least in its most influential versions, it ends in failure.[80] Odysseus, Heracles, and Aeneas emerge from Hades with what they came for, be it information or the infernal hound. The sorrowful theme of the Orphic narrative underscores the futile quest to

[77] A3 and A4 in Edmonds 2011b: 4.

[78] For further discussion see Bremmer 2014: 342.

[79] Ustinova (2009: 106–7) surveys the evidence including a fifth-century vase depicting an oracular consultation with a severed head.

[80] Using cross-cultural comparanda, Graf (1987: 81–2) suggests that Orpheus belongs to a category of shaman figures who perform the ritually enacted journey to the beyond to get information or to fetch back a soul through the power of music. Classical poetry has imbued the tale with a more tragic nuance.

retrieve what is irretrievable, a departed loved one; we are left with the melancholy conclusion that mortal life is as ephemeral as music.

Persephone

This survey of descent myths concludes with an overview of Persephone's *descensus ad infernos*, an unusual variant for several reasons. Persephone is immortal, while the catabatic heroes, with the exception of Dionysus *qua* Heracles, are not; she returns to the terrestrial world and then back to Hades repeatedly, but mortal heroes go only once before they die. Korē, "girl," as she is known in association with her mother Demeter, does not descend willingly (at least not the first time), but is abducted by her uncle, the god Hades, in what is essentially a marriage by capture. It goes without saying that Persephone is also different by virtue of her gender from male heroes who visit the underworld, and this distinction is realized most tellingly in her lack of agency as she is depicted in the *Homeric Hymn to Demeter*. Hades snatches her when she is innocently picking flowers in a meadow; her mother orchestrates her return, although Zeus has condoned his brother's choice of a bride without consulting his sister Demeter. Marriages in ancient Greece were contracts between men, and mothers had no legal authority to prevent or promote a particular match. In this respect Persephone's story is very much a reflection of the Greek and Roman societies that produced the *Homeric Hymn* (composed by an anonymous poet, *c*.650–550 BCE) and Ovid's two versions in *Metamorphoses* 5.341–661 and *Fasti* 4.417–620 (*c*. first century CE).[81] These are the best-known renditions of her story, although earlier treatments of the myth can be traced as far back as Hesiod (*c*.700 BCE).[82] It is difficult to discern if the Roman poet Ovid consulted the *Homeric Hymn* for his treatment of the myth, or was relying on other versions that were circulating, but since the basic structures of the stories are similar I will focus on the *Hymn*. It is

[81] Parkes (2015: 474) reads the *Metamorphoses* version as more epic. She discusses its influence on the unfinished version by fifth-century CE author Claudian, *de Raptu Proserpinae*, which also seems to be engaging with Ovid's version of Orpheus, especially his description of the underworld.

[82] Hesiod's reference (*Theogony* 913–14) suggests that the story was traditional. See Richardson (1974: 74–86) for an extensive catalogue and discussion of ancient literary versions of the myth, including lost and fragmentary sources; also Suter (2002).

important to note, however, that much of the *Hymn* deals with events leading up to the establishment of the Eleusinian Mysteries, one of the most popular cults in the ancient world; Persephone's abduction, which motivates Demeter's visit to Eleusis, is only one episode, although an important one, in the poem.[83]

The *Hymn* was composed no later than the mid-sixth century BCE to judge from its style and language, although there is no consensus on its precise date, or the circumstances of its original recitation; performance at a public festival, possibly at Eleusis (just outside of Athens), seems most likely.[84] *The Homeric Hymn to Demeter* occupies a unique place in the corpus of epic poetry, since it focuses on the experience of women, their homosocial relationships (not only that of Demeter with her daughter, but also with the women Demeter encounters in Eleusis), and the emotional trauma felt by a mother after her daughter's marriage.[85] The spotlight is on Demeter's reaction to her loss, but unlike mortal mothers, the goddess of agriculture and harvest has powerful leverage to bargain for the restoration of her daughter. By inflicting a famine on humanity she is able to short-circuit sacrifices that the gods require, and Zeus finally agrees to her daughter's return. Lucia Nixon has interpreted the myth in light of a cluster of European folktales that recount how a woman can improve her daughter's marriage situation. As she points out, in the ancient Greek asymmetrical construction of gender, girls' stories usually end with the birth of a heroic son; Persephone, who bears no children, is unique in this important respect.[86] But her story does represent a young woman's acceptance of marriage, symbolized by the pomegranate seeds that she takes from Hades, thereby insuring her return to him.[87] To consume food in the underworld is to accept a place in it.

[83] Bowden (2010: 26–48) offers an accessible, and up-to-date survey of the activities involved in the Eleusinian Mysteries, and its relationship to *The Homeric Hymn*.

[84] Richardson (1974: 10–12) reviews the evidence for dating and original context, which he suggests might have been at athletic games at Eleusis.

[85] O'Higgins (2003: 37) presents a clear-sighted analysis that acknowledges the probable male composition of the *HHD* but also discerns historical evidence of women's cultic activity in the text.

[86] Nixon 1995: 88–92.

[87] See Foley (1993: 107–12) on how the myth of Persephone treats marriage as a symbolic death of a girl's social identity, and how certain aspects of Persephone's time in the underworld mirror the nuptial rites of antiquity (for example, eating the pomegranate seeds, which resembles an Athenian marriage custom).

Much scholarly energy has been invested in understanding the descent of Persephone in terms of harvest customs. To be sure, in antiquity Demeter and Korē were connected with agriculture; perhaps they are different manifestations of the same goddess, for that matter. The exact correspondence with fertility is somewhat oblique, however, although contemporary versions of the myth make a rather simplistic equation between Persephone's disappearance and her subsequent reunion with Demeter in terms of the seasons; it is winter when she is gone and spring when she returns.[88] But it is more likely that for ancient Greek society the goddess's return from the underworld had a different significance. Based on the Mediterranean agricultural cycle, and the timing of the festivals associated with Demeter and Persephone in the autumn, scholars conclude that Persephone's time with Hades corresponds to summer months, when seeds would be stored underground.[89] Her association with both fertility and the realm of Hades may be connected to the recurring idea of the underworld as a type of womb, an analogy that will be evident at several points in this book. Persephone's reunion with Demeter, celebrated not only in the Eleusinian Mysteries, but also during Greek women's autumnal festival of the Thesmophoria, supports conceptual connections between women and fertility. But, while the festival no doubt had agricultural origins, it also celebrated the community of women, and gave mothers and daughters separated by marriage opportunities to reconnect temporarily. Although the story of Persephone is a metaphor for marriage and fertility, her reunion with Demeter is the backdrop for a ritual occasion when mothers and daughters spent time together at the festival.

Furthermore, we do need to recognize that the depiction of Persephone in this poem emphasizes her passivity, yet it is notable that she willingly eats the three pomegranate seeds that Hades gives her, and that he offers her specific honors in the underworld. She is not dissatisfied with this arrangement, and thus Demeter's negotiations and threats cannot achieve a complete reversal of her daughter's marriage; Persephone will descend and return forever. Finally, we must also acknowledge that the *Hymn* is one version of a story created for a specific context, although its exact purpose may be obscure. The maiden goddess may lack agency in this version, but

[88] Foley 1993: 58–9.

[89] Plutarch (*de Isis et Osiris* 70) connects Persephone's descent to both the disappearance of fruit and the storing of seed corn.

there is an abundance of evidence, for example the gold lamellae mentioned above, that give a different picture of a powerful chthonic deity whom souls must supplicate when they reach their final destination.[90] In the *Odyssey*, Hades is her domain; according to Circe she allows Tiresias to remain sentient, and sends the heroines to Odysseus; he leaves when he fears that Persephone might send the Gorgon. Indeed in the tales told by Vergil and Ovid it is Persephone whom Orpheus must convince to let his wife come back to earth. In Hades Persephone has power.

Despite her authority as the queen of the underworld according to the myths of antiquity, it is the story of her abduction that has furnished materials for contemporary retellings of the Persephone myth. The story has become increasingly popular since the 1777 discovery of a medieval manuscript of the *Hymn*.[91] Scholars have catalogued a wide range of adaptations of the story of Persephone's rape. Helene Foley surveys the popularity of the theme in poetry from the Victorian period to the present, including Margaret Atwood's "Double Persephone." Andrew Radford examines its resonance in late nineteenth- and early twentieth-century fiction such as Thomas Hardy's *Tess of the D'Urbervilles* (1891), and D.H. Lawrence's *The Lost Girl* (1921). According to Radford's thesis, these popular novels negotiate a more woman-centered approach to classical antiquity initiated by the late nineteenth-century scholarship of Jane Harrison and the Cambridge ritualists, who argued for close connections between myth and ritual, and the importance of a female element in both. Holly Virginia Blackford's monograph (*The Myth of Persephone in Girls' Fantasy Literature*, 2012), which begins with an excellent overview of the Persephone story's influence on poetry, opera, drama, art, and other cultural products since the eighteenth century, surveys how the *Hymn to Demeter* shapes children's fantasy literature of the past century. She notes in particular how Persephone's abduction can be used as a symbol for the psychic individuation of a girl

[90] The syncretism of mystery cults results in a conflation of Orphic and Eleusinian aspects, thus Orphic ritual texts absorb elements of the Persephone myth.

[91] The discovery in Moscow is credited to Christian Friedrich Matthaei. Schwab (2016: 346–7) describes it as "one of the most valuable documents for the reconstruction of ancient Greek religion," especially the Eleusinian Mysteries. He argues that its reception by a German commentator (who translated it into Latin) bears some evidence that he was influenced by his theory of the influence of Eastern mysticism on Greek religion and identifies it as the song of a priest in honor of the Eleusinian Mysteries.

from her mother.[92] These are only a few examples among many, but they illustrate how deeply the Persephone narrative has seeped into countless crevices of contemporary culture, from sophisticated poetry and novels to popular children's fiction.

The myth of Persephone's marriage to Hades is considerably different from the heroic exploits of Odysseus, Heracles, and Aeneas, although it does address emotional issues familiar from the myth of Orpheus. Significantly, however, the Greek and Roman versions of Persephone's story do not elaborate on her point of view, nor do they provide the physical details of the underworld's occupants or geography, or stage a series of trials for the young woman to accomplish. Nonetheless these missing ingredients do appear in recent versions of her story. So before proceeding to an exploration of contemporary descent adaptations, let us take stock of elements and themes that serve as signposts of the trip to the netherworld.

Elements of the Underworld Narrative

When the poet Tibullus, a contemporary of Vergil, melodramatically imagines his own death, he offers a sixty-five line description of the underworld (1.3.57–82) to which he will descend. It is a concise iteration of the Vergilian Dis albeit in a different order, starting with the perfumed fields of Elysium populated with youths and maidens, and ending with the depths of Tartarus filled with the familiar monsters and sinners: Tisiphone the Fury, Cerberus, Ixion, Tantalus, and (wishes the poet) anyone who spurned his love. The topography and denizens of Hades were by now well established and have survived in some form ever since. They can be deployed in ways that would be meaningful to particular storytellers and audiences, for irony (for example, Tibullus), or ideology (as in Vergil's *Aeneid*). The narrative context in which a catabasis occurs will always affect its meaning, whether it is a deliberate citation of a classical predecessor, but in a different genre like that of Tibullus, or changes the time and place of the adaptation, as most of the authors that we examine do.[93]

[92] Foley 1993: 97–103 and 150–69; Radford 2007; Blackford 2012. For further discussion of the influence of the Persephone myth see Richardson 1974: 68–86.

[93] Hutcheon (2012: 142–3) outlines the "vastness of context" in her work on adaptation by discussing the effect of a change in material, and various elements of presentation and reception.

Stories about the kingdom of the dead are a special kind of adaption since they can advertise an author's cultural capital to intimate membership in an elite poetic lineage, but the hereafter is usually a reflection of the here and now, as the following chapters will demonstrate.

The list below is a very general summation of the themes of descent myths, but *caveat lector*: our contemporary authors seldom adapt only one ancient prototype. It is typical of postmodern poetics to present a hybridized version of culture that, in terms of underworld narratives, will position different ancient versions against one another as a comment on authenticity, cultural hegemony, and the role of marginalized genres or peoples in the literary tradition. The following elements, when they show up—and not every story will have every theme—will often destabilize the very traditions that they evoke.[94]

1) An extraordinary individual takes a journey, often passing through a special portal, a secret door in a wall, a Devil's mouth entrance to a funhouse, a path into a forest, across or down a river, down a cellar or a hole in the earth, for the purpose of gaining knowledge or bringing back someone or something from a version of Hades.
2) A descent to the underworld, or a consultation with ghosts, grants wisdom, insight, or knowledge of the future from a mentor figure in the underworld. The traveler may have assistance, corresponding to the instructions of Circe or the Sibyl, before, and even during the trip.
3) The journey is usually arduous—despite Vergil's claim (*facilis descensus Averno*, *Aen*.6.128) that it is easy—often in a westward direction (for example from Troy to Italy, or from India to America). Bravery, therefore, is the defining feature of the mortal who makes the voyage.[95] The quality is also essential because the underworld can be a place of terrors, including hybrid monsters, snakes, gorgons and other female demons.[96]

[94] Readers can also consult Falconer (2005: 43) and Calvo Martínez (2000: 67–78) for their lists of elements in the catabatic narrative.

[95] Santamaría Álvarez (2015: 118–19) discusses the important requirement of a catabatic hero's bravery, and provides further examples of ancient sources that identify the terrors of the underworld.

[96] A fragmentary text of Plutarch (fr. 178 Sandbach) purports to describe the soul's experience as it enters the realm of the dead and sees *ta deina panta* ("all the dreadful things") therein. According to the Greek travel writer Pausanias (10.28.7), these were described in the *Nostoi* and *Minyas*, two Greek poems that (in addition to the *Odyssey*) featured a catabasis; see Horsfall (2013: 254) for problems associated with dating the *Minyas*, although he tentatively suggests the fifth century BCE.

4) Hades is vast, populated by innumerable souls, who live in a community often with distinct regions.[97] It is presided over by a king (called Hades by the Greeks, Pluto or Dis by the Romans) and/or a queen of the dead (usually some variant of Persephone), and naturally an extensive community of souls who dwell together in a city or a house.
5) The underworld is associated with the past, since visitors may see members of their own family, deceased comrades, historical and mythical figures, but it also contains information about the future.
6) A visit to Hades changes the individual who succeeds in returning above ground. Odysseus becomes a new type of hero whose survival depends on telling stories. Heracles is inducted into the Eleusinian mysteries; Aeneas transforms from refugee to ancestor of the first Roman imperial dynasty; Orpheus becomes the figurehead of a cult; Persephone transitions to marriage. Contemporary analogues include writers such as John Barth and Elena Ferrante, who use the *Nekyia* to authenticate their metamorphosis into adult authors; immigrant narratives by Amy Bloom and Salman Rushdie that configure their passage to America as either an ascent or descent; coming-of-age stories, including Toni Morrison's *Song of Solomon*.
7) Hades is a literary space, constructed from intertextual building blocks, alluding to other versions of itself, renewed by the hero who succeeds in leaving.

For at least the past 3000 years literature has imagined the underworld as a repository of narrative traditions. The selection of material in the following chapters focuses on the past fifty years of culture, a thin slice of history, but an era of great changes in society, including shifts in geopolitics, innovations in technology, and a fluctuating sense of global citizenship and personal identities. And yet just as it always has, the idea of a spectral world that exists parallel to our own, one that can be accessed through our dreams and imagination, holds a special appeal for the seeker of wisdom.

[97] The notion of Hades as a vast city is found in Mesopotamian literature. West (1997: 153) notes that Irkalla, ruled by Ereshkigal, means "great city."

2

The Ghost of the Father

Spirits of the Postmodern

ad genitorem imas Erebi descendit ad umbras.
He descends to the deepest shadows of Erebus to seek his father.

(*Aeneid* 6.404)

An intertextual Hades offers provocative opportunities for postmodern authors John Barth and Neil Gaiman to confront their literary paternity in fiction that symbolically stages a conflict between fathers and sons. Such are the possibilities of a tradition in which the underworld exists, after millennia of imaginary visits, as a nexus of literary allusions. To descend into it is to enter the realm of story, and a successful return guarantees that the visitor will have a story to tell. Its chthonic spaces produce that consummate spinner of tales, Odysseus, whose bardic abilities, showcased by the account of his descent, hold his Phaeacian audience in such a grip that they insist on staying awake to hear it. The Homeric episode has engendered a convention by which subsequent poets and writers lay claim to the *Nekyia* in order to authenticate their position in a poetic lineage.[1] In Dante's Limbo, modeled on Vergil's Elysium (where Aeneas meets his father), five canonical poets of antiquity, including Homer, Vergil and Ovid, legitimize Dante as the sixth member in their "bella scula" (*Inf.* 4.94–102).[2] The trope survives in modernist poetry six centuries later. In 1930 Ezra Pound began his *Draft of XXX Cantos* (now the introduction to *The Cantos*) with an adaptation

[1] Hardie (2010: 184), for example, remarks on how Spenser uses the underworld as "a resource for poetic traditions and makings."

[2] Jacoff (2010: 151) discusses how Dante thus "stages his legitimization by the great poets of antiquity."

of *Odyssey* 11; the consultation with Tiresias segues into Aeneas' golden bough to create a sense of continuity that by association extends to Pound.[3] By foregrounding and incorporating the *Nekyia* his poetry advertises an affiliation with the epic tradition consonant with the physical properties of the first editions of *The Cantos*. Produced in the manner of an illuminated medieval manuscript, the book is implicated in "a tradition of monumental codices," as Michael Thurston observes, which "materially enact the poetics of transmission that is the poem's chief innovation and achievement."[4] As the first section of this chapter argues, Barth's "Lost in the Funhouse," the central story in his 1968 work of the same title, revisits the cliché of the necromantic authentication of an author to suggest that it is both exhausted and infinitely renewable.

Gaiman's *The Sandman* (1989–93) is indebted to another ancient underworld tradition that aligns the *descensus ad infernos* with cultural production. Because the skills of Orpheus open the gates of Hell, he represents the pinnacle of artistic achievement. His status in the mythopoetic universe needs no further evidence, but it is worth noting that Ovid cleverly constructs his tale so that the stories of *Metamorphoses* 10 are composed and sung by Orpheus after his descent, suggesting that his underworld experience (like that of Odysseus) honed his artistry even further. The second section of this chapter explores how Gaiman deploys this myth against the backdrop of Milton's *Paradise Lost* so that the fiction of a journey to the kingdom of the dead becomes a catalyst for an author's engagement with his literary patriline.

Barth's self-reflexive parody and Gaiman's dark fantasy series may seem an unlikely pairing: a collection of fiction directed at the literati, and a popular comic book consumed by mass audiences. Nonetheless their texts are similarly haunted by the ghosts of authorial forefathers whom both writers confront with alternating gestures of homage and rebellion. In a work that typifies the ironic stance of postmodernism, Barth offers a critique of modernist literature by stepping over it and looking back to its Homeric rootstock. Gaiman's series makes a bold

[3] An earlier version (1917) of Pound's *Nekyia* occurs in *Three Cantos* 3. Thurston (2009: 23–30) considers the effect of the *Nekyia* (i.e. the invocation of the spirit of Tiresias) according to its variable positions in the *Cantos* as they underwent revision.

[4] Thurston (2009: 30) comments on the illustrated, expensively produced, early editions of *The Cantos*.

break from the traditional comic book format, and in the process recalibrates cultural hierarchies by citing such respected predecessors as Vergil and Milton. Provocatively, playfully, and with no small degree of polemicism, these two authors exemplify postmodernism's delight in blurring distinctions between high and low culture. Insinuating an ancient text beneath the surface of their work, they create the sense of a palimpsest—the term coopted by Gérard Genette for literature in the "second degree"—and by implication a conflict between texts, a sense of dissonance or disorientation.[5] In the case of our two authors those subterranean texts include the catabatic stories of classical poetry in addition to the traditions they have engendered. The effect is what Linda Hutcheon, in *The Politics of Postmodernism*, describes as:

> [the] paradoxical postmodernism of complicity and critique . . . that at once inscribes and subverts the conventions and ideologies of the dominant cultural and social forces of the twentieth-century western world.[6]

Barth and Gaiman epitomize Hutcheon's concept of the "presence of the past," that goes beyond nostalgia for older literary models to work "within the very system [they] seek to subvert."[7] Both writers orchestrate their acts of subversion with a blend of high and low culture that disputes the notion of authority, authenticity, and literary hierarchies. Their programs of "complicity and critique" call into question the self-validating literary personae of modernist giants, among other cultural icons. Pound declares his membership in this elite tradition of poetic necromancy by identifying with Odysseus throughout *The Cantos*, although as Lillian Feder notes he repeats his descent in the "Hell Cantos" (XIV to XV), surpassing even Odysseus who descends only once.[8] At the center of *The Waste Land* T. S. Eliot situates the figure of Tiresias and, as Thurston notes, "establishes and justifies a new poetic project built upon an avowed interdependence with the literary tradition."[9] Sarah Kennedy, in her sensitive reading of Eliot's engagement with both Homer and Pound, writes of, "the repeated symbiotic encounters with ghosts who themselves are inhabited by an older

[5] Genette's *Palimpsests* (1997) includes a study of Barth's *Lost in the Funhouse.*

[6] Hutcheon 1989: 11. [7] Hutcheon 1988: 4.

[8] Feder (1971: 107–21); see further Thurston's analysis (2009: 55–85) of Pound's "Hell Cantos" as a form of cultural critique and their influence on subsequent poets.

[9] Thurston 2009: 35.

revenant speech."[10] The postmodern author, I shall argue, questions these signifiers of cultural authentication by disturbing a sense of history and poetic lineage.[11]

Not every poet has taken this tradition seriously. In *The Culex*, a poem attributed to Vergil (probably incorrectly), a mosquito, appearing in a dream to the shepherd who killed it, recounts its heroic voyage to the lower world.[12] The poet takes advantage of readers' familiarity with epic underworld adventures to sustain his amusing conceit, but Barth thrusts his barb more deeply. His parodic Hades, a tacky amusement park, is a wry caricature, but through it Barth specifically reassesses the tradition of a consecration of an author. He refashions the catabasis by setting it in a lower cultural register, and has it perform the same metafictional tasks that it did in the Odyssean *Nekyia*—to reveal how a storyteller comes into being—but he also suggests that modernists have rendered the convention banal. A symmetrical process takes place in Gaiman's *Sandman* series, which elevates the comic book to high art by citing the catabatic tradition from Vergil to Milton as part of an elaborate reflection on the production of narrative, but also contests the notion of the linear continuity of literary history. Yet as both authors understand, the trip to the netherworld offers a lexicon of well-established symbols linked to the concept of cultural memory and narratorial power. That lineage begins with Homer borrowing from Near Eastern traditions and pre-existing tales of the descent of Heracles; Vergil combines Homeric elements with diverse philosophic and literary catabatic models; Dante and Milton reinterpret a classically inspired underworld as a Christian Hell; Gaiman borrows from them all, and then some. Literary underworlds both past and present are formed by citation and recombination to produce something fresh and vigorous from the realm of death, but this new growth seems to be of a different order.[13]

[10] Kennedy 2018: 219.

[11] Cf. Hutcheon (1988: 11), "When Eliot recalled Dante or Virgil in *The Waste Land,* one sensed a kind of wishful call to continuity beneath the fragmented echoing. It is precisely this that is contested in postmodern parody where it is often ironic discontinuity that is revealed at the heart of continuity, difference at the heart of similarity."

[12] Barrett (1970) argues that *The Culex* is Vergil's early work, in which he rehearses the themes of the descent before he wrote *Aeneid* 6, but the prevailing view ascribes it to a later poet. See further Seelentag (2012). Other parodies of descents, i.e. by Aristophanes, Lucian, and the Elizabethan satirist Maurice Arthur, are mentioned in my Introduction.

[13] A defining feature of postmodern culture is the use of bricolage to create art from preformed material generating new meanings by the assemblage. Ulmer divides the process

The urgency of these radical new poetics seems to burst forth from the formal restrictions of the past; the effect is one of discontinuity and fragmentation. Patricia Waugh has identified this characteristic of postmodernism: "Either it sees the world fragmenting or it sets out to discover modes which will fracture and dissolve old and supposedly exhausted unities."[14] In accord with this aesthetic, Barth's volume of fourteen pieces of fiction, as Max Schulz submits, presents itself as "a novel pretending to be a book of short stories."[15] Thematic links and recurring characters contribute to the overarching suggestion of a gradual disintegration of authorial identity, quite the opposite of the authentication of a powerful literary persona established by Pound and Eliot. Fragmentation is also the dominant aesthetic of Gaiman's treatment of the Orphic descent in his *Sandman* comic books. Obviously the graphic novel or comic is by its very nature a fragmented form; its panels, in the words of Scott McCloud, "fracture both time and space, offering a jagged, staccato rhythm of unconnected moments."[16] *The Sandman* accentuates this effect with a range of different artistic styles throughout each volume, thereby dissolving the notion of a single creator.[17] Its borrowings from canonical literature produce a montage that is both a tribute to tradition and a challenge to its prestigious status. The descent myth is woven through the principal narrative of the series, which traces the trials and character development of its protagonist Morpheus, the lord of dreams and embodiment of stories who, like his son Orpheus, also visits the underworld. In order to re-master the myth Gaiman breaks the Orphic narrative apart so that it occurs in different stories within a single volume, and also throughout different volumes. Like Orpheus himself, the tale of his life is dismembered and scattered in a kind of literary sparagmos.

into four distinct categories: decoupage (or severing), "preformed extant messages or materials"; assemblage (montage), which can produce a discontinuity or heterogeneity; collage is the transfer of materials from one context to another; and "montage" is the presentation of this assortment of material through new organization or arrangement. (adapted from Ulmer 1985: 82).

[14] Waugh 1992: 190; Donald Barthelme, famous for his short stories and often associated with postmodernism, had the narrator of one of his stories state that, "Fragments are the only form I trust" ("See the Moon?" 1964).

[15] Schulz 1984: 404. [16] McCloud 1993: 67.

[17] Gaiman's artistic team included multiple comic artists and writers, most prominently Sam Kieth and Mark Dringenberg.

By making his protagonist Morpheus the father of Orpheus, Gaiman engages with issues of literary paternity on several levels. His own revision of the story is an act of defiance against the established literary elite, reflected by the contentious relationship between Orpheus, a mythic poet, and his father, Morpheus, aka Sandman, both of whom participate in a *descensus ad infernos*. Orpheus' visit to Hades defies the authority of his father, just as Gaiman's telling of it defies the age-old tale that engendered his version. In a similar vein Barth also rebels against his literary forefathers, including James Joyce, and throughout *Lost in the Funhouse* he challenges the paradigms of twentieth-century novels. Just as Aeneas descends to the deep shadows of Erebus to find his father, the incipient author Ambrose Mensch, Barth's alter ego in the title story, discovers an old man at the center of his underworld, although the outcome is very different from what we might expect. An engagement with fathers and father-figures in both these postmodern tales, the following discussion argues, acknowledges the tradition in which the hero visits Hades to come in contact with an ancient literary genealogy, but also suggests a creative autonomy that supplants that convention. To accomplish this, each author deploys techniques of self-reflexivity, narrative fragmentation, and a blending of high and low culture, but most importantly he thematizes issues of paternity and filial discord to suggest a productive displacement of literary influence.

Finding the Way in John Barth's Underworld

Lost in the Funhouse represents Barth's response to what he perceived as the tired forms of modernist fiction which gained hold in the late nineteenth century as a reaction against a Victorian aesthetic and the proliferation of popular literature; accordingly modernism makes sharp distinctions between high and low culture. Putting theory into practice Barth's fifth novel, if we can call it that, follows his influential essay in *The Atlantic Monthly*, "The Literature of Exhaustion," that critiqued the "the used-upness of certain forms," especially in modernist fiction with its plot and character based narratives, and commended the virtuosity of writers such as Jorges Luis Borges.[18] In a later essay, "The Literature of

[18] Barth (1967: 29–30) specifically extols *Labyrinths* (1962), a collection of short stories by Borges.

Replenishment," Barth clarifies some of his criteria. He gives as an example the Italian writer Italo Calvino's *Cosmicomics* (originally published in 1964), a series of fables based on scientific knowledge such as cosmology and evolution, but drawing on motifs from the Italian Renaissance writer Boccaccio. *Lost in the Funhouse* claims to offer this new form of fiction, which is conspicuously rooted in the literature the past—as the following discussion demonstrates, it bears a structural similarity to the *Odyssey*—but uses humor, parody, irony, and a mixture of mythic and twentieth-century scenarios to engage and entertain the reader. Although not every reader will get the esoteric allusions to its ancient prototypes, it is impossible to ignore the frequent interventions by a narrator who insists on keeping us aware of his control. Amusingly, however, the text seems to slide out of his grasp in the eponymous central tale, so that we are led through a maze of narratorial reflections corresponding to a labyrinthine funhouse.

Barth parodies Joyce's stream of consciousness style in *Ulysses* (1904), an exemplar of high modernist fiction, but at the same time he reaches back to a much deeper past than the early twentieth century as if to assert a direct link with Homeric epic.[19] To establish this connection, an "Author's Note" tells the reader that the compilation is derived from the idea of the Greek epic cycle, a collection of narrative poems dealing with the Trojan War that circulated in antiquity. We are instructed to read the stories that follow as a connected series. Yet while he evokes a Homeric precedent throughout, the author also wants to revolutionize storytelling. The full title, *Lost in the Funhouse: Fiction for Print, Tape, Live Voice*, suggests new forms of media for fiction, at least in the late 1960s context. More importantly the collection is an innovation in the presentation of a narrative; intensely self-reflexive, ironically intertextual, and with fragmented forms that disrupt any illusion of reality and closure, it gleefully defies the standards of modernism.

Taking account of these polemics and innovations, the first part of the following discussion identifies the thematic strands that lead to Barth's version of the trip to Hades, and charts a narrative momentum driven by ancient poetry, especially Homer's *Odyssey*. In the second part of my analysis I explore how the author's experience in the infernal abyss, the

[19] McHale notes (1992: 42–55, with appropriate bibliography) that *Ulysses* is often cited as an example of High Modernism.

destination ordained by the Homeric paradigm, suggests the initiation of an author, but also upends that tradition in the most fitting way possible for "a prime mover of postmodernism."[20]

The birth of the author

Three of the stories in the first half of the book feature the childhood of an author-to-be, Ambrose Mensch, although his presence is felt in other tales where he is not named. To fully appreciate his metaphorical journey to the underworld, we will survey the installments treating his youth, which collectively form a *Künstlerroman*, an account of the maturation of an author or artist. There is an allusion here to Joyce's alter ego Stephen Dedalus, protagonist of *A Portrait of the Artist as a Young Man* (1916) and a character in Joyce's *Ulysses* (1922), where he stands in as Telemachus to Leopold Bloom's Odysseus. Barth refers to this connection by casting Ambrose, the future author, as an Odysseus figure, and by repeating certain phrases and perceptions from Joyce.[21] Ambrose's epiphany occurs in "Lost in the Funhouse," the centerpiece of the collection, corresponding to the *Nekyia's* position in the epic poem; like Odysseus he emerges as a storyteller in a revised portrait of the artist as a young man. As Schulz observes, this sequence is an "act of literary renewal" that grafts "local realism to postmodernist metafiction using Greek mythology as the common transplant."[22] In contrast to Joyce, however, Barth uses myth not as a structural foundation, but rather as a form of history. For example, Ambrose is directly connected

[20] Reilly (2000: 589) uses the term in his preface to an interview in which Barth acknowledges his status in the movement but now questions what exactly the term means. It seems somehow very apt that a novelist who is heralded for his contribution to postmodernism should question its existence. It should be noted that it is difficult to determine when postmodernist literature is supposed to have begun: using the metaphor of Orpheus' dismemberment and regeneration, Hassan (1971) argues that its roots were in changes in culture and thought that began in the eighteenth century. McHale (1987: 4–7) begins his book on *Postmodernist Fiction* with a discussion of the problematics of the term.

[21] Hindon (1973: 108) comments on"the recycling of Joycean/Homeric materials" and the Daedalus-labyrinth motif in "Night-Sea Journey," "Lost in the Funhouse," "Echo," and "Menelaiad." For a discussion of the *Nekyia* (and *Aeneid* 6) theme in Joyce's *Ulysses* (a funeral and an encounter in a cemetery in episode 6) see Platthaus (2004: 142–55).

[22] Schulz (1984: 406): "Whereas Joyce and his generation of writers had mistakenly added ancient myth as a layer to their stories in the hopes of thereby ordering and enriching their experience of immediate reality with an overlay of the universal, Barth contends rather that myth is the direct reflection of reality and therefore the ongoing product of the writer's attention to 'actual people and events'."

to a Homeric bard whose story ends the collection and whose water-borne message reaches the youth on the shores of New Jersey some 3000 years later.

The first pages of the book herald a new form of intertextual mythologizing with a visual pun that concretizes the opening lines of the *Odyssey*: *ἄνδρα μοι ἔννεπε, μοῦσα, πολύτροπον* ("Tell me Muse of the man of many twists and turns," *Od.* 1.1). "Frame-tale" consists of a band at the edge of two pages that reads, "Once upon a time there was a story which began"; beside it are instructions to twist the paper and join the ends to form a Möbius strip. The gimmick is a simple one, suggesting that storytelling is a cyclic activity, full of twists and turns and infinite retellings.[23] It also signifies the narrative structure of Barth's book of tales, and of its central story, "Lost in the Funhouse," which always seems to be turning in on itself, its tail in its mouth, so to speak. In this respect, too, "Frame Tale" alludes to the complex structure of the *Odyssey*, with its embedded stories and interwoven narratives, and of course it refers to the hero of the tale, a man "of many twists and turns" (*polytropos*) who is also a storyteller.

What Barth offers here is "an ontogeny of the book and a phylogeny of Western fiction," to cite Schulz again.[24] The second story-chapter is another case in point: "Night-sea Journey" is a miniature *Apologia*, with the role of Odysseus assumed by a self-reflexive sperm, presumably one half of the Ambrose-zygote, who is aware that he is "transmitting the heritage" (3–4), but has a somewhat defiant streak.[25] The sperm, prone to existential musings, considers the possibility of a Father god responsible for his presence, a speculation with both biological and literary implications. He scoffs at the possibility of a not-He, a Her towards whom he and all his companions (or rival suitors?) are swimming. Like Odysseus he will be the only one to survive, drawn inexorably towards the egg, a conflation of Penelope and the irresistible Sirens. This seminal narrator genetically coded, as it were, with a narrative tradition, becomes

[23] Although no Muse is mentioned explicitly in "Frame Tale," they turn up in the other stories; for example, as Thalia (the Muse of Comedy), the lover of a set of Siamese twins, one of whom pens a querulous letter in the sixth story, "Petition." Thalia is a contortionist in a circus, a fitting Muse for Barth, and the personification of his Möbius-like story.

[24] Schulz 1984: 408.

[25] As Schulz notes (1984: 404), the sperm-narrator figures as the latest in a long line of quest heroes.

Ambrose, whose story is told in three other sections of the collection, all of which manifest their Odyssean DNA. For the moment the sperm, his existence about to be subsumed by the egg, seems to speak to us from a position just outside the story immediately prior to the conception of Ambrose and the loss of the sperm's individuality as he makes his passage through a "tunnel of love," a version of which Ambrose himself will encounter in the funhouse.

The third story in the collection, "Ambrose His Mark," deals with the naming of the infant author-to-be, whose recollections include life within his mother's womb, and at her breast, a parody of Joycean realism.[26] Ambrose's naming also alludes to important motifs of (re)birth and naming in the *Odyssey.* Like Odysseus at several points in the epic, Ambrose is nameless: affectionately called *Honig,* or Honey, by his family, the baby remains informally named for months after his birth. As a christening is in progress at a nearby church, a swarm of bees lights on a bee-shaped birthmark on his head and is then herded into his grandfather's hive. Thenceforth he is Ambrose, after the saint, who had a similar visitation, but the name is prophetically significant: bees and honey are associated with the Muses and poetry throughout Greek literature, and there is a decidedly Alexandrian tone to the allusion here.[27] The bee motif might also refer to the Aristaeus episode in Vergil's *Fourth Georgic* with its allusions to *Odyssey* 4, part of which informs a later story in the collection, "The Menelaid." Like Aristaeus (*G.* 4. 453–527), Ambrose's grandfather suffered a collapse of his hive, which regenerates in the context of ritual, the bugonia (a peculiar rite performed over a dead heifer) for Aristaeus, and the christening for his Barthian counterpart.[28] The story of Ambrose's naming thus establishes contiguity with the "Menelaiad," in which Menelaus recounts his hallucinatory experience with ambrosia (based on an episode in *Odyssey* 4). In Barth's version Menelaus' account of his capture of Proteus is surrounded

[26] For example, Joyce replicates the development of Stephen Dedalus' consciousness from infancy to his early adulthood.

[27] The learned Alexandrian or Hellenistic poets, discussed briefly in the previous chapter, flourished in the period between the death of Alexander the Great in 323 BCE and the mid-first century CE. An example of the equation of bees and honey with poetry can be found in Callimachus *Aetia* fr. 1, 21–8 Pf. For further examples and discussion see Fletcher 2002: 70 and Petridou 2016: 82–3.

[28] Since water is another symbol for poetry in Hellenistic literature, this adds yet another layer of allusion to the Ambrose stories, which also use the ocean as a symbol for literature.

by nine sets of quotation marks at one point, acknowledging a long heritage of citationality, and also the embedded narration of *Odyssey* 4. Menelaus' tale is a perfect metonym of Barth's protean narrative, and a vehicle for a meditation on the nature of the authorial voice.[29] This complicated network of recondite allusions, both internal (other stories in the collection) and external (Homer's *Odyssey* and Vergil's *Georgics*) suggests that the entire collection can be cross-referenced in many ways, creating a Möbius-like narration, and an endless continuum of stories.

The tale of Ambrose's naming is one component of a shape-shifting enterprise that mutates from generation (and genre) to generation. Rebirth or regeneration, and a change from one state to another are the thematic links of the Ambrose stories, but also reflect the central catabatic chapter, suggestive of the social rebirth implicit in descent myths, and thus the final phase in Ambrose's transformation. This initiatory theme is presaged in the fifth story, "Water·message," which also connects with the final story in the collection, "Anonymiad," told in the voice of an *Odyssean* bard. Ambrose, now a young lad, endures his daily trips home from school fraught with trials including dogs and social misfits whom he nicknames Scylla and Charybdis, the sea monsters that Odysseus must elude after his underworld encounter, and the title of an episode in Joyce's *Ulysses*. Portentously, Ambrose finds a mysterious message on the ocean shore, a letter in a bottle, whose text has been washed away, except for its salutation, "To Whom It May Concern," and valediction, "Yours Truly." The faded epistle beckons Ambrose to his position in an authorial lineage, although that tradition is apparently much diluted, or to use Barth's terminology "used up." The final story, "Anonymiad," reveals who has been casting messages into the sea: the bard left behind by Agamemnon to watch over his wife Clytemnestra when he left for the Trojan War, but who was sent to a desert isle by her lover Aegisthus (*Od.* 3. 267–71). Thus Ambrose is materially connected to an ancient, nameless poet, a figure from Homer's *Odyssey*, who seems

[29] In *Odyssey* 4, the words of Proteus are embedded in Menelaus' narration to Telemachus, which is recounted by the Homeric narrator. In Barth's "Menelaiad" the center of the story is the word "Love"—Helen's reason for being with Menelaus. Genette (1997: 342) suggests that Barth's "Menelaiad", which he describes as a "Russian doll of a narrative," is a nod to the archaic Greek lyric poet Steisichorus' palinode, which recounts that Helen did not go to Troy because she loved Menelaus. McHale (1987: 114) cites "Menelaiad" as a tour de force of the "recursively nested narrative" favored by postmodern writers.

to summon the boy to his authorial destiny. And therein lies an ontological paradox. The elision of narrative levels between Ambrose on the twentieth-century Jersey shore, a seemingly realistic setting, and a character from the fiction of the past, encapsulates what Brian McHale argues is the essence of postmodern fiction, setting it apart from realist fiction with its boundaries between the possible and impossible.[30]

Homeric parallels in "Water-message" connect Ambrose to this ancient literary past as well, although the connection with the ancient bard gives a different cast to the metaphors and similes in which, for example, he is "Odysseus steering under anvil clouds" (45) committing feats of daring. "Water-message" reveals that there is something special about Ambrose, beckoned to the ocean of literature directly by a voice from the past that seems to circumvent a tradition of authorial lineage. A sense of cultural genealogy, already implied by the seminal motif of "Night-sea Journey," is reaffirmed in "Anomymiad," whose narrator is on intimate terms with the Muses, nine amphorae that he fills with semen/texts. The story and the book end at noon (an auspicious time in Alexandrian poetry) when the bard casts his "last lay," the amphora Calliope (the muse of epic poetry) now filled with his final text, into the sea. An ocean of textual genealogies, or as the anonymous bard puts it a sea "a-clink with literature" (196), awaits Ambrose whose biography implies the investiture of the poet, a convention in Alexandrian literature. Taking their cue from Hesiod, who recounts his inauguration by the Muses, the Alexandrian poets Theocritus, Callimachus, Vergil, and Propertius all describe an induction into the art of poetry (and so does Dante, as mentioned above); water is a common symbol for this literary baptism.[31] Ambrose's experience on the shore, connecting him with the

[30] The ideas of postmodern recursivity and ontological paradox run through McHale's book, but the phenomenon that I describe here is best expressed by his notion of heterocosms (alternative universes) and possible worlds (1987: 31–3).

[31] The motif of the "consecration of the poet" occurs most prevalently in the Alexandrian poets, whose irony and allusiveness resemble that of Barth. Borrowing from Hesiod, who is visited by the Muses while pasturing sheep on a mountain (*Theogony* 1–34), Theocritus' *Idyll* 7 features a visitation to a herdsman-poet, Simichidas, by an Apollo-like figure at noon (the time of Ambrose's visitation by the bees; see Williams 1971: 137–45). In Vergil's *Eclogue* 6, Linus, son of Apollo, hands the pipes of poetry to Gallus (see Ross 1975: 18–39). Water is a prevalent motif in these poetic consecrations: Callimachus drinks from a fountain of poetry; he delicately avoids attempts at epic, which he admires but likens to an Ocean (*Hymn to Apollo,* I07). Propertius (3.3.51) tastes of the "water of Philetas" (i.e. elegiac poetry, see Luck 1959: 140–4 I).

Homeric bard, suggests as much. Barth is channeling an ancient literary moment here, and its crowning flourish will be that universal coming-of-age symbol, the descent to the underworld, the final stage of this *Künstlerroman*. Not surprisingly it will happen at a place called Ocean City.

The death of the author

By naming himself "Nobody" when he escapes the Cyclops, Odysseus disavows his identity. It is a significant negation, since in essence he will become a nonentity, stripped of his ships, companions, status, and finally even his clothing, when he washes up on the Phaeacian shore where he will tell the story of his wanderings. Some scholars detect elements of rebirth in his sea passage from the island of Calypso to the Phaeacian kingdom; his earlier visit to the underworld thus symbolizes the death of his social identity as a warrior, his Iliadic role.[32] As the previous chapter argued, his most important metamorphosis after the *Nekyia* is into the role of storyteller. It is a notion that Dante embellishes when his poetic self encounters the canonical poets of antiquity who inaugurate him into their distinguished group (*Inf.* 4.100–2), and Pound repeats with his modernist version. Barth is alive to these nuances when he creates a biography for his author-to-be that concludes with a catabatic experience symbolic of rebirth. While the entire collection is imprinted with classical antecedents, the spirit of the *Odyssey* manifests most palpably in its focal story, "Lost in the Funhouse," structured as a trip to the underworld, an event that Falconer has described as forging a sense of self in Western narrative; in this case, however, that visit ultimately shatters any sense of authorial wholeness.[33]

[32] Newton (1984: 5–20) has noted a birth metaphor in the hero's penultimate journey from Ogygia, the island of Calypso, to the shores of Scheria, where he is met by the Phaeacian princess Nausicaa. He likens this to the birth process: a journey through water (another night-sea voyage), in which Odysseus casts off even the clothing he is wearing and, naked as a newborn, falls at the feet of a nubile young woman (Nausicaa) to whom he later says: "You gave me life" (8.466). Cf. Kardulias (2001) who detects an initiatory motif in the same journey. In general, as Segal (2001: 13) remarks, the entire poem "deals recurrently and in many different forms with death and rebirth, and the loss and resumption of identity."

[33] Falconer (2005: 2–3) argues that Dante's journey ("Midway on the journey of our life, I found myself in a dark wood," *Inf.*1.1–2), in which "I" is both personal and archetypal, is the most influential prototype of this concept of catabatic selfhood. As she goes on to say, "Western culture is saturated with the idea of a self being forged out of an infernal journey."

Ambrose Mensch, now an adolescent, accompanies his family to an amusement park in Ocean City, a place-name redolent of the Homeric hero's nautical wanderings, the sperm's night-sea journey as he "transmits the heritage," and the ocean-borne message in a bottle summoning Ambrose to that heritage. His epiphany occurs in a carnivalesque journey through the underworld, a funhouse that is "a place of fear and confusion" (69). The formative interlude in his young life is the culmination of the initiatory motifs of the preceding chapters. Already the youth realizes that he has "antennae" and that "the world winks at him through its objects" (88), but this day, Independence Day, will see him complete the definitive ordeal. At first Ambrose descends under the boardwalk, littered with detritus, where he interrupts a couple having sex, but he will need to descend to even more fetid depths. He imagines a squalid funhouse where predecessors have vomited or defecated, yet where he can be like Ulysses struggling "past obstacle after obstacle" (87). When he enters the funhouse, a garish simulacrum of the underworld, it is through the traditional grim portal, in this case a Devil's mouth, leading to tunnels that wind "around the right part like the snakes on Mercury's caduceus" (83) as if the divine psychopomp had become part of the structure in which Ambrose imagines a "longhaired filthy monster that lived in some cranny" (86). Like other visitants to Hades, Ambrose pays a special price: just as Odysseus offers blood to the shades of the underworld, and Aeneas gives the golden bough to the Cumaean Sybil, Ambrose accidentally but symbolically gives the witchlike ticket-taker a disc with his name stamped on it. His coming of age and new identity are akin to the rebirth of Odysseus, and although the underworld/womb from which Ambrose emerges is materially different, the effect will be the same.

Barth is taking a shot here at Joyce's *Portrait of the Artist*, with its theme of the investiture of the author and the young writer's sense of a great destiny before him.[34] Joyce's Stephen Dedalus, as his name suggests, becomes the creator of a labyrinth, although he is lost in a series of psychological and spiritual mazes until he sees his way clear by formulating an aesthetic theory that fits with his alienation from religion and

[34] Hindon (1973: 108), with the observation that the title story cites Joyce twice (at 71 and 85), describes *Lost in the Funhouse* as "an elaborate parody, revival, and refutation" of *A Portrait of the Artist as a Young Man*.

other social forces. Barth's young author is lost in a physical and a narrative labyrinth; he too will emerge as an author, although of a different kind of fiction. During his wandering through the funhouse (and all its imaginary variations) Ambrose recognizes and accepts his identity as an incipient author, the operator of "a truly astonishing funhouse" (97). His catabasis is woven through a narrative that emphasizes its status as fiction and position in the history of fiction, while subverting a conventional structure with its non-linear sequence. The tale begins with an excursus on the editorial conventions of using italics. Then the flow is interrupted by a technical discussion of metaphors and similes. Five pages into the story, the narrator criticizes himself for giving details of the family car trip when the real topic should be the funhouse. Like other heroes who must travel far to reach Hades, Ambrose endures a long and arduous journey to its portal thanks to the narrator's solipsistic rambling. At one point he acknowledges that the story should be "much farther along" (78), and predicts that "our protagonist" will never get out of the funhouse. With its stops and starts, and musings about the process of telling a story, this tale is really a story about storytelling, exemplifying the characteristic metafictional reflexivity of postmodernism.[35] As Carol Shloss and Khaching Tololyan observe:

> In his [Barth's] hands, the hidden costs of writing assume the status of a plot. Intent on making the invisible visible, Barth ensures that those who are usually absent from a text—writer and reader—are dramatized, and that the processes by which they communicate are exposed.[36]

Mortals can often lose their way in the underworld (which is why the ancients carried directions on gold tablets to the grave), and readers of Ambrose's catabasis experience a similar perplexity. Incomplete sentences pop up and dissolve as the tale lurches from events that precede the entry to the funhouse, to Ambrose's ordeal in it, and back in time to the car ride, with no transitional indicator. Different complications and resolutions

[35] Worthington (2001: 114). On metafiction see Hutcheon (1984: 48) where she identifies Barth as "one of the most overt metafictionists." Waugh's (1984) *Metafiction: The Theory and Practice of Self-Conscious Fiction* also offers a comprehensive survey of metafiction in postmodern fiction and, more broadly, in the history of literature.

[36] Shloss and Tololyan 1981: 64; cf. Hutcheon (1984: 52). Waugh (1984: 95) observes that the persistent references to the conventions of editing and production undermine the validity of the text itself.

appear at random. In one version Ambrose is led out of the tunnel by a little blind girl. In another, he dies of starvation telling stories to himself. Unbeknownst to him, a pretty girl transcribed his every word realizing that here "was one of Western Culture's truly great imaginations, the eloquence of whose suffering would be an inspiration to unnumbered" (96). Countless stories co-exist in Ambrose's imagination, and he is momentarily aware of "all the stories behind all the people on the boardwalk" (87). Thoughts of heritage and ancestors are woven throughout the meandering tale: in its opening paragraphs the narrator dilates on the social and family tradition of visiting the shore, and anticipates future visits in flying "Autogiros" (70). This narrative richness is what happens in Hades, as it did for the Homeric Odysseus, who hears the stories of the dead and emerges as a storyteller. In the postmodern version of this important transformation, however, stories run parallel to each other regardless of continuity; mutually exclusive plot fragments follow one upon the other. The idea that the underworld can be a trove of stories, as it was for Odysseus, has now become a frenzied, out-of-control, illogical sequence of possible endings, a "garden of forking paths."[37] This instantiation of Hades, while adhering to the ancient convention that the underworld is a repository for a multitude of narratives, is also a display of the poetics of postmodernism, from which a new type of writer will ascend.

And ascend he does, finally returning home with his family, but then he dissipates, never to appear as himself in the remainder of the book. Even if he only imagines his own demise, Ambrose undergoes a symbolic death to be reborn as a mature creator himself.

> He wishes he had never entered the funhouse. But he has. Then he wishes he were dead. But he's not. Therefore he will construct funhouses for others and be their secret operator. (97)

Taking over the role of builder and operator of another funhouse, Ambrose will replace a very old "somewhat sad and tired-appearing" man who resembles his grandfather or uncle, and whom he sees operating the gears and machinery. The formulaic mentor at the center of Hades—Tiresias or Anchises—is now reduced to a symbol of "used-upness." Indeed all of Ocean City, Ambrose realizes, is "worn out" (89), a place

[37] The term is Borges', cited in McHale (1987: 107), who gives other examples of this phenomenon in postmodernist fiction.

for fathers and grandfathers. He realizes too that he despises his father, who probably felt the same way about his father "and so on" (86), an infinite regress of filial contempt that blends adolescent recalcitrance with a postmodernist subversion eschewing traditional narrative and literary paternity, also a thing of the past. This, the keystone story of the collection and the last explicit reference to Ambrose, has generated what Brian Edwards reads as: "the postmodernist hero whose task is to discover not answers but uncertainty itself."[38]

Lost in the Funhouse was published at the same time as Roland Barthes' influential essay "The Death of the Author."[39] The coincidence is not lost on Bran Nicol who observes that Barth instantiates Barthes' notion that the author is not a divine creator but comes into being through the agency of the reader.[40] Roland Barthes' revolutionary ideas are tinged with the civil discord and rebellion in France during 1968. Correspondingly John Barth represents a countercultural tendency in American novelists of the 1960s and 70s (for example Kurt Vonnegut, Thomas Pynchon, and Robert Coover), who equated literary realism with official structures of power. In response they produced fiction that was about fiction, and often used myth and fairytale to emphasize the literariness of their work.[41] *Lost in the Funhouse* is typical of this post-modern defiance of realist forefathers. And yet it does not represent a complete break from the past, but acknowledges a genealogy of story-tellers. In "The Literature of Replenishment," Barth acknowledges that:

> My ideal postmodernist author neither merely repudiates nor merely imitates either his twentieth-century modernist parents or his nineteenth-century pre-modernist grandparents.[42]

But the father that Barth claims for his new form of creation is much older than the modernist Joyce. Stories are like sperm, microscopic versions of Odysseus, transmitting their primordial DNA, as "Night-sea journey" has already established, but also existing somewhere beyond history.

[38] Edwards 1985: 272.

[39] The essay was later included (translated into English by Stephen Heath) in Barthes' 1977 anthology, *Image-Music-Text*.

[40] Nicol 2009: 78.

[41] Nicol (2009: 72–98) gives a lucid summary of the political motivations of "US Metafiction."

[42] Barth 1980: 203.

It is by conceptually melding birth with death, and myth with reality that Barth envisions a new status for fiction: one in which the postmodern novelist unseats his immediate literary forefathers, such as Joyce, while aligning himself with an ancient heritage, parodied yet still recognizable. The *Nekyia* thus becomes a locus of contestation where postmodern fiction confronts its Joycean predecessor, a literary forefather whose authority does not hold sway as it does for the chthonic mentor figures in Homer and Vergil. Unlike Tiresias or Anchises, the old man operating the machine has no wisdom to impart. Nor, as Ambrose querulously notes, did his father reveal to him any secrets about the funhouse, and the multitude of stories within its depths. And so rather than claiming membership in the lineage that includes, Dante, Pound, and Eliot, Ambrose will depose an etiolated remnant of that tradition. And he is conspicuously isolated in this chthonic realm; he sees the old man through a crack in the wall; his family seems to have found their way out before him. The hordes of ghosts that converse with or appear to catabants of the past, are replaced by distorted reflections of the traveler in funhouse mirrors. In a new sparsely populated otherworld where fiction of a different order comes into being, where narrative chronology is replaced by fragments of dislocated, contradictory tales—the little girl who guides him out, his death within the funhouse—Barth's Funhouse-Hades animates an ancient tradition of forging a storyteller in a subterranean archive of fiction, but then has that creator disintegrate into the remainder of the volume, his identity effaced by the text that he will create.

The Anxiety of Influence in Neil Gaiman's Underworlds

Barth aspired to a new form of fiction that would reinvigorate what he saw as the moribund condition of the modernist novel. Two decades later Neil Gaiman confronted his own intellectual paternity with a hybrid medium, the comic book, in which several versions of Hell, each citing separate underworlds of the literary past, collectively produce a postmodern bricolage defying boundaries between genres and media.[43] As

[43] A characteristic of postmodern poetics as observed by Hutcheon (1988: 9) is the effacement of "disciplinary boundaries and boundaries between genres."

represented by Gaiman, Milton's Hell is another place entirely than Vergil's, and while literary history can chart a genealogy that links the pagan Hades to the Judeo-Christian Hell, both seem to exist simultaneously, yet independently, in *The Sandman* cosmos. Gaiman upsets the epic conventions of underworld chronologies, epitomized by Pound and Eliot, in which the poet or author is an integer in a constantly developing, but linear, cultural sequence. His disruption is symptomatic of a shift in the concept of time that characterizes postmodern aesthetics. As Frederic Jameson has argued, technological changes in media have played havoc with our sense of historicity; the "random cannibalization of all the styles of the past" bombards us, as in the use of advertising to stimulate consumers' appetites, reflected by a postmodern aesthetic that combines elements from different historical periods in a single piece of art, for example.[44] An examination of the relationship between representations of a descent to a Miltonic Hell and Orpheus' descent to Hades reveals how Gaiman creates a different sense of literary chronology consistent with this aesthetic, a mash-up of historical periods and literary genres challenging the notion of continuity. That impression is amplified, but also complicated, by making the Orpheus myth into a tale about a son rebelling against his father.

And yet the literature of a descent to Hades is tightly bound to notions of history, memory, and tradition. Voyagers to the netherworld encounter both the past and the future, although paradoxically time ceases to exist within these subterranean spaces. The infernal otherworld, as Macdonald sums up, is: "the place of and for eternity, a place outside of time and process."[45] This ahistoricity is evident in the four ditches of Circle Eight of Dante's *Inferno* (24–30) in which a heterogeneous collection of sinners cohabit regardless of their historical existence: a fictional character from the past such as the treacherous Sinon of *Aeneid* 2, who conned the Trojans into accepting the Greeks' wooden horse, is suspended in the same misery as Florentine shysters and counterfeiters

[44] Jameson 1991:71. A good example of the postmodern aesthetic from the visual arts is David Salle's *Muscular Paper*, 1985, a triptych that incorporates Picasso's 1931 sculpture *Bather* and elements from the 1642 painting *The Club Footed Boy* by Jusepe de Ribera. The work critiques the "grand narrative" of art history because it disrupts the idea of linear history. See Hutcheon (1989: 60–5) on postmodernism's critique of "totalizing" narratives that attempt to impose order and continuity on history.

[45] MacDonald 1987: 74.

of Dante's own day.[46] While the dead coexist simultaneously in the afterlife, the tradition of the descent narrative inevitably and paradoxically highlights themes of history and memory; the ancient sages of the underworld give advice that presumes both a past and a future in the terrestrial domain. But, as we have just noted, Barth's carnivalesque construction of that literary space disrupts the sense of linear history, in part by creating an underworld that contains different versions of Ambrose's story. Conventionally narratives unfurl in time; even flashbacks and embedded tales presume a consecutive order of events. But in the postmodern literary cosmos time does not unfold sequentially; for Barth it is a Möbius strip, forever turning in on itself, even possibly inseminating itself. Both Barth and Gaiman disturb narrative temporality by fragmenting storylines, although there are certainly obvious differences in their techniques.

On a purely functional level Barth's Hades is symbolic, parodic, and allusive, while Gaiman's are emphatically explicit with their pictorial depictions of the netherworld. The reader, seduced by the sequential, albeit fragmented, framework of the comic book, expects a logical movement through events, but such anticipation is thwarted in *The Sandman* cosmos. Narrative time, and especially infernal narrative time, exists as separate threads, suggestive of parallel universes, rather than a Möbius strip. Yet both authors acknowledge and incorporate a dominant humanist tradition, and thus a sense of the past, within a new form of fiction that represents a rupture from that tradition and a different future. Modernist poets such as Pound and Eliot, as Thurston recognizes, confront the convention of the necromantic consultation with Tiresias to offer innovations, yet still position themselves within that tradition. As he notes, Pound and Eliot "sought to reinvigorate poetry to a mode of experimentation and invention deeply dependent upon the resources inherent in the literary tradition."[47] By acknowledging their cultural ancestors, the modernist poets situate themselves in time as part of a creative continuum that they will change and yet keep in progress. In what follows I argue that, like Barth, Gaiman contests the logic of this continuum.

[46] As MacDonald (1987: 13) notes, they are "often made to consort in arresting combinations."

[47] Thurston 2009: 23.

Gaiman's *Sandman* series is a disturbance of a different tradition as well. A commercially successful mass media production, it is a game changer in the world of comics: a wide distribution by DC puts it in the mainstream category, but extensive allusions to high prestige literature, and complex storylines were more typical (in the 1990s) of alternative, single-issue, graphic novels.[48] The central figure, Morpheus, also known as Dream, Oneiros, or the Sandman, is one of the Endless, seven siblings who represent various universal forces, including Destruction, Delusion, and Death. The issues feature stand-alone tales, but also a continuous storyline that leads to the death of Morpheus and the end of the series, yet another deviation from comic book conventions. The episodes within individual volumes can be in different visual styles; a stable of accomplished artists adds to the effect of heterogeneity and cultural eclecticism created by the fragmented literary allusions. Some stories are set in a timeless fantasy world, but are just as often in discernible historical periods such as the French Revolution, Augustan Rome, ninth-century Baghdad, the contemporary Western world, or in the literary worlds of Vergil, Dante, Milton, and Shakespeare.

In Gaiman's underworlds—and it is essential to remember that there are several in *The Sandman*—classical and renaissance poetry inform a fantasy world populated by such traditional literary characters as Milton's fallen angels, Lucifer and Beelzebub, who rub shoulders with figures from the Sandman universe, to create Gaiman's distinctive "recursive fantasy" worlds of "intersecting strata of realities."[49] The topography of Hell is familiar enough for the literate reader, but while Vergil and later poets create vivid word pictures with descriptions of the sinners, monsters, and landscapes of the underworld—Dante

[48] *The Sandman* series was under the auspices of a mainstream corporation, DC comics. Between 1989 and 1996 it was released in installments of seventy-five monthly comic book issues, and again as ten trade paperback editions spanning over 2000 pages. For further production details see Pustz (1999: 85) and Wagner, Golden and Bissette (2008: 30–1). The series earned Gaiman notable awards including the World Fantasy Award (the first comic to win). Its success led DC to the formation of the Vertigo imprint. Since there are no page numbers in comics, all discussions cite material by referring to the title of individual stories within the Vertigo editions.

[49] The terminology comes from Wagner, Golden, and Bissette (2008: 30) to describe the recasting of pre-existing fictional characters in *The Sandman*. Characters from other comic series also make an appearance in the series. Castaldo (2004: 97) observes that a generic feature of comics is their "persistent metatextuality, as characters regularly cross over into other universes." See Marshall (2011) for other examples of this phenomenon.

often providing a real-world specificity that helped his audience to visualize the enormity and horror of some of his monsters—Dream's visits to Hell are pictorially augmented.[50] The comic book, a unique mixture of word and image, offers rich possibilities in this regard. To give one memorable example: a two page spread in "A Hope in Hell" (*The Sandman* 2.4) displays Lucifer and Morpheus licked with flames atop a volcano as they survey an assembly of slavering, fanged demons, dislocated eyeballs, and slithering reptilian mutants. It is conventional comic book artwork, although of a very high order. There is but one speech balloon in this expansive picture, a solitary question floating above the congregation to accentuate the enormity of Hell: Lucifer asks Morpheus to identify the demon that took his helmet, a seemingly impossible task. The speech balloon, as David Carrier notes is "a great philosophical discovery," in that it "defines comics as neither a purely verbal nor a strictly visual art form, but as something radically new."[51] Text becomes part of the imagery; images do the work of text. Lucifer's single utterance thus dramatically and economically illustrates the vastness of Hell. All this is in accord with the genre; the twist throughout the series is that Morpheus' words are lettered in white against a black bubble, allowing the reader to recognize him in all his shape-shifting manifestations with minimal narratorial intrusions. The absence of language, when it occurs, becomes especially evocative, since the several descents to the underworld are largely graphic, spanning several pages of wordless panels to convey a sense of great depth and distance, but also of the ineffable.

The serial format, the innovation here, allows Gaiman to play the long game, stretching out themes and ideas, such as the Orpheus story, over several volumes, a strategy that exploits the ongoing nature of the comic book genre, but also goes beyond its confines. At the time of the series' initial release, comics were generally episodic, with each issue featuring a finite narrative. *The Sandman* is far more intricate, and although there are still discrete stories, the complex ordeal of Morpheus is a sustained narrative arc beginning with his escape from confinement in the first

[50] See MacDonald (1987: 60–1) on how Dante relates elements of Hell to his contemporary audience's lived reality, for example giving the precise dimensions of one of the fallen giants in the last circle of Hell (*Inf.* 31.58–66).

[51] Carrier 2000: 4.

volume, his fraught relationship with his former lover Nada, whom he has condemned to Hell, and his tragic interaction with his son Orpheus, which finally leads to his own death. The fact that the series does end, rather than existing potentially ad infinitum, changes the valence of the sequential format. On the one hand, Morpheus conforms to the paradigm of the comic book hero: an exceptional individual whose special abilities are the source of his own suffering.[52] On the other, Gaiman goes beyond static characterizations of the typical superhero in his portrayal of Morpheus as a powerful, albeit flawed and vulnerable entity, to depict a being who experiences learning, comes to terms with his own abilities and weaknesses, and ultimately gives up his powers. There is a tragic dimension to his personality, and an increasing self-awareness that is more literary than the narratives of most comic book characters.

The delineation of his role as the Prince of Stories is accentuated by lavish intertextual references including Vergil's *Fourth Georgic*, Ovid's *Metamorphoses*, Dante's *Inferno*, Milton's *Paradise Lost*, and Shakespeare's *Midsummer Night's Dream*. Setting this dark gothic figure in such a bookish environment inevitably imbues him with a profoundly nuanced identity, and Gaiman thus ostensibly situates his postmodern epic within a celebrated tradition: for example when Morpheus visits Hell to find his lost helm, he is led past the Woods of Suicides, an allusion to *Inferno* 13 (itself a reference to *Aeneid* 6), the seventh circle of Hell where Harpies roost on trees, transmogrified mortals who took their own lives. We have already noted that trees in the underworld can be symbols of the literary tradition; here we are invited to associate Morpheus with a heroic lineage of beings that descend to and return from the underworld. These allusions to traditional catabatic moments are not just superficial flourishes, however, or an attempt to elevate popular culture to high art; they do important thematic work. Accordingly, our examination of the Morpheus stories will focus on his relationship to various underworld narratives: he descends like Dante's pilgrim, but into a Miltonic Hell, and yet he also bears similarities with Lucifer. The Lord of Dreams functions as a creative force who confronts, colludes with, challenges, absorbs, and at times transforms that epic tradition of descent and necromancy. He is a shape-shifter who sends dreams to all living beings, and is thus

[52] Castaldo 2004: 97.

the archetypal creator. His engagement with the inherited catabatic archive is so powerful at times that he seems to take over stories, which are a form of dreaming, and are therefore within his sphere of power.

But his ability does not extend to the tale of Orpheus. Retrofitted into the Sandman universe by making Orpheus the son of Morpheus, the tale is derived from a composite of Vergil's and Ovid's versions. The interaction between father and son illustrates Morpheus' character flaws—he has a problem letting things go, to put it mildly—and also his eventual development into a more compassionate and self-aware individual.[53] But the Orphic narrative has a much more important function than serving as a backdrop to Morpheus' acquisition of insight. For one thing it creates a thematic resonance with the earlier story of his relationship with his lover Nada, whom he condemns to Hell, but who comes back eventually to the land of the living. But because Orpheus is also a poet and a creative force he becomes a challenge to the authorial control of his father, who tries to prevent his story from happening. And so we come to realize that the Orpheus tale has something to say about the limits of Morpheus' power and perhaps that of all authors to control their adaptations. As scholars recognize, Gaiman's engagement with the Miltonic Lucifer facilitates a reflection on the conflicting notions of free will and determinism.[54] Gaiman's manipulation of the Orpheus myth has ramifications for this metaphysical debate, but entrenches it within a metatextual commentary on an author's engagement with tradition. But before contemplating how Morpheus' unsuccessful attempt to forestall the Orphic myth informs these tensions, let us consider another version of the *descensus ad infernos* that can illuminate some of the interwoven themes of the Morpheus/Orpheus sequences.

A catabatic cat

Although the comic book is by its very nature fragmentary, the *Sandman* series also exemplifies the rhizomatic nature of postmodern culture. Like grass or ivy, a plant whose "root system is coextensive with

[53] Emphasizing Morpheus' tragic characteristics, Marshall (2011: 63) sums him up as: "a sullen workaholic with a string of bad relationships and a history of poor family communication."

[54] Porter (2013) and Jahlmar (2015).

the plant itself," the series offers numerous entrances and exits from the narrative, which thus has the potential to expand infinitely.[55] Barth's representation of Ambrose's catabasis as wanderings through the funhouse suggests this multiplicity with its non-linear narrative and different potential endings, and it reflects the structure of *Lost in the Funhouse*, which offers multiple points of entry; each story can be read as a discrete unit. Congruently there is a traditional narrative arc to Gaiman's *The Sandman* (just as there is to the Ambrose stories), but the series also features numerous stand-alone tales. Various nodes divert and contradict a sense of linear time, pulling the story through wormholes into different narrative worlds, although Morpheus' stern persona remains constant.

One such node is "A Dream of a Thousand Cats" (*The Sandman* 2.18), a twenty-four-page sequence included in the volume *Dream Country*, which also contains the first reference to Orpheus in the preceding story, "Calliope," about his mother.[56] Much loved by the series' fans, the cat's story functions as an overture to the Orphic tale, and encapsulates the descent narrative with many of the component parts listed at the end of the previous chapter. An exponent of the wisdom tradition, this is the story of a feline catabasis, told by a Siamese cat to an audience of other cats in a graveyard at night. She recounts how her owners drowned her kittens, and in an effort to deal with the loss she has a dream in which she takes a a journey to enlightenment, walking through a "wood of ghosts, where the dead and the lost whispered continually." Like her human counterparts she gains important knowledge in the kingdom of the dead: that cats could be the rulers of the world, and that dreams have the power to change the world. She is by no means the only animal to make the descent, if we recall *The Culex*, but unlike the tragic insect of the Latin poem she does return above ground.

The tale reflects some of the themes of the series, but is a self-contained story in its own right. Without a hint of parody the poignant

[55] Lucy 1997: 186. This idea was developed by French philosophers Gilles Deleuze and Felix Guattari in their two-volume *Capitalism and Schizophrenia* project (1970–82), and contrasts postmodernism with a hierarchical tree structure of culture growing into a multi-branched structure from originary roots.

[56] Originally published in 1991 "A Dream of a Thousand Cats," is the second story in the volume, *Dream Country*, the third volume in the Vertigo compilations.

tale exemplifies a feature of postmodern poetics that Hutcheon identifies as a "miniaturization of monumental forces."[57] The same principle is evident in Barth's Odyssean sperm, but there is no sense of comedy in Gaiman's story of the Orphic cat. This nameless creature's tale exerts the decentering pull of postmodern culture against the hegemonic narratives of the androcentric Western canon. To the seemingly "homogenous monolith" of the canon's purview Gaiman would add "human."[58] The story is tragic, revelatory, and ultimately horrific, with a frame depicting a giant cat with a small man in its mouth, a dream that could become reality if enough feline minds imagined it. In many respects the cat's story is programmatic, rehearsing some of the major themes of the series in a minor key, and commenting, perhaps ironically, on the place of the descent story in the Western tradition, to which Morpheus and his son will add. Like Odysseus the cat must travel great distances to reach Hades; like Aeneas she passes through a distinctive portal; this one is flanked by the same demons that guarded the Hell that Morpheus visits. And like both classical heroes she seeks knowledge from a wise being at the center of Hades. That turns out to be Morpheus in the shape of a cat, indicated by his black speech bubble. Like those of Orpheus and his father Morpheus, the cat's descent is motivated by loss, and although she does not entertain hopes of retrieving her loved ones—in this respect she illuminates the reality that Orpheus cannot accept—she does achieve a form of knowledge about the power of dreams. Like Odysseus her encounter with a mentor in the underworld has given her compelling narrative powers, and she is able to communicate her tale to an enthralled audience, although there is also a whiff of insurrection here that offers the possibility of a species rebellion. And one final but important point: the topography of the underworld in this feline catabasis shows no evidence of human culture once the cat passes through its fantastic portals—no demons, no mythical sinners, no ghosts of mortal men and women. This is the underworld of a cat, and is shaped according to her relationship to the natural world, not to that of human culture. It is one of several versions of Hades, each discrete and noncontiguous, coexisting in the Sandman cosmos.

[57] Hutcheon (1988: 4) uses the term in relation to architecture, but it suits literature well.

[58] Enumerating the categories as white, Western, middle class, and heterosexual Hutcheon (1988: 12) writes, "The centre no longer completely holds."

The mutating underworld

In "A Dream of a Thousand Cats" Morpheus demonstrates both his shape-shifting abilities and authorial powers by manifesting a version of Hades tailored specifically to the being who visits it. The story also insinuates a revolution against authority consonant with Gaiman's genre-blending challenge to the canonical status of those cultural products that he adapts. A different manifestation of these defiant poetics occurs in the tales of Morpheus' descents to Hell. His initial catabasis occurs in the first volume of the series (*Preludes & Nocturnes*), although it is evident that Dream has visited the underworld before the story began. Now he finds it much changed, with the Miltonic Lucifer sharing his rule with two other demons. "A Hope in Hell" (*The Sandman* 2.4) is a quest narrative in which Morpheus goes in search of a lost object, a helmet, which he retrieves in a battle of wits against the demon Choronzon in order to cement his power. The two opponents can manipulate the realm of Hell to suit their battlefield needs, for example turning it into a nightclub: "The landscape of Hell is mutable, if one has authority. And I have certain authority, even here," declares Morpheus before he makes his next visit to Hell in a subsequent volume (v. 4, *Season of Mists*). Like Gaiman himself he has the power to reconfigure the underworld, but the tradition does set some limits.

Morpheus descends again, this time to release his former lover Nada whom he dispatched for 10,000 years, and the changes in Hell are even more dramatic. Lucifer has decided to close the place down evacuating all its occupants and handing the keys over to Morpheus.[59] The seven linked episodes of *Season of Mists* grapple with a weighty question: why must there be a Hell? Gaiman offers an answer to a theological conundrum, but in order to do so he dismantles the notion of the underworld, making explicit allusions to its existence in the literary canon, to explore a possibility that it can be created and destroyed at the whim of its chief

[59] Gaiman (1999: 78) explains the inspiration for this idea as the remark of Abbe Mugnier that he was obliged to believe in Hell because Church doctrine said it existed, but that he did not have to believe that anyone was in Hell. The abdication led to a Vertigo spin-off series, *Lucifer*, running from 2000 to 2006. In a reading of *Seasons of Mists* through Derrida's concepts of forgiveness, Al-Tabaa (2012: 130) suggests that Lucifer abdicates because of the pointlessness of a task that offers no purpose. The revised Hell offers redemption and therefore purpose.

executive. If Hell is a literary space, can it be written *out* of existence? And its existence as a cultural construct is emphasized by Lucifer himself, who, in his retort to Morpheus' emissary, Cain, cites the tradition that produced him by quoting, "Better to reign in Hell than serve in Heaven" (*Paradise Lost* 2.263), attributing it properly to Milton, and then undercutting the citation by adding that, "We didn't say it. Milton said it. And he was blind." The fallen angel thereby acknowledges his own position as a literary creation and the power that the canon gives him, an authority from which he now wishes to abdicate; he is after all the quintessential defier of authority, even his own. On a metatextual level, Gaiman also seems to be saying that Milton had it wrong, a challenge that he supports, as Adam Porter argues, by undercutting Milton's version with elements of the Jewish tradition of legends known as the *Aggadic Midrash*. If Porter is correct, and he certainly presents a lucid argument, then Gaiman may be following the representation of Lucifer in Jewish folk tradition to provide an alternative to a more familiar Christian version espoused by Milton.[60] For example, Gaiman never calls Lucifer "Satan" (the name Milton uses for the fallen angel after his expulsion from Heaven) which may be an acknowledgement of a Jewish tradition.[61] So while Milton's *Paradise Lost* supplies the overarching framework of *The Sandman*, Gaiman disorders the stability of texts and authors by setting Milton's epic against older, but less familiar, narratives. And yet with this gambit he may be playing the same game that Milton did. It is beyond the scope of this chapter to delve into how *Paradise Lost* interacts with the epic tradition, but it is worth noting that Milton's citations of his predecessors suggest his own antecedence, as Harold Bloom argues.[62] For example, the passage from *Paradise Lost* that Lucifer quotes ("Better to reign in Hell . . . ") is a revision of Achilles' response to Odysseus in the underworld that he would rather be a serf tilling the ground, but alive, than rule among the dead (*Od.* 11. 489–91). Milton disputes and revises Achilles'

[60] Porter 2013: 181.

[61] Porter (2013: 180–3) interprets this nomenclature as a comment on Milton's use of a long tradition that associates Satan's fall with his attack on humanity. "Gaiman's Lucifer, on the other hand, reigns over Hell but has little interest in humanity," which for Porter implies that Gaiman rejects Milton's story of the Fall.

[62] MacDonald (1987: 175–6) builds on Bloom's concept of metalepsis in Milton's *Paradise Lost* (1975: 125–43), i.e. the use of something later in place of something earlier, to argue that Milton cites his predecessors in a way that suggests that he actually comes first in that tradition. For the device in postmodern fiction see McHale 1987: 190–1.

assessment of Hades to give priority to that of Lucifer, which now occurs at the beginning of creation, and obviously earlier than Homer. Gaiman, however, responds with an act of ventriloquism that uses Milton's own character, Lucifer, to challenge his creator. But of course this assumes that Milton has already written *Paradise Lost*, and we find ourselves in a strange narrative loop, distorting the chronology of that narrative.

By suggesting that he is deposing Milton with his own creation of Hell, Gaiman is exemplifying Bloom's concept of the "perverse, willful revisionism" that provokes authors to produce new literature. In *Anxiety of Influence: A Theory of Poetry* (1973) Bloom posits an Oedipal impulse that compels poets to contest their literary forefathers; the theory applies equally well to all exponents of the literary tradition. Rather than receiving and preserving their heritage, authors contest it, often misrepresenting it in order to notionally correct it.[63] Bloom's model for a poet in conflict with another creator is Milton's Satan, whose rebellion manifests as Hell, his poetic creation as it were. In the most willful revision possible Gaiman's Lucifer would now dismantle the version of Hell that he has occupied.[64]

Yet Morpheus, for all his dark sensibilities, is not willing to assume the role of king of the dead despite Lucifer's abdication. As other powers, including Egyptian and Norse gods, vie for control of Hell, an angel delivers a message from "the creator":

> There must be a Hell. There must be a place for the demons; a place for the damned. Hell is Heaven's reflection. It is Heaven's shadow. They define each other. Reward and Punishment; hope and despair. There must be a Hell, for without Hell, Heaven has no meaning.

There must be a Hell and it resembles its former manifestation, but with a new redemptive purpose. No longer only the site of torment and

[63] Bloom (1973: 14) offers several different categories to describe poets' engagement with their predecessors, but the most applicable in this case is *clinamen*, "which is poetic misreading or misprision proper; I take the word from Lucretius, where it means a 'swerve' of the atoms so as to make change possible in the universe. A poet swerves away from his precursor, by so reading his precursor's poem as to execute a *clinamen* in relation to it."

[64] Bloom might be appalled to have his theories of poetry applied to popular culture. As he complained to one interviewer: "At Yale, I am surrounded by professors far more interested in various articles on the compost heap of so-called popular culture than in Proust or Shakespeare or Tolstoy." Excerpted from "Bloom and doom," Harold Bloom interviewed by Ken Shulman, *Newsweek* v124, #15 (Oct. 10, 1994) 75. It may be a coincidence, but Gaiman (1999) invokes the metaphor of compost for his use of myth.

punishment it becomes a place of potential rehabilitation, a kind of Purgatory now under the supervision of two reluctant angels. Gaiman has disassembled Hell to answer the question of why it exists. Before "the creator" sent his message, Lucifer had given a similar explanation:

> This realm is Heaven's shadow, remember. Or, more precisely, Heaven's dark reflection—like a landscape hanging inverted in the waters of a lake.

Hell's status as a simulacrum, one upon whose presence its "original" depends, is closely tied to the notion of authorship. Hell will not close down, but its survival as a literary product of an authorial creator is advertised in this new story. Gaiman rewrites Hell, handing it over to a different supervisor who asserts that "rulers of Hell [are] only answerable to our creator." Neither Lucifer nor Morpheus can obliterate a tradition, although they can modify it within prescribed terms. The omnipotent creator, never explicitly named, may be the literary canon or it may be Gaiman himself, who has manipulated the conventional tale of a descent to the netherworld to engage in a self-reflexive comment on his own creative powers, but also on the inevitability of the tradition that he has deconstructed and put back together again. This restoration of Hell, however, implicates *The Sandman* in a metaphysical dialogue with Milton about free will.[65] Milton seems to place responsibility for their fall squarely on Lucifer/Satan and humanity: "freely they stood who stood and fell who fell" (*Paradise Lost* 4.66–7). Gaiman's Lucifer, however, suggests that the creator wants Hell to exist, and that even his rebellion was part of a master plan. Since he is restoring the Hell of literary tradition, we might speculate that Gaiman makes a gesture to tradition's authority inasmuch as that authority must exist for any author to challenge it.

For all that, we must acknowledge that the forces of alterity and impossibility swirl throughout the realm of Morpheus. Before he descends to search for Nada, the Prince of Stories takes great pains to protect his immense library, which includes a collection of books dreamt by renowned literary figures but never written.[66] Consigning it to the care of

[65] Porter (2013: 177–8) puts this debate, and Gaiman's response to it, in the context of Jewish narrative traditions.

[66] Soledad Souza e Palma (2006: 141–3) makes interesting associations between Sandman's library and Borges' concept of the labyrinth and garden of forking paths.

his librarian Lucien he ensures that all its doors are secure before he goes down to Hell where all doors are now open. Although Morpheus is not yet aware of Lucifer's plan to abdicate when he takes this precaution, he does feel a responsibility for those imaginary volumes in the event that he fails to return to the Dreaming, his realm. The containment of the unwritten stories and the dissolution of the written underworld, however, set up a provocative symmetry. The Dreaming has intriguing similarities with the underworld: a gothic castle with a graveyard in its backyard, manifesting a connection between death, dreaming, and narrative. As one of the several underworlds in the Sandman, it functions here very explicitly as a repository of stories, although these are spectral narratives that do not enter the waking world, and are all the more enticing for that.

Relatedly, Morpheus' quest to release Nada, a beautiful African queen who rejected a life with Morpheus, seems to "un-write" the Orpheus and Eurydice tale. Nada, whom Morpheus condemned to eternal damnation, had beseeched him to pity her on his first visit to Hell. When he descends to bring her back, he discovers that like all the other souls she has been released. Not the least bit interested in reviving their relationship—thousands of years of suffering have firmed her resolve—Nada agrees to be reincarnated as a baby boy far from Dream's orbit. Their story reflects the failed quest of Orpheus—"like a landscape hanging inverted in the waters of a lake"—but Morpheus is decidedly different from his poetic son. His severe, unyielding nature lends a different tone to the lover's journey to Hell: he is the cause of the woman's imprisonment; unlike Eurydice the object of his quest does not share his desire for reconciliation; and unlike Eurydice she does actually leave the underworld. While the Nada story ends in *Season of Mists*, it acts like a "dark reflection" of the romantic tale of Morpheus' son, told in a later volume, and tragically entwined with the story of Morpheus. Because the Orpheus myth is so deeply fixed in Western culture, it can function here as a synecdoche for traditional narrative in a metafictional program that involves a conflicted relationship between Dream, proprietor of untold stories, and the traditional tale that he wishes to "unwrite," the story of his son's voyage to the underworld. For just as the Miltonic version of Hell cannot be made to disappear, neither can the classical underworld and its traditions be erased. The story of the Orphic descent is preordained, and while Morpheus can mutate or modify it, he cannot make it go away any more than Lucifer can make Hell disappear.[67] Orpheus would not be Orpheus without the underworld. There is a sharp glint of defiance in this rewriting of the poet of myth as a version of the rebellious son (whose father is in a sense Gaiman's alter ego), a defiance countered by that mythic figure's insistence that his descent takes place as written in its classical sources.

Orpheus remastered

In the Sandman universe Orpheus is the son of the Muse Calliope, in accordance with ancient traditions, but Morpheus is his father, rather than Apollo or Oegreus of Thrace (both are attested in ancient sources). The modification produces a revised mythology that uses a conflicted father–son dynamic as a meditation on narrative authority and the inevitability of tradition, ideas that predicate Gaiman's adaptation of the Miltonic Hell.[68] The name of Orpheus had been uttered at the end of the first story in *Season of Mists*, when a demented twentieth-century novelist suffering from writer's block had kept Calliope captive. Like Barth's nameless Homeric bard, who fills nine amphora-muses with semen, his form of creation is an act of sexual congress, but in this case a violent rape of the muse. (It would seem that the goddess of inspiration and epic requires masculine potency to produce a story, but cannot control her own.) After Morpheus intervenes to release his ex-wife, the writer is left trying to remember him: "Morpheus, Orpheus?" The confusion is significant since father and son share certain aspects; the son's name is embedded in that of his father, just as his story now represents part of his father's. Gaiman develops a loose connection between the two figures suggested by Ovid in *Metamorphoses* 11, which continues the story of Orpheus at its beginning and ends with the appearance of Morpheus, the god of sleep and dreams. There is also a subtle connection to Milton behind all this: Book Seven of *Paradise Lost* (33–9) compares the poet's own heavenly source of inspiration, Urania, with Orpheus' mother, the muse who could not prevent that "Thracian bard" being ripped apart by maenads. Without naming Calliope directly Milton

[67] On the "tragic inevitability" of Orpheus' story see Butler's elegant analysis (2009: 59).

[68] *The Song of Orpheus* was released by DC as a Sandman Special in 1991, but an analysis of its integration into the main story arc is best accomplished by considering it as part of the Vertigo compilations.

declares that his heavenly inspiration is superior, since the pagan goddess is but "an empty dream." Charles Martindale comments on the "tortuous illogic of the lines," since Milton denies that Calliope and the story of Orpheus ever existed.[69] The illogicality, however, seems an appropriate predecessor of the paradoxical elision of fictional levels in Gaiman's Orpheus story.

The major elements of the tale appear in the sixth volume of the series, *Fables and Reflections*, which begins with an episode from towards the story's conclusion, although this is a coda invented by Gaiman to suit his frame narrative. Orpheus appears first as a disembodied head in "Thermidor" set during the French revolution, a period when he was but one of many severed heads. He is returned to Naxos for safekeeping where he asks about his father and learns that Morpheus still refuses to see him. Even before the story begins, then, it highlights the theme of intergenerational conflict. Furthermore, the reader is put on alert that this story will feature the blurring of ontological boundaries that McHale identifies as a crucial element of postmodernist fiction: a character from myth intrudes into a historical moment. And if that is not disorienting enough, when the tale reemerges, we find ourselves within Orpheus' prophetic nightmare: he is still only a head, now floating down a river calling out for Eurydice, a scene taken from Vergil. But dreams are stories according to the dominant conceit of the series, and Orpheus will soon bring his into the waking world. It is his wedding day, and his father is trying to awaken him from within the dream (Figure 2.1). The different levels of reality are nothing new as far as the series is concerned, and besides we know by now that Orpheus' father is the lord of dreams. But in this case Morpheus is trying to end the dream, as if to curtail its fulfillment.

Gaiman's adaptation, set in ancient Greece, combines elements of the Vergilian and Ovidian renditions with his own variations that necessarily draw attention to his artifice and inventiveness. As we know, the story of Orpheus had different endings before this; it too is mutable, but not completely. Yes, Morpheus embodies stories, and shapes the dreams of storytellers, but even he must operate within the scope of tradition—such

[69] Martindale (1985: 324) goes on to say that the word "dream" suggests the source of his inspiration. Cf. MacDonald (1987: 138): "if Orpheus' muse is an empty dream, it is still true that Urania inspires the poet narrator, i.e. Milton, in his dreams."

Figure 2.1 Morpheus in the Dream of Orpheus. Neil Gaiman, *The Sandman* v.6. *Fables & Reflections* (1993), art by Brian Talbot, et al.

was the lesson learned in his own confrontation with the Miltonic underworld. He enters his son's dream with the knowledge that it is a prophecy, and that try as he may, he cannot change that story entirely. For the moment, however, he and his siblings have adapted to this new story-scape wearing Hellenized versions of their usual garb and adopting Greek names for the occasion of their nephew's wedding: Morpheus as Oneiros, Death as Teleute, Destruction as Olethros and Destiny as Potmos, etc. While these modifications adapt the Sandman narrative to its new setting, they also draw attention to issues of authenticity, cultural proprietorship, and history.

As a series produced for a mass market, *The Sandman* comics are products of and for a culture immersed in imitations of reality. Theorists such as Larry McCaffery identify the influence of market driven, consumerist ideologies on postmodernism's challenge to the idea of authenticity.[70] How can we speak of an Ur-version of a text when thousands of reproductions of comics are in circulation? The sheer volume of *The Sandman* issues (not to mention the different combinations and reissues of the series), and their popularity in mainstream culture combine with the bold, eclectic appropriations of the literary canon to force questions about the genuineness of the story. Related to this sense of indeterminacy about origins is the question of reality. If we are surrounded by simulacra, or if there is no stable originary text, where do we draw the line between fiction and the real world? Self-reflexively postmodern literature enmeshes this question within its fiction, creating an ontological dilemma: what are we to accept as part of the "real" world that fictional characters inhabit, and what is fictional in relationship to this world? Barth connects Ambrose Mensch with a Homeric bard as if to remind his readers that an author can be a product of fiction as much as a producer of it, thereby effacing divisions between fictional levels. Gaiman's strategy is to elide myth and history: the head of Orpheus in the context of the French Revolution, and then in a dream, melts the divide between fantasy and history, and toys with the notion of historical truth. Moreover by transporting Morpheus and his siblings into a well-known myth, in a way that acknowledges its prior existence as a work of fiction by two

[70] McCaffery 1991: 4.

classical authors, Gaiman is challenging the concept of authorial identity, which is also a product of history.

The entire volume in which the main part of the Orpheus tale occurs, *Fables and Reflections*, is an implicit admission of the social construction of time and history: "Three Septembers and a January," is set in eighteenth-century America; "August" in the Roman principate; the opening story of Orpheus' head is titled "Thermidor," a month created specifically for the French revolution; and the final story bears the name of another, "Ramadam," the Islamic month of revelation. From revolution to revelation these references to time (and its cultural labels) frame a series of tales that engage with historical moments featuring "authentic" figures such as Augustus, Marco Polo, Robespierre, and Haroun-al-Raschid, all of whom encounter Morpheus in some form, usually in their dreams. The Orpheus sequence sits in their midst and blends the historical with the mythical, a postmodernist commentary on the concept of time. A visit to Hades is about stopping time and perhaps, Orpheus would hope, about reversing time. But the story "Thermidor" is not only a reminder that Orpheus will meet his prescribed end, it also inserts his fantastic narrative within a specific historical event, the French Revolution. Like his father, who flickers in and out of different narrative traditions and historical periods, he exists in a narrative space that blends myth and history. Nonetheless, the telling of his story suggests a familiar temporal continuum beginning in ancient Greece during some heroic past, inserting Orpheus' head in the French Revolution, and his mother Calliope (after her breakup with Morpheus) in the twentieth century. As logical as that historical sequence may seem, there is a temporal disjunction in the story of Orpheus that upsets the notion of linear time. While the appearance of the Endless in a mythic version of Greece suggests that they existed there simultaneously with Orpheus and Eurydice, that notion is shattered when Orpheus visits his aunt, Teleute, the power responsible for the death of his wife on their wedding day. His aunt's intervention insinuates what McHale describes as a "transworld migration" between two different fictional worlds, emphasized by a sudden jolt of the present.[71] When Orpheus visits her she lives in a twentieth-century apartment with armchairs and a goldfish bowl, "so strange to

[71] McHale 1987: 36.

my eyes," that Death changes it to what she thinks would look more appropriate to her nephew. The collapse of a linear chronology is disconcerting, but then again, as we have already noted, death can change the quality of time.

The tale of Orpheus, it would now seem, emanates from the embodiment of death herself, who represents nothing if not the inevitable. For despite the jarring insertion of the comic book characters into the world of myth, the story remains essentially the same. It begins when Teleute takes over as a force of narrative agency, setting the story in motion by leaving the wedding festivities to attend to Eurydice's death. A viper's sting as the new bride flees from the amorous Aristaeus—here he is a satyr, as if to emphasize the mythic quality of the events—conforms to the Vergilian account. When his father refuses to help him enter the underworld to bring back Eurydice, which is to say he tries to make a different story happen, conflict between father and son is thus a conflict between a new form of the myth in which Orpheus accepts his loss (although Morpheus knows this is not possible) and the fulfillment of the narrative as represented by Orpheus' desire to bring Eurydice back. In retaliation for his father's refusal, Orpheus disowns him, as if to set the story free from his father's control. Teleute is reluctant to grant Orpheus' request even though he cites that conventional catabatic prototype, Heracles, to argue for its possibility.[72] But his aunt eventually relents: he can come back from Hades because she grants an override that will (horrifically) guarantee his continued existence even after decapitation. The tale follows its classical course from here; all modifications (i.e. the appearance of the Endless) have been in the terrestrial realm. In the subterranean kingdom, where time no longer exists, the story of Orpheus and Eurydice remains in its apparently ossified form. There is the familiar long and arduous journey to the subterranean portal, located in Taenarum. Twenty-one frames spanning six pages with minimal speech or narration convey the immense depths through which Orpheus travels. The standard elements of the Greco-Roman catabatic tale are all visible: a Vergilian Charon accepts a golden bough; Cerberus is a three-headed shadow, then a slumping mass; an infinite multitude of shades fill the cavernous depths along with the

[72] Teleute claims that, "Herakles was full of it. He just got dead drunk for a couple of weeks in Phrygia and told everyone he'd been to the land of the dead."

familiar sinners charmed by Orpheus' song, and the giant forms of Hades and Persephone, who receive the request—the details confirm what hardly needs confirming, and, as expected, Orpheus turns to see Eurydice receding into the distance. The story of Orpheus' descent is thus another example of pre-determination, and yet another response to the free will debate articulated by a narrative as fixed and preordained as death itself.

The penultimate installment in this volume (Chapter 4) ends with the inevitable decapitation by a band of maenads, bringing us back full circle to the head of Orpheus floating down a river calling for Eurydice, and actualizing the dream that Morpheus tried to end. The macabre epilogue features another encounter between Morpheus and his son. Ever conscious of propriety he has come to say goodbye ("It seemed the right thing to do"), and has arranged for his son's head to be tended by priests as an oracle; the story closes where it began on the island of Naxos. The biography of Orpheus, enclosed here in a ring composition (as if to suggest an eternal cycle), is presented as an intergenerational conflict within the story itself, but also epitomizes (inversely) a conflict between literary fathers and sons.[73] Gaiman, like Barth, acknowledges the tradition that has engendered him, but simultaneously creates a postmodern paradox in which an authorial figure, Morpheus, is unable to control, or "rewrite," the fictional space of the underworld. On the other hand Gaiman uses the classical version of the Orpheus tale to enhance the tragic nature of Morpheus' life; so while the story can be read as a stand-alone tale Gaiman extends it by having Morpheus visit his son's head to obtain a prophecy. In return he promises to end Orpheus' miserable life; the mercy killing results in the prosecution of Morpheus by the Furies, and his death. In the final volume of the series, Orpheus and Eurydice are reunited in the underworld, as they are in Ovid's *Metamorphoses*, a place which Morpheus will never enter.

In the Sandman universe father and son descend to different versions inflection, while for his son it is equipped with classical gods and mythic personnel. These distinctions confirm the underworld as products of culture and literature (except for cats), and although Lucifer's Hell is a descendant of Vergil's underworld in literary history, the two remain

[73] "Inversely," because the rebellious son insures the fulfillment of the traditional tale, while the authorial father, Morpheus, attempts to stop it from happening.

distinct and disconnected in Gaiman's appropriation. Thus while Dante and Milton are each adapting Vergil's underworld, thereby implying a continuum in which they play an important role as transmitters, Gaiman acknowledges no such literary genealogy. Because Morpheus' descent to Milton's Hell precedes Orpheus' descent to Vergil's Hades, it contradicts whatever impressions we might have about their relationship to each other.

Let us return to Bloom's *Anxiety of Influence* for a moment; although a discussion of poetry, it offers useful tools for analysis of both Barth's and Gaiman's underworlds. Bloom contends that poets, and by extension we can say authors, engage in what he calls "an act of creative correction that is actually and necessarily a misinterpretation."[74] In this version of the father–son dialectic, the "ephebe" as Bloom calls the incipient writer, engages in a revisionism that is always a form of rebellion against earlier creators. This "act of creative correction" in Gaiman's case is an overwriting of Milton's Hell, but it also something more complex. Gaiman refuses to play along with the idea of the historical evolution of a tradition: Vergil's Hades does not turn into Milton's, but exists in some separate universe. Yet authors, including Morpheus, cannot change a tradition whose elements are apparently predetermined. Along the same lines, Barth's parody of Joyce engages in a diminution and caricature of his predecessor's novels in order to notionally supplant them with his own, but the author-to-be, Ambrose Mensch is directly connected to a Homeric bard, convoluting any sense of time and tradition.

The postmodern underworld

For both Barth and Gaiman the underworld represents the past, as it does for Odysseus when he confronts his former Trojan comrades. But both authors complicate the notion of the past: literary traditions are plotted along a Möbius strip or disrupted by detours through parallel worlds. As we are led through these impossible worlds we see familiar landmarks that remind us of the ancient story. For ancient catabatic travellers, access to the realm of death is a way of achieving knowledge and insight, which allows them to tell their tales by engaging with and moving beyond the past. Like Odysseus, Ambrose Mensch is

[74] Bloom 1973: 14.

transformed into a storyteller after spending time in a different form of Hades; so is Gaiman's catabatic cat. His Orpheus exists as a talking head with the gift of prophecy after his descent, a different sort of narrator. Morpheus, the prince of stories, must make a symbolic descent to Hades, but his realm, the Dreaming, with its immense library of untold tales, is a version of Hades unto itself. And while these diverse ancient and post-modern iterations of the *descensus ad infernos* corroborate the metaphor of Hades as a literary space, Barth and Gaiman engage with the catabatic tradition on two different levels. Each author acknowledges the classical version of the tale—the Odyssean *Nekyia*, and the descent of Orpheus—but then spars with literature "in the second degree" (to borrow from Genette)—Joyce's *Ulysses* and Milton's *Paradise Lost*. These they set in juxtaposition to their source texts in a complex performance of self-reflexivity that allegorizes issues of intellectual paternity and the anxiety of influence.

3

Engendering the Haunted Text

ὃ δ' ὑπὸ ζόφον ἠερόεντα
ἁρπάξας ἵπποισιν ἄγεν μεγάλα ἰάχουσαν.

And seizing her as she screamed
he took her down in his chariot to the murky darkness below.

(*The Homeric Hymn to Demeter* 80–1)

ἐμὲ δὲ χλωρὸν δέος ᾕρει,
μή μοι Γοργείην κεφαλὴν δεινοῖο πελώρου
ἐξ Ἀΐδεω πέμψειεν ἀγαυὴ Περσεφόνεια.

And pale fear seized me,
lest from the house of Hades, revered Persephone
might send the head of the Gorgon, terrible monster.

(*Odyssey* 11.633–5)

How do women fit into the literary spaces of the underworld? Ghostly heroines, gorgons, and revered Persephone occupy the infernal landscapes of classical myth, but female visitors to Hades are few and far between. Certainly their descents, when they happen, are transformative, but women tend to emerge as brides rather than heroes and storytellers. This chapter analyzes how two feminist novelists, A.S. Byatt and Elena Ferrante, contest a legacy of descent mythology in which gender roles are prescriptive and stereotypical. For classical heroes such as Odysseus or Aeneas, the descent is a voluntary act of courage, while Persephone, or Proserpina as the Romans called her, is snatched screaming from the terrestrial world. Although she has authority among the dead as the bride of Hades, the best-known account of her descent emphasizes her passivity and terror. In early versions of the Orpheus myth, his wife makes it back to the land of the living, but her story, if she ever had one, is lost.

Apparently the myth of her return was familiar to the fifth-century BCE audience of Euripides' play, *Alcestis*: Admetus, whose wife had volunteered to die on his behalf, wishes that he had "the voice and music of Orpheus to charm the daughter of Demeter and her husband, and bring you back from Hades" (*Alc.* 357–60). All ends well because Heracles wrestles with Death at Alcestis' tomb to restore her to life. Like the wife of Orpheus she does not make the descent while alive, and may never have arrived in Hades according to Stamatia Dova, who deduces that "[Alcestis'] seemingly conventional end of life, followed by her removal from the grave before she is given a chance to visit the underworld, deprives her of the opportunity to embark on a true *katabasis*."[1] The drama concludes with her presence as a veiled, silent bride; revived from the dead, she is now a gift from Heracles to Admetus, a commodity exchanged between men.[2]

Apuleius' tale of Psyche's catabasis (*Met.*6.10–21) in his second-century CE Latin novel *Metamorphoses*, also known as *The Golden Ass*, gives a more energetic role to a mortal woman, although predictably she too returns from the underworld as a wife. The tale within a tale, told by an old woman to the narrator, recounts how the pregnant Psyche, now separated from Cupid, must appease his mother Venus by performing four tasks so that she can be reunited with her beloved. The final challenge requires her to visit Proserpina to fetch a special beauty treatment for Venus—a twist on the classic underworld quest.[3] Like Vergil, Apuleius recounts the catabasis in his sixth book, which features a number of allusions to *Aeneid* 6 including the use of a soporific cake to calm Cerberus. The tale is distinctive with its complex list of instructions and interdictions required for Psyche's descent and ascent: for example, she must decline a lavish banquet offered

[1] Dova 2012: 180; Johnston (2017: 17–36) surveys accounts of myths of returns from the dead, which include the story of Alcestis. Cf. Plato's account omitting the intervention of Heracles (*Symposium* 178a–180b).

[2] Rehm (1994) describes and analyzes the conflation of marriage and death for women in Greek tragedy.

[3] Cupid had fallen in love with the beautiful maiden Psyche, but kept her ignorant of his identity by only visiting her in the dark. She lights a lamp to see his face while he is asleep, but drops hot oil on him. He sends her away in anger, and Venus takes over by reducing Psyche to slave status, and setting the tasks, all of which she is able to complete with the help of various animals and forces of nature. Finkelpearl (1990: 333–47) explores the Vergilian allusions in the descent story. See further Toscano (2010) who emphasizes the atypicality of Psyche's descent (i.e. her gender), but also notes some parallels with the Persephone paradigm.

by Proserpina, and refrain from looking into Proserpina's gift once she returns. But she finds herself incapable of this final act of self-control, opens the jar, and instantly falls into a death-like coma to be awoken, not by the kiss of her handsome prince, but by a prick of his erotic arrow. Her successful *descensus ad infernos* is thereby jeopardized, and it requires male intervention to bring her back to life. In a fairytale ending, Jupiter ordains that the couple is to be wed in a formal ceremony, and Psyche is granted immortality. Thus the extraordinary tale of a heroic, voluntary catabasis by a woman has a resolution familiar from the story of Persephone-Proserpina; she becomes the wife of a god.

Throughout the Western tradition, with a few exceptions, the catabasis and its narration have typically been male endeavors.[4] Rachel Falconer, commenting on this phenomenon, points out that the patriarchal imaginary understands the underworld itself as feminine. This gendered construction shapes the psychoanalytical theory of Freud, who was influenced by Greek myth in his tri-partite construction of the psyche with a subconscious beneath the ego. Freudian theory subsequently influenced Lacan's concept of the Symbolic Order, which includes language, law, and culture; psychic development thus involves leaving the maternal sphere to enter the patriarchal world.[5] By gendering the realm of death as feminine, Western thought has historically celebrated the male voyager's ability to separate from it. And while such an underworld is understood to be a literary matrix comprised of earlier versions of itself, the aspiring storyteller, in order to revive it as literature, must ascend to the Symbolic Order.

More recently, storytellers have begun to write female characters into the heroic descent, although within limits. In her study of the subterranean motif in French and English children's literature of the nineteenth century, Kiera Vaclavik notes that while men and boys can have underground adventures in popular novels such as *The Journey to the Center of the Earth* (Jules Verne, published in English 1871), or *King Solomon's*

[4] One exception includes a seventeenth-century French fairytale by Countess Marie Catherine d'Aulnoy, *Serpentin Vert* ("Green Serpent"), a complex romantic adventure influenced by Apuleius' Cupid and Psyche. It concludes when its heroine, princess Laidronette, must visit the underworld and appeal to Proserpina to find her husband, a green serpent. He is restored to human form; the couple returns to earth, and live happily.

[5] Falconer 2005: 144–6. Likewise Lesser (1987: 126) outlines Freud's debt to classical myths of a trip to the underworld in his layered concept of the human psyche, with the subconscious beneath the conscious, and the id below that.

Mines (H. Rider Haggard, 1885), the only females who have access to the subterranean realm are girls like Lewis Carroll's Alice or George MacDonald's Princess Irene (*The Princess and the Goblin*, 1872). Vaclavik observes that children's fantasy narrative of the Victorian period offers "a privileged space in which to reconfigure or at least to rethink the gender roles and relations of traditional katabatic narratives."[6] The following discussion examines authors who have carried that project through to more recent cultural products, with revisions of underworld themes that bring women into the tradition both as subterranean travelers and terrestrial storytellers. Among other strategies, A.S. Byatt and Elena Ferrante make children's culture a platform from which to survey issues surrounding women's identities as authors. Their feminist adaptations of the Odyssean *Nekyia* and the tale of Persephone's descent epitomize a combination of citation and defiance characteristic of postmodern culture, although feminism is not necessarily correlative with postmodernism.[7] The preceding chapter has argued that works by John Barth and Neil Gaiman frame a postmodernist appropriation of classical descent stories as an Oedipal challenge to a patrilineal tradition, but this metaphorical intergenerational conflict has little relevance for women authors.[8] If they are to be the unruly daughters of such a lineage, they must either declare the tradition to be meaningless for women, or insert themselves in more active roles than those left open for them by literary precedents.

The first of these options is represented by the multi-award winning American poet Adrienne Rich in "Diving into the Wreck" (1973), one of the most influential poems of twentieth-century feminism. As a retort to a cultural history in which women have been largely absent, the poem uses the image of a deep-sea diver, who, having read a book of myths, descends

[6] Vaclavik 2010: 84–5; Lesser (1987: 153–72) devotes a chapter to "The Child's Underground," which begins with discussions of some of these works.

[7] Hooks (2002: 422) remarks that postmodern theory is dominated by: "white male intellectuals . . . who speak to and about one another with coded familiarity." Cf. Morris (2002) on the scarcity of women theorists in the early postmodern movement. Klimenkova (1992: 283) draws parallels, from a philosophical standpoint, between the two movements, but points to their differences as well, noting that postmodernism fights "against universalism, while feminism is more interested in the social and cultural aspects of criticism." Nicol (2009: 140–63) devotes a chapter to postmodern fiction by women such as Margaret Atwood and Cathy Acker. He begins with a useful survey of the debates about gender and postmodernism.

[8] Armstrong (2006: 100–1) summarizes critiques of Bloom's *Anxiety of Influence* in the context of women novelists.

a ladder, and sinks into the depths of the ocean. The descent is masterfully and beautifully described, culminating with the diver surveying the treasure, decayed instruments, and wreckage of a rotting ship at the bottom of the sea; the poem ends by returning to the book of myths, which the diver is carrying, but in which "our names do not appear." "Diving into the Wreck" has spoken to decades of feminist scholars for whom it represents Rich's program of re-visioning a history that has excluded or trivialized women's accomplishments. Alicia Ostriker, for example, notes that the "watery descent inverts the ascents and conquests of male heroism." For Cheri Colby Langdell the diver's descent symbolizes an attempt to "decolonize, reexplore, revise, and excavate a history that contains the drowned voices of all early women in particular and marginalized people generally."[9] If, however, we think specifically of the tradition of male descent poetry, we can read in Rich's diver a suggestive critique and repudiation of the necromantic convention that has erased women from its transmission. The diver encounters no wise truth-teller at the bottom of the sea, but rather drowned faces, and a mermaid and merman, who, along with the diver, enter and explore the wreckage of what Michael Thurston identifies as the patriarchal literary tradition. For Thurston "Diving into the Wreck" evokes the myth of descent, not to engage in a filial appropriation of the myth, as the modernist poets Pound and Eliot do, but rather to passively declare it otiose for a female poet. Adrienne Rich, along with the poets H.D. and Edna St. Vincent Millay, as Thurston writes:

> enact and implicitly advocate a poetics of passivity, winning the struggle with a patriarchal poetic tradition by opting out of it, and at the same time, announcing this strategy through their own allusions to narratives of Underworld descent.[10]

The second alternative is a form of appropriation: Byatt and Ferrante recuperate a patrilineal trope that turns on an Oedipal anxiety of influence, not only by making women the protagonists of underworld-themed fiction, but by giving them the roles of authors. Both novelists engage with and reinterpret a stereotype that configures the underworld as a cultural space visited by heroic males. In A.S. Byatt's *Angels and Insects*, one subaltern woman tells a story that has its origins in Homer's *Odyssey*, and draws attention to the fact that she is marginal to the tradition that produced it. Another melds the characters of Penelope

[9] Ostriker 1982: 71–2; Langdell 2004: 113.

[10] Thurston 2009: 46.

and Odysseus in a revision of the *Nekyia* that gives her similar narrative power. The two novellas that comprise *Angels and Insects* domesticate the descent myth by adapting it for children's culture or the genteel parlors of Victorian England. An underworld motif dominates several works by Elena Ferrante, including her children's book *The Beach at Night*, in which dolls make symbolic voyages into a mythic abyss. These remarkable tales transcode the Demeter–Persephone narrative within texts that explore women's homosocial bonds while also granting subjectivity to versions of the chthonic female monster. Beyond this, Ferrante reworks the idea of the birth of the author as an ascent from Hades in a brilliant adaptation of an ancient narrative device that is reinvigorated specifically for the genesis of a female writer.

Between the analyses of these two authors is a discussion of Henry Selick's adaptation of Gaiman's *Coraline*, which functions as a segue between them: most obviously it features the catabasis in a product of children's culture, which aligns it with both writers. It also splices the Persephone motif of Ferrante with the Odyssean intertexts of Byatt. And finally, and most provocatively, both the novel and film reanimate the figure of the female monster, a familiar denizen of classical underworlds, by setting her in the place of the father-mentor of male-focused descent stories. Other Mother is a creative power, but one with dangerous capabilities that require her to be vanquished. This problematic notion in the context of female agency will set the stage for a close reading of Ferrante's recuperation of women's roles in the lineage of underworld fiction. Thus, in the course of this chapter my analyses progress from Byatt's vision of the female narrator who tells tales of the underworld to Ferrante's disturbing revision of the chthonic woman in a story of a female catabasis that results in the making of an author. Dolls, cats, ghosts, insects, and fairies make appearances as accessories in these works, thus adding interpretive dimensions to underworld traditions that make spaces for female curiosity, courage, and narrative power.

Mutations and Hauntings: A.S. Byatt's *Angels and Insects*

Angels and Insects (1992) fits together two tales set a decade apart in nineteenth-century England: the first begins and the other ends with the figure of a shipwrecked man, one of many clues to the novellas' shared Homeric intertexts. The two tales epitomize the postmodern genre christened by Hutcheon as historiographic metafiction: "those well-known and popular novels which are both intensely self-reflexive and yet paradoxically also lay claim to historical events and personages."[11] Byatt developed her craft during a period of experimentation born of frustration with the realist tradition of postwar British fiction; a similar dissatisfaction led to Barth's new forms of storytelling in *Lost in the Funhouse*.[12] Like Barth and other postmodern writers, Byatt uses myth and fable to overcome her aesthetic discontent, although she is also concerned with critiquing the concept of historical authenticity. With her 1990 Booker Prize winning *Possession* she creates a "postmodern Victorian" romance encrusted with fairytales and poetry, and framed by a twentieth-century contemporary campus novel and detective story. The pastiche of literary forms, the sense of fragmentation, the metafictional devices, intertextuality, and juxtaposition of different historical periods of *Possession* are typical features of the postmodern novel shared with *Lost in the Funhouse*. But while Barth's authorial figure is male—so much so that he is first presented as a sperm carrying on the tradition—Byatt succeeds in forging, as Jane Campbell elucidates, a continuity between past and present in a way that highlights the literary heritage of women authors.[13]

Angels and Insects exhibits many of these same characteristics, but dispenses with the complementary twentieth-century frame tale. Instead, two stories within the same historical period share similar themes, and continue the project of critiquing literary history by incorporating the possibility of female authors. With a superb display of learning, Byatt blurs divisions between different genres and discourses in her twinned tales: the scientific knowledge of the insect world and its Swedish taxonomer Linnaeus; a theological debate born of Darwinism; an authentic sounding Victorian fairytale; a discourse on the vein of spiritualism developed by Swedenborg; and an exegesis on nineteenth-century lyric

[11] Hutcheon 1988: 5.

[12] Wallhead (2007: 34) notes that while in the 1970s the author still leaned toward "Leavisite and Murdochian moralism . . . in her Continental inclinations and fascination for language, [she] comes to accept that 'classic realism' relies on an untenable theory of language."

[13] Campbell 2004: 146.

poetry. Of special note is the complex network of literary citations in both stories. Most pertinently "Morpho Eugenia" and "The Conjugial Angel" are bound together by their allusions to the Odyssean underworld, a device that illuminates Byatt's concerns with gender and narrative authority, the nature and function of metaphor, and the semiotics of storytelling. The underworld motif serves two contrasting discourses of the Victorian era: that of the rational scientific community (the entomological Darwinism of "Morpho Eugenia") and that of spiritualism (the séances of the Swedenborgian sect featured in "The Conjugial Angel").

The following analysis treats the underworld theme of each novella within the context of its Homeric allusions, but also as a manifestation of the overlapping intellectual and philosophical ideas shared by both stories. Byatt integrates the two modalities—the rational and the irrational—within a penetrating meditation on anthropomorphism that digs deep into the storyteller's toolbox of metaphor and analogy. These ideas are explored as aspects of gender in a way that recreates and then unsettles Victorian notions of women's role in society. More broadly her program can be understood as a critique of a binary deterministic opposition between male and female, a precept that Byatt vigorously and effectively dismantles in both her fiction and discursive essays.[14] Richard Todd has observed how the author, "reinscribes . . . those voices, often but not exclusively those of women, that have been excluded by patriarchal and colonial tradition, canon formation and interpretation."[15] To this end Byatt has made the female narrator a key figure in both novellas, linking storytelling with female agency. A tendency to privilege the creative and artistic ability of women typifies her challenge to the essentialist notion that the creative forces of the universe, culture, and society are male, while matter is aligned with the female.

As a challenge to a patriarchal control of discourse within a circumscribed Victorian society (and perhaps also our own), Byatt offers Matty Crompton, a nanny in a wealthy aristocratic household, in "Morpho Eugenia," and Lilias Papagay, a medium working amongst the landed gentry, in "Conjugial Angel." Both are marginalized women surviving on

[14] Byatt has argued (2001: 192) that feminists should be more critical of the male as Nous and female as matter analogy. For a survey of her critical positions on feminism and post-structuralism see Franken (2001: 1–32).

[15] Todd 1994: 104.

the fringes of their respective milieux. Their ability to tell stories, as a fairytale in one case and through the séance in the other, evokes the Odyssean underworld within a female-focused framework, but also transforms various narrative elements of the entire epic. These two female storytellers are artful reminders, perhaps, of the late Victorian scholar Samuel Butler's hypothesis that the author of the *Odyssey* was a woman. Byatt's narrators, both of whom possess Odyssean qualities themselves, are thus constructed as a reflection of a real controversy during the Victorian period.[16]

Mutations: "Morpho Eugenia"

In "Morpho Eugenia," set in 1860, the year after the publication of Darwin's *The Origin of the Species*, the concept of anthropomorphism informs a debate between William Adamson, a young scientist, and his eventual father-in-law Sir Harald Alabaster. Returning from the Amazon, William has lost most of his own insect specimens in a shipwreck off the coast of England. Virtually destitute, the young botanist accepts the job of cataloguing Sir Harald's unwieldy collection, an occupation that involves a gentlemanly exchange of theological and philosophical ideas. William is critical of Alabaster for anthropomorphizing God but he does the same himself when he studies and writes about insects. Michael Lackey has argued that "Morpho Eugenia" evinces the importance and inevitability of anthropomorphism in the construction of knowledge, especially self-knowledge.[17] It is an unavoidable way of negotiating reality, a lesson that William will learn and profit from when he reads Matty's fairytale. On the other hand both the narrator of "Morpho" and William himself perform the reverse analogical process by thinking of humans in terms of insect qualities. The comparison is implicit at first, but grows stronger. Sir Harald's chapel, for example, is arranged like a honeycomb, but more pronounced is the description of his corpulent wife, swollen like a queen bee or ant, fed and cosseted by a colony in which males play only minor roles. William falls in love with her

[16] *The Female Authoress of the Odyssey* (1897) was probably a parody of the Homeric scholarship of Butler's day, including speculations about the authorship of the *Odyssey*, although several scholars took him quite seriously.

[17] Lackey 2008: 136–7.

daughter Eugenia, an incarnation of the eponymous butterfly of the story, Morpho Eugenia, and a woman whom William, professional specimen collector that he is, obsessively longs to possess ("I shall die if I cannot have her," 15). But he finds himself living an insect-like existence, reflected and rectified by Matty's story, which casts William's entrapment among the Alabaster colony in terms of an Odyssean descent to an underworld occupied by moths, spiders, and ants.

It is not until Matty's story that the Odyssean intertext comes into clear view, but its subliminal pulses are felt from the first moments of William's arrival. Bredely Hall, home of the beautiful, privileged Alabasters, rephrases the pleasures of the utopian island of Scheria, where elite dancers display their skill for Odysseus (*Od.* 8.253, 370–80), now an elegant Victorian ball for another shipwrecked guest. William's interaction with Lady Alabaster, who admires how well her son's evening wear fits the newcomer, reenacts the exchange between Odysseus and the Phaeacian queen Arete, who notices that his clothing is from her own household (*Od.* 7.237–96). Like Arete, whom Odysseus was instructed to supplicate, Lady Alabaster is "a source of power in the household" (27). And most importantly there is her nubile daughter, Eugenia, who corresponds at first blush to the Phaeacian princess Nausicaa.

The Homeric signals grow stronger and more sinister. Edgar, Eugenia's half-brother (and secret lover), corresponds to Nausicaa's brother, Euryalus: he vaunts his social status and equestrian abilities, scorning his sister's fiancé, the lowly son of a butcher, as "underbred," an echo of Euryalus' sneer at what he assumed was Odysseus' mercantile status, and suggestion that the epic warrior was no match for him in athletic prowess (*Od.* 18.365–86). Matching Odysseus' trenchant response, William informs his future brother-in-law that surviving ten years in the Amazon and fifteen days at sea in a lifeboat should be proof enough of his courage. At the same time Edgar's aggressive insults evoke a parallel encounter between Odysseus, in his disguise as a beggar, and Penelope's suitor Eurymachus.[18] Just as Edgar is a composite of Nausicaa's brother and Penelope's suitor, Eugenia embodies both Nausicaa and Penelope—at

[18] As Murnaghan (1987: 97) notes, the leading men of the Phaeacian kingdom are characterized as Nausicaa's jealous suitors, which mirrors the situation that Odysseus encounters when he returns to Ithaca.

least initially—a congruence enhanced by her eventual marriage to William who prevails in what seems to be a contest for her hand.

Eugenia's correspondence with Penelope is heightened by her own morbid creation: she is making a "kind of a quilt" from William's insect specimens, pinning them down in embroidery patterns. Then again, there are more threatening female textile workers in the *Odyssey*: the intertextual presence of Calypso and Circe troubles the idea that Eugenia has metamorphosed from Nausicaa to Penelope. Eugenia possesses a binding power equal to that of Calypso: "I am yours to command, Miss Alabaster," William tells her, half jokingly, but soon feels like a "fairytale prince trapped by invisible gates and silken bonds in an enchanted castle" (21). It is symbolic that Eugenia pins down William's specimens in her "quilt." Her act of fixation, predicated on death, contrasts with William's gesture of mobility, the clouds of living butterflies and moths that he creates for Eugenia on the day of his marriage proposal. Yet like those pinioned specimens, he is immobilized by Eugenia and her family, making it impossible to resume his forays into the South American jungle. It is not long before he feels profound unhappiness and loss of purpose like the despondent Odysseus held in captivity on Calypso's island. Or to put it another way, William the entomologist has become a drone in a human hive.

"Things Are Not What They Seem"

Insects metamorphose, changing from one state to another; so does Eugenia and so will the drab nursemaid Matty Crompton, whose transformative potency manifests most forcefully in her authorial ability. Indeed stories metamorphose, *mutatis mutandis*, an idea integral to the novella. The *Odyssey* has become "Morpho Eugenia," whose Darwinian theme implies that narratives go through a mutation and evolution analogous to that of organic matter. It is an idea neatly encapsulated in Hutcheon's theory of cultural memes in her work on adaptation.[19] Arguing that there are no new stories, she uses an evolutionary model to explain the process by which stories evolve like genes. Thus an adaptation can "transcode" another work; this might happen by putting the story in a different medium, but also by setting it in a different

[19] Hutcheon (2012: 177): "Memes are not high-fidelity replicators: they change with time, for meme transmission is subject to constant mutation."

context.[20] Byatt presents us with a narrative embodiment of the theory: Matty's story, "Things Are Not What They Seem" (119–39) is a metamorphosed version of the Odyssean *Apologia* in which insects play a major role. Matty is thus the keeper of the interpretive key to "Morpho," even though she seems to be only a marginal figure in the household, an apparently dull ancillary to the glamorous story that unfolds around her. Her precise status is unclear, but she is somehow involved with schooling the growing brood of children, and assumes the important position of storyteller. Unlike the governess Miss Mead, whose tale of Cupid and Psyche is interrupted by William before its heroine reaches the gates of Hades, Matty composes a story of such power that William feels "uneasy, in ways he could not quite analyse" (140). To achieve a sense of purpose, he agrees to her suggestion that they co-author an illustrated children's book documenting an ant colony, the proceeds of which will finance their eventual escape from Bredely. Storytelling helps William, like Odysseus, survive, but Byatt also empowers the female narrator in this metamorphosed *Odyssey*. Matty's short story, which she eventually publishes, is the most explicit reference to the *Odyssey* in the novella. By structuring her fable as a descent narrative Matty invites her readers, both internal and external, to understand William's experience as a living death from which he must escape.

Alexa Alfer and Amy J. Edwards de Campos have noted that Byatt's fiction tends to incorporate "many features of the intellectual world it inhabits."[21] Replicating and merging three related characteristics of Victorian literary culture, Matty's story is a case in point. "Things" reflects the era's fascination with fairies, which became a passion of the Victorians, especially in art and fiction consumed by the middle class. In his introduction to an anthology of Victorian fairytales, whose authors include such literary celebrities as Charles Dickens and Oscar Wilde, Jack Zipes identifies their frequently didactic moralism and allegorical nature. Matty's story evinces both these qualities, ostensibly serving as instruction about the insect world, but also functioning as a symbol for William's situation. Zipes also notes how fairytales challenge the construction of gender in Victorian society, and give female characters the same heroic virtues as males, especially in the works of women authors

[20] Hutcheon 2012: 17–18. [21] Alfer and de Campos 2010: 119.

such as Mary de Morgan and Edith Nesbitt.[22] The wise Fairy-beyond-the-wall in Matty's tale is an implicit celebration of female authority, while Matty's role as an author who publishes her fairytales reproduces the successes of women such as de Morgan and Nesbitt that made them financially independent.

The second historically accurate element of "Things" reflects an intense interest in Homer among Victorian scholars. Renditions of the *Odyssey* by Alfred Lord Tennyson, Richard Jebb, and other significant figures exemplify the passion for Homer found in nearly every aspect of Victorian culture. The figure of Circe (mentioned in Matty's story) held a special allure for artists such as Edward Burne-Jones and John William Waterhouse (who painted her twice). In her study of the influence of Greek literature on women authors of late Victorian England T.D. Olverson discusses how writers such as Mary Elizabeth Braddon (*Circe, Or Three Acts in the Life of an Artist*, 1867) reimagined the sorceress in contemporary contexts.[23] Thus Matty's learned interest in the Homeric Circe is an entirely realistic touch on Byatt's part that acknowledges the epic's powerful influence on nineteenth-century culture. Furthermore Matty's tale is intended for children, and thus reprises adaptations of the *Odyssey* for juvenile readers in works like C.M. Bell's *The Cruise of Ulysses and His Men: Tales and Adventures from the Odyssey for Boys and Girls* (1880).[24]

The third related phenomenon that Byatt imitates is the proliferation of underworld tales in fiction for children of the period. In her study of the theme in English and French children's literature Vaclavik, taking her cue from Wendy Lesser, has identified the nineteenth-century's fascination with the underworld as a by-product of commercial, technological, and scientific endeavors. Excavations for subways, the mining industry, and forays into archaeology made the physical underground a visible, palpable reality that provoked the Victorian cultural

[22] Zipes 1987: xxii–xxvi.

[23] Scenes from the *Odyssey* inspired several other artists of the period such as William Turner ("Ulysses deriding Polyphemus," 1829), and John William Waterhouse ("Ulysses and the Sirens," 1891).

[24] Olverson 2010: 45–53. For a more general discussion of the influence of a classical education on Victorian women writers such as George Eliot, see Hurst (2006), who argues against the misconception that access to Greek and Latin literature was limited to boys.

imagination[25] Vaclavik surveys the catabatic theme in prose and poetry targeted at children (or which became popular among young audiences).[26] Lewis Carroll's *Alice's Adventures in Wonderland* (1865) is the most famous among the many novels that reflect the subterranean themes of the popular culture of the day, and the trend survives up to the present, as we shall see later in this chapter. The fairytale that Byatt's narrator creates not only imitates these three strands of Victorian culture, but melds them with an interest in botanical science inspired by Darwinism. It is quite a powerful concoction.

"Things Are Not What They Seem" is both a miniaturized metaphor (or *mise-en-abyme*) of William's sojourn among the Alabasters and a catabatic fairytale that secures a connection with the *Odyssey* insinuated by the frame tale. In other words, the contours of Homer's *Odyssey* are only suggested in the William/Eugenia plot, while "Things" makes specific allusions to the Homeric source text. These unambiguous citations not only illuminate the intertextuality of the frame text, but also align the internal storyteller Matty with the narrator of the novella. She possesses a preternatual ability to replicate and explicate the Odyssean allusions of the story in which she is a character, exemplifying the collapse of ontological boundaries that is for McHale a fundamental characteristic of postmodern fiction.[27] "Morpho Eugenia," the frame narrative, only makes opaque allusions to the *Odyssey* by recasting different episodes in a genteel Victorian setting that culminates with William imprisoned, as it were, on Calypso's island, an Elysium from which he cannot leave.[28] "Things," by making the allusions explicit in the embedded text affirms the allusions of the frame narrative, and offers a message of liberation from its strictures.

The protagonist of Matty's tale is Seth, the archetypal hero, who must leave home to seek his fortune.[29] Like William and Odysseus he travels the oceans until he is shipwrecked, in this version on an island that

[25] Vaclavik 2010: 3.

[26] See also Stevens (2015) for an analysis of the influence of *Aeneid* 6 on Verne's conception of the underworld in *Journey to the Center of the Earth*.

[27] McHale 1987: 14.

[28] Even in the Odyssey, the hero's time with Circe and Calypso is an underworld of sorts. Odysseus' sojourn with Circe, which is introduced by Hermes, and his subsequent departure from Calypso, activated by Hermes the psychopomp, can also be understood as a "long amorous" catabatic adventure, as Dova (2012: 39) puts it.

[29] Seth was the son of the biblical Adam, and William's last name is Adamson.

combines the Amazonian jungle of William's research (with its monkeys and tropical vegetation), Bredely Hall, and Circe's island, to mention the most obvious. A walled enclosure unlocks to reveal a luxuriously appointed castle featuring a table laden with food. Seth's companions greedily consume the feast, just as Odysseus' companions cannot restrain themselves from eating the cattle of Helios, but also like the greedy suitors on Ithaca. (And given that Miss Mead was telling the story of Psyche's descent earlier in the frame story, perhaps we should also remember that Psyche had to refuse Persephone's feast in order to return from Hades.) Only Seth refrains, although he is tempted into swallowing a few pomegranate seeds by the fairy enchantress, Mrs. Cottitoe Pan Demos, who turns his companions into pigs but spares the abstemious Seth, whom she appoints as her swineherd in an underground prison.

But Seth has allies, as heroes on quests always do: a benevolent ant provides seeds that make him tiny enough to escape, an allusion perhaps to the ant that helped Apuleius' Psyche fulfill one of Venus' challenges. And in many respects Seth's anabasis from the caverns is akin to the ascent from the cave in Plato's *Republic* (514a–520a): unshackled from the land of shadows (where things are not what they seem) the seeker moves upward to enlightenment. The now miniaturized Seth is in a state of heightened perception: colors are more vivid; he can hear noises, especially the sounds of insects moving and eating, that he could not in his normal size. A diminutive fairy, Mistress Mouffet, gives him instructions from here. She identifies herself as "the recorder of the Garden, or you might say the Spy, for Dame Cottitoe does not know of my existence" (150), so in another sense she is an author, the analogue of Matty herself. She also reveals her connection with Swedish scientist and taxonomist, Carl Linnaeus, who gave the insects their Greek names, "like delightful poems" (150). Linnaeus' reverence for the Homeric poems, as Byatt writes in an expository essay, inspired him to name insects after epic heroes. From the Linnaean inventory Matty has selected insects that bear names associated with the underworld: for example a Hawk-moth caterpillar Deilaphila Elpenor who functions as a threshold guardian on the garden wall, was named after "a Greek sailor, who was turned into a swine by a relative of Mistress Cottitoe, named Circe" (150).

The references to two characters so closely associated with the Homeric *Nekyia*—Elpenor who greets Odysseus at the mouth of Hades, and Circe who gives him directions on how to get there—are signposts of

Seth's subterranean voyage to come. The tiny hero learns that he must visit the Fairy-beyond-the-wall, a journey to the underworld in search of knowledge. The Sphinx moth, whose death-head markings make it an appropriate psychopomp, will carry Seth down to her cave.[30] Its full name is evocative, Sphinx Acherontia Atropos, which Mistress Mouffet glosses: "And Acheron is the River of Pain in the Underworld, where you must go, and Atropos is the Fate who snips the thread of life" (152). The descent is vividly described:

> They flew on, and on, over oceans, cities, rivers and forests, and then began a long, slow descent in a ravine between rocks that went on and on so deep, that about them the stars appeared to vanish. And as the sky and the moon and the stars vanished, another world was revealed by another light, a black world washed by flickering silvery fires, and shot with rainbow colors whose source he couldn't see. (156)

When they finally reach their destination, "a temple cut in a rock face, surrounded by a thick grove of silent watching black trees," they are greeted by another moth, appropriately named Proserpinus Proserpina. After a ritual sleep prescribed by a moth named Morpheus, Seth can address the mysterious power, whom he beseeches to help him and his comrades. When the all-powerful Fairy, like a Sphinx, poses her riddle Seth inadvertently names her "kind," and is rewarded with the power to release himself and his comrades from Cottitoe Pan Demos with the same drug, moly, that enabled Odysseus to defend himself against Circe.

Nomenclature is an important motif in the frame narrative, including William's desire to have an insect named after him, another way that it relates to the embedded tale. The names of insects in "Things," for example the moth Proserpinus Proserpina, emphasize the catabatic motif of the story, and its Greek mythological sources. As Mouffett puts it:

> Names, you know, are away of weaving the world together, by relating the creatures to other creatures and a kind of *metamorphosis*, you might say, out of a *metaphor*, which is a figure of speech for carrying one idea into another.
> (150, italics in the original)

The commentary provides a clue to William and the reader of the different interpretive levels in her story. It is, most obviously, a metaphor for William's experience among the Alabasters—not only Eugenia, who

[30] For ancient representations of the sphinx as a psychopomp see Petit 2016.

has bound William with "silken bonds," but also his life and experience at Bredely, have kept him trapped in a version of Cottitoe's underground chamber.

Matty/Mouffett's unequivocal didacticism also insinuates a complex tissue of allusion that binds the three stories: the embedded fairytale, the frame tale "Morpho Eugenia," and the *Odyssey* are thus variants of one another. The straightforward references to Circe, insect names associated with the underworld, and the shipwrecked sailor's descent to gain knowledge from a wise seer, all point to the Odyssey's *Nekyia*. Even though the descent is a generic characteristic of heroic myth, and Matty's version mutates and conflates different elements of the *Odyssey* (just as "Morpho" did), the Odyssean template is now firmly established and guides the interpretation of events that occur in "Morpho," both before and after Matty writes her tale.[31] At the center of her story is the Sphinx-like creature spinning a tissue, a powerful authorial figure (another version of Matty), who creates a new story for Seth and thereby for William. Events that lead to his release occur after the story, but also because of it. The embedded story is a performative metaphor that causes change in the frame tale.

It is significant that Mouffett links metaphor with the process of metamorphosis. A chrysalid, by her account, is a house, a cradle, a coffin, or even a shroud. Death is a form of "transfiguration": the Hawk-moth caterpillar Elpenor sleeps in something like a mummy case, which if broken reveals, "a yellow soup, like egg-yolk, which looks like putrification and is the stuff of life and the rebirth itself. For things are not what they seem, and you must always remember" (152). Mouffet's homily can be read as a metafictional disquisition on the Odyssean elements of *Angels and Insects*, for both novellas are reincarnations of the Homeric epic. Most significant is how Byatt has utilized the ancient catabatic pattern, letting the narrative dissolve and reconstitute as a new story-form, but one whose genetic code is apparent. The caterpillar that melts into a "soup" will always emerge as a Hawk-moth, just as the transfigured story will follow a particular pattern. In this case it is the descent narrative in which the hero gains knowledge from a necromantic encounter before ascending back to life above the ground.

[31] Tiffin (2006: 60) notes that the embedded narratives in Byatt's fiction encourage the reader to see parallels between the realist frame tale and the fairy tale.

A brief survey of how Byatt uses the catabatic motif elsewhere provides some background to her understanding of the wisdom tradition. Byatt's education, including her acknowledged study of Vergil's *Aeneid* 6 and a postgraduate year at Bryn Mawr College that involved courses in Classics, is evident in much of her work, and particularly in her deft use of classical descent themes. For example, Stevens identifies the influence of Aeneas' catabasis in *The Children's Book* (2009), which makes a direct reference to *Aeneid* 6 as a component of its characters' early education.[32] Scholars have also noted how *Possession*, which ends with a dramatic revelation exhumed from a poet's grave, evokes classical underworld tropes including the Persephone myth.[33] *Possession* also deploys the underworld motif in a Platonic vein with the character of Roland Mitchell, a struggling young academic, who is studying in the basement library of the University of London when he makes the life-changing discovery of a set of love letters between two Victorian poets. His subterranean revelation sets the complex plot in motion, but his true epiphany occurs, as Lena Steveker observes, when he starts to distance himself from his earlier obsessive academic interests and individuates into a creative poet himself. With this revelation Roland leaves his dank basement apartment and enters a hitherto forbidden garden where he feels a creative poetic force welling up within, a transformative moment that Steveker likens to the allegory of Plato's cave.[34]

This is only a brief survey, but it demonstrates the sophistication and erudition of Byatt's engagement with classical descent traditions, which she obviously knows very well. *Angels and Insects* is, of all her fiction, most indebted to that story pattern, and "Things" is clearly influenced by the catabatic teleology of enlightenment and wisdom. Matty's tale is an especially resonant and imaginative version of the catabasis that deploys

[32] The novel begins in the late 1800s and ends with World War I. Following the "dark" readings of the characterization of Aeneas, Stevens (2016 b) identifies a Vergilian intertext that culminates in a play named *Tom's Underground*. He concludes that just as Aeneas' experience in Dis is a metaphor for his own damaged psyche, Tom exists in a form of living death.

[33] References to the Persephone myth occur at the beginning and end of *Possession* (Cox 2011: 137, cf. Slater 2003). Although Cox is more concerned with Vergilian themes, she perceives a Demeter/Persephone motif in the Frederica quartet: Frederica's sister, Stephanie, who is killed in a household accident (*Still Life*, 1985), fantasizes about the underworld, especially in the context of her marital relations.

[34] Steveker 2009.

the entomological motif of the frame tale as a metaphor modeled on the wisdom tradition. It exerts a performative and interpretive force that ricochets back into the frame tale.[35]

A hybrid Odyssey

If Matty's story invites the reader to interpret the novella as a version of the *Odyssey*, particularly Books 5–13 (the Wanderings), then "Things" itself corresponds to the *Nekyia*, although a *Nekyia* mutated and evolved (with a few grafts from Apuleius' *Metamorphoses* 6). Like Odysseus consulting with Tiresias, Seth seeks knowledge from the benign Fairy/Sphinx. The "transexuation" (to use Genette's terminology) of the wise seer reflects the gender of her creator and analogue Matty, who like the Fairy can pose liberating riddles. During a game of anagrams with William, Matty slyly changes "insect" to "incest," a hint of the revelation to come. Moreover the reader is invited to participate in the game: when William produces "Phoenix," as Campbell deduces, he had "Sphinx" before him.[36] The Fairy-beyond-the-wall, who identifies herself as the Sphinx, offers the possibility of a phoenix-like regeneration both for Seth and William. The semiotic playfulness in which the reader becomes part of the game is a microcosm of the larger game in which we are invited to view "Morpho" as a rearrangement of the components of the *Odyssey*. Correspondingly, just as Seth is released from Dame Cottitoe Pan Demos, and Odysseus from Calypso, so William is released from Eugenia when he follows a mysterious summons to her bedroom where he finds his wife in bed with her half-brother Edgar.[37] Freed from any sense of obligation to Eugenia and her children, and enabled by the proceeds of his book, he can make his escape.

Matty, whose scientific curiosity, intelligence, and cunning combine with William's expertise to produce the book, is the very opposite of the decorous, docile, amoral Eugenia. She is William's equal; but if he is a

[35] Tiffin (2006: 61) observes that Byatt's fairytales can have effects on the frame stories in which they occur by serving as cautionary tales or warnings, or offering insights or suggestions to characters in the frame narrative and thereby empowering them.

[36] Campbell 2004: 158.

[37] Eugenia's incest recalls the story told by the Phaeacian bard Demodocus *(Od.* 8.266–366) in which Hephaestus is summoned to the lovemaking of Ares and Aphrodite (also half-siblings); indeed William has compared Eugenia to Aphrodite. As Byatt reveals (2001: 194), "Morpho is one of the ways of naming Aphrodite Pandemos, the earthly Venus."

version of Odysseus, then is she his Penelope? Unlike her Homeric predecessor she has the capacity to accompany her man on his sea voyages, and has Odyssean features herself. Characters in this story are crossbred rather than cloned: Eugenia is a fusion of Circe, Calypso, and Nausicaa; Matty combines attributes of Penelope and Athena, the goddess who enables Odysseus to escape Calypso's island. As William prepares to leave, Matty goes through her own metamorphosis. She has corresponded to all the tutelary figures in her catabatic fairy story—the ant, Mistress Mouffett, and the Fairy-beyond-the-wall. She somehow slid in amongst the Alabasters, an Athena to William's Odysseus, and is now ready to leave with him. There is a thrilling moment of "recognition" when the former mild-mannered, plain nanny morphs into a powerful agent of change. With funds from the publication of her fairytales, she has booked passages for them both to Brazil. William demurs, and in a final rearrangement of the game pieces, Matty takes on the role of Odysseus, demanding to be recognized, and (as Odysseus did when he revealed himself to his wife), names herself.

> "You have no idea who I am." . . . He hardly recognised the practical Miss Crompton of earlier times . . . "My name," she said, "is Matilda . . . *Look at me*."
> (156–7, italics in the original)

As a narrator whose stories provide a sea-passage to freedom, she is a version of Odysseus, who earned his passage from the Phaeacians with his storytelling, most notably of his time in Hades. The last we hear of William and Matty they are onboard the *Calypso*, whose name is the final quotation mark on this revised tale of descent and escape.

Byatt's poetics of hybridity and adaptation fit well with Hutcheon's theory of the meme, a replicating unit of culture that is analogous to a gene. Every living organism has a genetic code, but we are all unique fusions of inherited genes, which can mutate and thus evolve, and specific environments. Correspondingly, a meme is never simply a clone, but manifests blends of traditions and context. "Morpho" inherits its "genetic code" from the *Odyssey*, and yet it is set in a Victorian context. It has mutated and evolved into a different version of the story, a process that exemplifies Hutcheon's theory of adaptation and cultural production. Contingent on these ideas is the conviction that there is no stable origin of a text, in other words there is no "perfect" source text, but rather only a series of cultural products adapted to their specific contexts.[38] While the genetic metaphor of "Morpho" exemplifies the concept of the inherited story that adapts to its environment, the second novella, "The Conjugial Angel," is a form of textual haunting that questions the notion of authorship. Conversations with ghosts and voices from beyond the grave exert a decentering pull on the text, confusing the notion of the individuality of the authorial voice.

Hauntings: "The Conjugial Angel"

Lilias Papagay, the focal character of "The Conjugial Angel," is a spiritualist whose reflection that the séance is a form of "communal authorship" perfectly expresses the notion that texts are complex tissues of references and citations. Byatt shifts her metaphor in this tale of otherworldly voices, but her theory of literature is consistent. The two novellas share but a single character, and one who appears only briefly at the end of each. The sea captain Arturo Papagay sails away with William and Matty to Brazil at the end of "Morpho Eugenia," and returns from the sea in the final pages of "The Conjugial Angel," twice-wrecked, as he tells his wife Lilias, introducing some doubt about the fate of the two lovers in the previous story. The novellas are linked in more subtle and significant ways, however: the binding ingredient is a shared Odyssean intertext, again associated with a female voice, a narrator whose presence and agency contests the alignment of masculinity and formative power. While the first novella is infused with elements of the wanderings of Odysseus including his Phaeacian interlude, the second has more affinity with events at home in Ithaca. In keeping with the ludic poetics signaled by the game of Anagrams, the important preoccupation of "Angel" is the séance, which "even at its most intense, visionary and tragic, retained elements of the parlour game" (202). The spirit world sends snatches of verse, Biblical quotations, and other enigmatic correspondence, which participants are invited to decode and interpret. The narrator of "Angels" thus plays games with the reader; we interpret clues, reassemble fragments of pre-existing texts such as Milton and Tennyson, and become aware of another narrative dimension, ghosts from other stories.

[38] As Hutcheon herself put it, her interest in adaptation was part of her "postmodern de-hierarchalizing impulse." See her interview with Bucknell (2006: 159).

The novella's title refers to the precept of the eighteenth-century Swedish philosopher/mystic Emanuel Swedenborg that angels combine male and female attributes and are thus"conjugial." Byatt's characters, influenced by his book on the afterlife, *Heaven and Hell* (1758), meet to commune with their departed loved ones through a series of séances in the home of Emily and Richard Jesse. In this context, and informed by Alex Owen's "feminist account of nineteenth-century mediumship," *The Darkened Room* (1988), Byatt brings to life the sister of Alfred Lord Tennyson.[39] Emily was briefly engaged to the poet Arthur Hallam before his premature death, which inspired her brother's *In Memoriam*, one of the most celebrated literary works of the nineteenth century.[40] The two young poets shared a deep emotional bond (Byatt's text hints at the homoerotic) strengthened by Hallam's engagement to Emily. Tennyson also wrote his *Ulysses* in response to his friend's death, a detail that creates an intriguingly subliminal resonance with Byatt's Odyssean intertext.[41] Using Emily's letters and piecing together references by contemporaries, who criticized her for marrying Jesse nine years after Hallam's death, Byatt has created her backstory. Emily's attested interest in spiritualism and her membership in Swedenborg's Church of the New Jerusalem guided the author to imagine a group dominated by Mr. Hawke, a repressive but lubricious proponent of the sect, who is given to citing Saint Paul's misogynistic strictures while letting his eyes wander over the bosoms of the two mediums, Lilias Papagay and Sophy Sheekhy. This "revisionist and feminist" untold story of Emily is the general framework for Byatt's reimagined *Nekyia*.[42] It is the two mediums, Lilias Papagay and Sophy Sheekhy, to whom we now turn our attention.

Sophy's talents are visceral; the spirits speak through her, and at times she sees, hears, and even smells them. These are not parlor tricks: there is an eerie scene when she is alone with the putrefying revenant Arthur Hallam who sends a message to Emily, a montage of biblical quotations and literary passages, as a reminder of her putative obligations to him. The contrast between corporeal impermanence and poetic immortality

[39] Byatt (2001: 184) provides the reference in her discursive essay.

[40] The poem is another link with the previous novella where it is quoted by Harald Alabaster.

[41] Tennyson wrote that *Ulysses* was composed "more . . . with the feeling of his [Hallam's] loss upon me than many poems in *In Memoriam*." See Ricks (v.1) 1969: 613.

[42] Byatt 2001: 184.

shapes this gothic encounter, but the séances also emphasize that, "poems are the sensuous afterlife of men."[43] The other medium, Lilias Papagay, is a Penelope figure cut from Homeric cloth—she wears "wine-dark" silk, the epic epithet for the sea—tailored to nineteenth-century specifications. With such citations and an emphasis on spiritualism, "Angel" evokes the *Nekyia* of *Odyssey* 11, now somehow transported to an English coastal town. Homeric allusions in the early part of the story add to the ghostly intertext. It is specifically around Lilias that the Nekyian references cluster: throngs of spirits who "squeaked and gibbered" in the night (195) and ghosts of men and women, poets and painters "who congregated thickly in the garden and trooped together up the stairs" (196), counterparts of the "gibbering" spirits of the Odyssean underworld (*Od.* 24.5–9) and the swarms of shades that Odysseus encounters at the entrance to Hades (*Od.* 11.42). Toward the end of the novella, before the final séance, Lilias seeks to reassure Sophy that it is a natural inclination for the living to want to speak with the dead. She includes in her list "Odysseus offering Tiresias beakers of blood" (319), a further clue to the Nekyian intertext. Lilias, who has a particular talent for automatic writing, seems to takes on the role of Odysseus, co-opting and blending two of his abilities: to communicate with the dead and to tell stories. And she is a spiritual go-between, who wears a winged hat like that of "Hermes in old pictures" (188), and whose vatic talents enable her to cross social boundaries and mingle with the upper class. Although her gender, economic circumstances, and a Victorian code of behavior keep her fixed at home, her clairvoyance and creative imagination grant admittance to other realities and reveal how "that world penetrated and interpenetrated this one" (188). She apprehends a subliminal world of angels, dead children, lovers, and poets coterminous with the narrative ghosts who haunt the pages of this story.

Like Penelope, Mrs. Papagay has been waiting patiently for the return of her husband, whom she has come to believe is lost at sea. She misses him deeply: theirs was a marriage of sexual fulfillment and personal compatibility. Arturo enchanted her "with tales of his deeds and sufferings in faraway places" (193), just as Penelope listened to Odysseus with delight when he told her "what cares he inflicted on men and what

[43] Byatt 2001: 191.

sufferings he endured" (*Od.* 23.306–7). But Lilias Papagay likes to create stories as well as hear them. Like Matty Crompton she is a storyteller. She spins tales from scraps of gossip and everyday life, and takes a shot at a literary career, weaving her husband's stories into a novel about a sailor who survives a disaster at sea, exists on a raft for weeks, and is "imprisoned by amorous Tahitian princesses" (201). But if her creation reads like the *Odyssey* (and even a little like "Morpho Eugenia"), it is an adaptation in which the sailor returns to "his Penelope" (202) only to find her married to his detested cousin. Like Agamemnon, who returned home to find his wife married to his cousin, Aegisthus, and who serves as a negative exemplum for Odysseus and Penelope throughout the *Odyssey*, Mrs. Papagay's sailor suggests alternate narrative universes where tales are told with different endings. Eventually she abandons the enterprise, but although a career as an author eludes her, she discovers a profitable outlet for her creative talents in the séance, which gives rein to her penchant for storytelling.

This second novella's focus on the Victorian séance highlights its essence as a haunted text, a descriptor that applies to many of the cultural products discussed in this book, but particularly apt here. The analogy of ghost and narrative is quite explicit in "Angel," in which the séance becomes a form of storytelling that channels the ghosts of past stories. The two mediums at times give voice to other texts, including the book of *Revelations* and the poems of Arthur Hallam. Furthermore, the possibility of a narrative possessed by the spirit of an ancient story challenges the concept of authorship. Lilias, whose surname is a based on the Spanish word for "parrot," and her accomplice Sophy Sheekhy become ventriloquists projecting disembodied voices from a hidden dimension. And having invoked the spirit of the *Odyssey* Byatt mischievously defies expectations by presenting divergent possibilities that allude to familiar details of the epic, a tendency that Mrs. Papagay's novel exhibited in microcosmic form, but then deviates from its anticipated conclusions. The citations are recognizable, but there is also a spectral fluidity about these ghost texts. For example, the famous fireside scene in which Penelope, apparently unaware of his true identity, questions her husband disguised as a beggar, seems to be the inspiration for Mrs. Papagay's fireside encounter with Mr. Hawke in her own parlor. A recent séance weighs heavily on her mind. Its message included a quote from Tennyson's *In Memoriam*, "his loved remains sail the placid ocean-plains" (204), which convinces

Mrs. Papagay that Arturo is now "ground white bones" (208). In her corresponding fireside scene Penelope (*Od.* 19.312–13) articulates the same conviction that her missing husband will never return, an irreplaceable loss, since like Arturo he is uniquely suited to his wife. Penelope and Odysseus are a perfect match, "of like mind." *Homophrosyne* is the word Homer uses (*Od.* 6.180–2); "conjugial" is its Swedenborgian equivalent.

It is the *Odyssey's* emphasis on marital compatibility that prompts Norman Austin to remark that: "The ideal of harmony between two persons is the keystone of the poem, the *telos* to which it moves."[44] The theme of a perfect love, two partners who are made for one another, is likewise integral to *Angels and Insects,* but there are false recognitions, so to speak.[45] William does not recognize his true soul mate, Matty, until the end of the tale. Lilias Papagay, after a decade of loneliness, has a brief moment of indecision when Mr. Hawke broaches the topic of perfect union between man and woman. According to Swedenborg, there is but one chance at true "conjugial love" for us all, "one perfect other half, whom we should seek ceaselessly" and to whom the Conjugial Angel will join us (242). But, wonders Mrs. Papagay, can a person be mistaken about the identity of their perfect soul mate? Is this unctuous little man her Odysseus after all? Apparently not, and the familiar narrative sequence is truncated as Mr. Hawke clumsily gropes Lilias, who pushes him away.

The story of Lilias and her commitment to Arturo counterpoints that of Emily Jesse and her lost love, Arthur Hallam, as the similarity of the two men's names suggests. Instead it is Captain Jesse, a sea captain and a teller of tales (like Odysseus) whom his wife Emily recognizes as her true love in another fireside scene that allows the epic moment to be reanimated. The denouement of Byatt's speculative reconstruction of Emily's life occurs when the elderly Captain, having believed throughout his marriage that his wife's "perfect other half" is the dead poet, is dumbfounded to hear that she would prefer to spend her afterlife with him, even though the spirit of Hallam has indicated (via Sophy) that she

[44] Austin 1975: 181.

[45] The question of whether Penelope consciously (or even subconsciously) recognizes Odysseus in his beggar disguise has long exercised scholars. Homer does not grant much insight into Penelope's thoughts, but Amory (1963) has argued that she intuits the beggar's identity soon after she meets him. Reece (2011: 109–10) surveys the scholarship on the topic.

should be his in eternity: "Captain Jesse shook his head, like a surfacing swimmer" (284). His recognition recalls the famous simile (*Od.* 23.232–9) in which the reunion of Odysseus and Penelope is likened to a shipwrecked man coming to shore. This final séance comes to a dramatic end when Lilias is inspired to do some automatic writing. Her pen, squirming as if possessed, produces a naughty poetic rendering of Sophy's message; it is a suitable historical replication of the obscene turn that the Victorian séance could take. The concatenation of "plumply limbs," "liquid oozing," "scarlet holes," and "golden cock," sends Mr. Hawke scurrying away, and emphasizes the creative talents of Lilias whose writings have the power to get rid of an unwelcome suitor.

The story of Lilias and Arturo parallels the happy recognition of Emily and Captain Jesse as true soul mates. Captain Papagay may share a name with Arthur Hallam, but he is very much the flesh and blood opposite of the ethereal dead poet. The "recognition" of Richard Jesse by his wife, and the image of the swimming man foreshadow the reunion of Lilias and Arturo. On her way home from the Jesses Mrs. Papagay realizes she is being followed. At first, like Penelope, she cannot distinguish the identity of her husband, but soon enough realizes that it is Arturo. The Odyssean swimmer evoked by the reunion of the Jesses has now materialized.[46] Their rapturous embrace is observed by Sophy Sheekhy who sees them "becoming more and more completely entangled in one," the perfect embodiment of the Conjugial Angel. On the other hand Mrs. Papagay herself is the embodiment of both Odysseus and Penelope, merging the attributes of husband and wife who are now "completely entangled" in her. She has waited patiently at home, resisting the advances of a suitor, but she has also communed with the spirit world in a domesticized version of the *Nekyia* that transforms her into a storyteller and thus appropriates Odysseus' most salient and salvational

[46] He wept as he held his beloved wife, steadfast of mind, as when the land appears welcome to men swimming because their sturdy boat has been smashed in Poseidon's sea and wracked by wind and thick waves—and a few escape by swimming from the salty sea to, dry land; with brine thickly caked on their skin and rejoicing they step on the earth, having escaped evil, so her husband was welcome to her as she looked at him.

(*Od.* 23.232–9).

characteristic. And while Odysseus' voyage to Hades is the most distance he will travel from home, Byatt artfully combines the *Nekyia* and home so that two contrasting narrative elements become "completely entangled" in this quaint, yet stirring, version of the heroic journey.

The postmodern Nekyia

Barth's *Lost in the Funhouse* and Byatt's *Angels and Insects* exemplify how well underworld narratives suit the definitive qualities of postmodern fiction including its preoccupation with narrativity, and intertextual pastiches. As one of the oldest and most adapted tales in literary history, the Odyssean *Nekyia* offers possibilities for defiant amendments of a story pattern associated with male heroic endeavors. Both authors exploit this prestigious heritage to disassemble the notion of authorial wholeness and hegemony. Barth exemplifies this fragmented aesthetic in the structure of *Lost in the Funhouse*, and its central catabatic story. Byatt's *Angels and Insects* represents the tendency in a different way with two separate stories, each citing the Odyssean *Nekyia*, including an embedded fairy tale, and fragments of other works. Moreover, as a *mise-en-abyme*, a miniature version of the frame tale, "Morpho Eugenia," Matty's fairytale, is another example of the blurring of ontological levels that McHale identifies as a foremost characteristic of postmodernist fiction.[47] This recursive abyss, the sense of infinitely receding worlds within worlds, makes the formal structure of the story an icon for its content (i.e. the infinite chasm of Hades), another version of the funhouse mirrors in which a reflection goes on forever.

Acutely aware of the recurring tradition that precedes them, Barth and Byatt subvert traditional configurations of the underworld while exploiting the implications of its lineage, now transcoded in a non-heroic context. In their fiction an ironic mixture of learned and prestigious literary allusions is juxtaposed with different forms of popular culture: an amusement park, a fairy tale, and a séance become vehicles for reimagined underworlds. In short, both writers critique cultural hierarchies with literary alloys that revitalize the tradition. Concomitantly, just as postmodern novels absorb

[47] McHale (1987: 14) "*Mise-en-abyme*, wherever it occurs, disturbs the orderly hierarchy of ontological levels (worlds within worlds), in effect *short-circuiting* the ontological structure, and thus foregrounding it." And (124) "one of the most potent devices in the postmodernist repertoire for foregrounding the ontological dimension of recursive structures."

aspects of popular culture, there is a corresponding phenomenon in popular culture that alludes explicitly to ancient catabatic narratives. This hybridization of highbrow literature and mainstream culture is also evident in mass-produced media, as Neil Gaiman's *Sandman* series illustrated.

The previous chapter treated this postmodern rebellion as a conflict within a patrilineal literary tradition that resulted in new types of storytellers. Byatt's adaptation of the *Odyssey* is a different sort of challenge that valorizes female narrators by insinuating them into the role of Odysseus. Moreover the underworld mentor in Matty's tale is also female: the Fairy-beyond-the-wall who corresponds to Tiresias in the *Odyssey*, but has an aura of Persephone about her as well. The Fairy is a creator figure from whom stories seem to emanate, like a spider's web, but we are not yet at the point where a female descends and becomes a storyteller. The next analysis will pave the way for a discussion of how Ferrante's catabatic female storyteller engages with a powerful chthonic other who embodies the potential of narrative production. The bridge will be Henry Selick's adaptation of Neil Gaiman's *Coraline*, a children's novel that features a heroic battle with an infernal female force, and proves to be a multifaceted and nuanced examination of issues of gender and identity within the tradition of underworld fiction. Like Matty's tale in "Morpho Eugenia," *Coraline* adapts a descent narrative for a children's story, which conforms to a well-established tradition. But the film is also another manifestation of the postmodern underworld with a blend of different intertexts that dislodges illusions of wholeness and continuity.

Persephone Interrupted: *Coraline*

The multiple award-winning children's novella *Coraline* (2002) recounts the adventures of an eleven-year old girl who discovers a tunnel to another world occupied by idealized simulacra of her busy, preoccupied parents in a more appealing version of home. The tale follows the structure of the portal narrative, a common convention in children's literature, for example Alice's tumble into Wonderland, which *Coraline* resembles in certain respects.[48] It epitomizes the gothic turn in children's

[48] As Gaiman has revealed, his inspiration for *Coraline* was a Victorian cautionary tale, "The New Mother," by Lucy Clifford, published in her collection, *The Anyhow Stories*,

literature with a clear demarcation of good and evil, a heroine from the everyday world, and a dark, unnerving tone.[49] As one reviewer put it, the story is permeated with the "charged and often horrific flotsam from the subconscious."[50] Accordingly it has generated a spate of psychoanalytic interpretations; two related approaches are particularly germane to the catabatic theme of the story. David Rudd and Richard Gooding have independently determined that Gaiman is animating Freud's essay on "The Uncanny," which analyzes the morbid anxiety described as *unheimlich*, the mirror opposite of *heim*, or "homely." Gooding surmises intentional allusions to Freud in *Coraline*, and remarks that:

> There are doubles, the dead, talking animals, toys coming to life, the constant threat of blindness and mutilation (not only in the black button eyes of the other parents but also in Coraline's blinding of the other father and the bargain she strikes with the other mother), the apparent reading of Coraline's mind, immediate wish fulfillment, and so on.[51]

This incisive analysis posits a double audience for *Coraline*, and indeed Gooding argues that the novella exemplifies the phenomenon of cross-writing, which activates a form of communication between an adult reader and his or her child self.[52] Along the same lines Rudd reads the novella as "a quite overt fictional representation of the Freudian uncanny," and pinpoints the fantasy of being buried alive, another fear included in Freud's theory.[53] This primal anxiety is encapsulated by the uterine imagery of Coraline's Other World, noticed in the analyses of Karen Coats and Holly Virginia Blackford. Coraline experiences an infantile regression, and the concomitant fantasy of maternal plenitude in which her every desire is fulfilled. Other characters gradually transform into fetus-like creatures in this alternative reality, for example Misses Spink and Forcible, who regress from their elderly state to more youthful versions of themselves, and finally into embryonic blobs.

Moral and Otherwise (1882), in which children are tempted by an enchantress to drive their real mother away so that a new mother can replace her.

[49] Coats (2008: 79) describes Gaiman's novel as "old school" gothic.

[50] Burkam 2002: 755.

[51] Gooding 2008: 394.

[52] Gooding 2008: 390–1. In her explanation of the appeal of myth in children's stories, Murnaghan (2011: 343) writes: "children stand for popular audiences in the sense that they stand for everyone, representing humanity in general, not yet molded by particular historical circumstances."

[53] Rudd 2008: 161–2.

In essence *Coraline* touches upon fantasies of returning to the womb, which in this case corresponds to an underworld occupied by ghosts and other terrors.

Coats, in her analysis of the gothic elements of the novella, points out that Coraline's first visit to Other Mother's lair (a dream apparently) occurs after a frustrating shopping trip with her mother for a dreary school uniform. In the womb-like space dominated by Other Mother she easily obtains the cool clothing denied to her in the real world, along with a nicer room, and better toys. Coraline's experience in this apparent paradise serves as an allegory for how children learn to negotiate and understand desire. From her time in a seemingly utopian world where all wants are immediately gratified, Coraline comes to learn that she does *not* want not to want. But having eaten Other Mother's delicious food, she finds it difficult to separate from her. Coats identifies the psychological dynamic here in terms of the mythological pattern established in the Persephone story, which represents "the ambivalences that plague all young girls: a desire to remain in a dyadic relationship with their mothers."[54] This "archetypal font of all Gothic fiction" provides a story pattern in which a young girl deals with her conflicting desires either to remain in an infantile mother–child bond or be with her husband or lover. Coraline of course is too young to consider marriage or romance, but at eleven she is approaching her teenage years when she will become increasingly independent. While Coats' use of the Persephone myth helps to explain Coraline's liminal identity, not an infant and not yet an adolescent, she goes no further in terms of the underworld theme of the novella. Blackford takes up the project by developing the Persephone analogy. Noting that Coraline's name aligns her with Persephone/Korē, she connects the womb and egg imagery with an impending menarche.[55] As she recognizes, Coraline undergoes a catabasis when she visits Other Mother, a signal of her transition.

The first of these descents occurs at night when she follows a psychopompic mouse that guides her to a previously locked door opening into a tunnel leading to a replica of her real home. Here she is now the center of

[54] Coats 2008: 85.

[55] Blackford 2012: 210. Although Gaiman (2012: xiv), in the introduction of his revised edition of *Coraline*, has stated that Coraline was a fortuitous typo for "Caroline," the name opens up a rich vein of interpretive possibilities.

the doting Other Mother's attention. Another visit during the daytime, however, reveals the predatory desires of the maternal replica, her true arachnid form, and the possibility of her dangerous irruption into the waking world of Coraline's home life. Although Other Father appears jovial and benign, it is soon evident that he is a cipher created by the monstrous Other Mother to help entrap Coraline. As Other Mother's prey Coraline would live among the ghosts of her previous child victims, and the girl's efforts to evade this fate are complicated when she sees her miniaturized parents imprisoned in the "Demetrian winter" of a glass snow-globe.[56] In order to release them Coraline must answer a riddle and play a game with Other Mother that, should she lose, would require her to accept buttons for eyes and remain locked in her lair forever: in other words she would die, or become a copy of the doll that Other Mother created earlier, which amounts to the same thing. The mysterious tunnel, which Blackford reads as a birth canal, and the ghosts of children locked in a kind of limbo certainly suggest that Other Mother presides over a smothering womb-like underworld. Be that as it may, allusions to the *Hymn to Demeter* are subliminal in Gaiman's text; it is not until Selick's animated filmic adaptation that the imprint of classical underworld myths becomes distinct.

Coraline *transcoded*

Selick's *Coraline* (2009) retains the essential plot and theme of the novella, but adds several elements to flesh out the narrative into a full-length, stop-motion, animated film. Its visual impact and strategic adaptations explicate and heighten mythic elements implicit in Gaiman's story by means of allusions to classical underworld adventures, with discernible references to the *Homeric Hymn to Demeter* and the *Odyssey*. The result is a hybrid tale that resists a narrative of passivity (the abduction of Persephone) to present a young girl with heroic agency analogous to that of Odysseus and other male catabants. The blending of two classical intertexts epitomizes the postmodern strategies of bricolage and pastiche, as well as the tendency for underworld narratives (such as *Aeneid* 6) to "mix and match" different traditions. In Selick's *Coraline* this admixture produces a tension between two ancient myths that intensifies the

[56] Blackford 2012: 212.

impression of Coraline's self-sufficient individuality, and also allows the Odyssean theme of homecoming to override the inevitable separation of parent and child that the *Homeric Hymn* strives to reconcile. Consequently the Odyssean allusions function as a counterweight to the Persephone story by emphasizing that this is a girl with heroic agency and intellect equal to that of the Homeric model. Rather than existing as a mute bride to be brought back from Hades by her mother, she is the savior of her parents, a significant twist to the *Homeric Hymn.* A mixing of genres, forms, conventions, and clichés (of epic poetry, children's texts, art, and animated films), offers both nostalgic and ironic perspectives on cultural history, while also suggesting a possibility of renewal or rebirth, a new type of story that is created from fragments of the old. Before embarking on an analysis of this dynamic, however, we need to survey how Selick elaborates the underworld theme with specific visual references.

In its early moments the film hints at Coraline's forthcoming infernal journey when she descends down a flight of stairs to visit the basement apartment of her new neighbors, the former actresses Misses Spink and Forcible, who live in a taxidermic mausoleum of former pets. (Stuffed Scotch terriers adorn the walls.) The barking terriers at the door, from her perspective (and ours), blend into a three-headed Cerberean Scottie Dog, an affirmation of the descent motif suggested in an earlier encounter with another neighbor. While she is water-witching, an activity that intimates her connection with the realm below the ground, Coraline meets Whybie, Death personified if his biking-gear is to be believed. The episode, one of Selick's additions, is a harbinger of things to come. The boy knocks Coraline down with his dirt-bike, suggestive of the moment when Persephone is abducted by Hades in his chariot and the earth opens up to receive the couple. Whybie, once he takes off his skull-embossed helmet, turns out to be a friendly ally, who helps Coraline find a well by scraping away the earth. Even though the episode reassuringly defangs the Persephone/Hades paradigm, it contributes to the film's chthonic motif and presages a more sinister encounter between Coraline and Other Father.

The counterpoint to Coraline's dreary reality—it is apparently autumn above ground and the landscape is covered by a persistent mist—exists in her dream world where she finds Other Father tending a dazzling garden as he rides an insect-shaped tractor. A panorama reveals that the garden is a floral portrait of Coraline, a flattering appeal to an eleven-year old's ego, and a visual allusion to Persephone/Korē, the "flower-faced girl" (*καλυκώπιδι κούρῃ*, *HHD* 8). In the *Homeric Hymn to Demeter* Persephone was gathering flowers in a meadow when she reached for a narcissus (6–10); the earth gaped open; Hades seized her and carried her off in his golden car (14–19). In Selick's vision Other Father's fantastic garden has the same seductive quality as the narcissus sent as a lure (*δόλον*, 8) to Persephone (Figure 3.1). In this case the garden is bait to get Coraline to stay with Other Mother and Other Father; later the threatening qualities of the garden become apparent as menacing flowers try to pull the child into an underground chamber, just as the "wide-pathed earth gaped open" for Persephone (*χάνε δὲ χθὼν εὐρυάγυια*, 16), before Hades made his lunge. There is a more ominous echo of Persephone's abduction when Other Father scoops up the little girl on his big mechanical grasshopper. Nonetheless he never seems to be the real danger in this story: as "a powerless phallus in the underworld," he is merely a puppet of the omnipotent creator, Other Mother.[57]

All of these visual elements invite us to read the film as an adaptation of the Persephone myth. Then again, the film develops themes of the

Figure 3.1 Coraline and the lure of the flower. *Coraline*, dir. Henry Selick (2009).

[57] Blackford 2012: 210.

novel that go beyond a singular allusion to the *Hymn to Demeter*. By means of a strategically positioned signpost, Selick splices the Persephone story with an Odyssean motif that aligns with the heroic implications of Coraline's adventure, and rejects the narrative trajectory of Persephone as a bride. Coraline's intrepid independence is a challenge to the ancient myth of Persephone's abduction, a challenge heightened by references to other mythical adventures that align the girl with more assertive male heroes: the Scottie-dog-Cerberus, recalling the infernal canine encountered by Heracles and Aeneas, has already signaled an active role for the young traveler. Another suggestive allusion occurs as part of the entertainment provided for Coraline in the Other World. Selick's revision features a tableau vivant of "Ulysses and the Sirens," a painting by Herbert James Draper (*c*.1909) depicting the hero tied to the mast, but now supplemented with Spink intruding as a "mermaid enchantress," vying for the stage with Forcible as Botticelli's Venus. This nod to the ruse that allowed Odysseus to hear the Sirens after his visit to the land of the dead, without falling into their trap, allows us to view the brave, canny, and resourceful traveler, Coraline, as another Odysseus. She uses her intelligence to resist the lure of Other Mother, who like the Sirens offers a seductive but deadly alternative to home. By evading her fatal snare Coraline not only saves herself, her parents, and the ghosts of children trapped by Other Mother, but she also accomplishes her return home, a *telos* achieved by Odysseus after his underworld experience. The descent to Hades is an intrinsic aspect of a journey homeward in the *Odyssey*, the farthest separation possible from loved ones, just as it is for Coraline, whose encounter with the *unheimlich* reveals her heroic fortitude.[58]

The pregnant intertextuality of these visual references to mythical antecedents also performs an important diegetic function. Gaiman's text, as Gooding points out, uses the device of psychonarration to describe Coraline's emotional state at various points in her adventure, but since there is no third-person narrator in Selick's film, mythic references serve as a non-verbal commentary on her actions. For example, in the print version when Coraline finally engages Other Mother in conflict, she musters her courage by remembering her father's heroic act of rescuing her from a swarm of wasps. Since the film does not

[58] On the antithesis of Hades and home in the *Odyssey*, see Dova 2012: 44, and de Jong 2001: 271.

provide flashbacks or interior monologues, the reference to heroic male paradigms such as Odysseus and Aeneas replace Coraline's interiorized identification with her father's bravery.[59]

This strategy of graphically associating Coraline with classical antecedents is also a shrewd way of relating her experience to the literary canon, making this more than a children's story. In this respect the film shares certain features with Barth's amusement park version of Hades, the various underworld narratives in Gaiman's *Sandman* comics, and most certainly with Byatt's catabatic fairy tale, all of which defy the concept of a literary hierarchy by referring to elite forms of literature within a product of popular culture. Using an underworld theme for a children's fantasy tale is not in itself revolutionary or unusual, since Coraline is one of many children in literature who make the descent. Aside from the fact that underworld narratives fit well with the coming-of-age theme (as it does for Ambrose Mensch), the journey to the netherworld is an opportunity to observe a strange mythic environment that has similarities with the child's own reality, but is sufficiently "other" enough to create suspense, danger, and excitement. Of course Coraline has been preceded by Lewis Carroll's Alice and other girl catabants, so her gender is not unique in this tradition. Nonetheless, as Vaclavik observes, earlier girl heroines are: "largely passive and their behaviour circumscribed."[60] Coraline resembles Alice in certain respects: she enters a womb like-space through a narrow aperture and encounters a dangerous female ruler. But she has a more independent and courageous streak.[61] Gaiman's novel achieved its popularity because of its fearless, resourceful protagonist, whose heroic characteristics set her apart from many of her female predecessors. Nonetheless the adventure has a very pronounced female focus that incorporates the womb–tomb analogy.

[59] On the patriarchal implications of Coraline's father, Parsons, Sawers, and McInally suggest that he: "embodies the symbolic law of the father via his commitment to following written recipes as ruling instructions and his suggestion that Coraline entertain herself by counting, categorizing, and making lists of real world objects" (2008: 377).

[60] Vaclavik 2010: 85.

[61] Lesser (1987: 128–30) provides a synopsis of theories about the motif of "birth trauma" in *Alice's Adventures in Wonderland*, and also recognizes its classical origins. See Brahen (2007: 146) regarding the similarities and differences between Carroll's Alice and Gaiman's Coraline, notably that the former is more a satire of society while the latter is a focused on a journey of development and learning. Borsellino (2007: 51–3) comments on Gaiman's general tendency to avoid gender stereotyping.

Consistent with the myth of Persephone, argues Blackford, Coraline's descent to the underworld represents a necessary stage in a pubescent girl's life when she starts to transform into a fertile woman. In an analysis that focuses on the transitional elements of the paradigm, she notes that Coraline is on the cusp of puberty, but her fantasy of another world with such adoring parents is way to prolong her childhood, although the transition is inevitable:

> But in the paradox of the Persephone motif, her underworld exploration of regression is a means to development. She might be wishing to prolong early childhood, but in the underworld she is pushed into a role of adolescent rebel.[62]

By comparing Coraline's challenge against Other Mother to a form of teenage rebellion Blackford makes the case that Gaiman's novel is concerned with a girl's incipient transition to adolescence. Undoubtedly Coraline will eventually enter a new phase of her life, but as we have just observed, the filmic adaptation challenges the Persephone paradigm by interleaving it with a more heroic, androcentric model, which suggests other possibilities for her adult life than motherhood. And the sophistication of the visual references is an invitation to situate the film in other underworld traditions, which include the heroic encounter with a wise prophet. But just as the Persephone tradition is altered by its Odyssean interjections, so too the conventions of the necromantic tradition take on a different hue.

These complications arise in part because the Persephone model is compromised by gender issues. Why is the attempt to abduct Coraline not performed by a male corresponding to Hades, but rather by Other Mother? As we have noted, the Hades figure (Other Father) is only a factotum, with no agency or desire of his own, although his act of swooping the girl into his chariot seems to assume an ancient prototype. Yet the power at the center of this underworld is a deadly female. What is her significance? Although there are elements of the *Homeric Hymn to Demeter* in this story—certainly the garden motif suggests growth and fertility—any analysis must include the resolution of Coraline's story, a reunion with her family in which she resumes her identity as a cherished child. Her encounter in the underworld might hint at the transition to come, yet it turns away from the Hades-as-bridegroom motif (with the

[62] Blackford 2012: 208–9.

benign figure of Whybie, and the weak Other Father). Instead the shape of this underworld myth is an encounter with a child-snatching demon, the sort of monstrous females that occupy classical versions of Hades, and whom heroes like Odysseus and Aeneas fear.[63]

Later this chapter will examine how Elena Ferrante adapts the idea of the bogey-women of classical myth in her female focused versions of the underworld. The next chapter offers an analysis of Ann Patchett's *State of Wonder*, which stages a similar confrontation between a woman and a child-snatching female demon. These chthonic fiends suggest that a female catabasis is not simply a relabeling of the male heroic descent story. The journeys to the realm of death undertaken by Coraline and other female catabants are infused with issues of maternity, and posit an infernal matriarchal core in which women encounter a monstrous version of femininity that represents both the negation of their own identity and a reflection of themselves. A better mythical model, perhaps, might be the confrontation between the Sumerian goddesses Inanna and Erishkegal, who represent forces of life and death. But Other Mother has a quality that sets her apart even from Ereshkigal. She is gradually represented as a deadly spider-woman, who spins everything in her realm into existence; she is a creator. This is more explicit in the novel, for example when Coraline finds herself in an empty space, which a talking cat describes as "the place *she* hasn't bothered to create" (72 emphasis in the original). As long as her creations are contained in a fantasy world, there is a possibility of escape, but Other Mother had already extended her power into the material world when she left the doll replica for Coraline. The film opens with her claw-like hand sewing the doll into existence and leaving it as a lure for Coraline to discover.

If realized, her ambition to make Coraline into a doll, replacing her eyes with buttons, would permanently install the child in the realm of the

[63] As already noted, the female bogey is a common feature of classical underworlds, e.g. Odysseus departs from Hades because he fears that Persephone will send the gorgon head (*Od.* 11.633–5); Aeneas raises his sword in terror against phantoms of the Gorgon (*Aen.* 6.282–90). In many ways Other Mother resembles their descendants, the wicked witches of fairy tales, although they are often obstacles to romantic fulfillment. Warner (1994: 218–19) has argued that such figures, familiar from *Snow White* or *Cinderella*, are projections of mothers-in-law, conventionally regarded as hostile to newly-wed women. The figure of Venus in Apuleius' version of Cupid and Psyche is a version of this hostility.

"unseen" (*a-idēs*), i.e. Hades, as a sightless replica of herself.[64] This is not a story about a creator emerging from a chthonic matrix, as it was for Ambrose Mensch, but rather one in which creativity is linked with unsettling repetitions of the real world. Nothing is solid in this liminal space, but created to entice the unwary into blindness and invisibility. Coraline battles against absorption into the chasm by enhancing her power of sight with a magic stone to detect the ghosts of children entrapped in Other Mother's kingdom. Her salvation comes with her ability to solve Other Mother's riddle: "In each of the wonders I've made just for you, a ghost eye is hidden in plain sight." True vision, the apprehension of what is real and what is hidden, is linked with survival; blindness and an acceptance of a world of replicas with death. The theme of sight, already present in the novella, is especially meaningful in a product of visual culture. The underworld narrative becomes a means of contesting the concept of authenticity because it offers an alternative world that bears a similarity to everyday life, although with horrifying aberrations. Yet the Other World is not sustainable: Other Mother gradually slips back into her insect shape; Other Father seems to melt away. Moreover Coraline's perception of the world of ghosts hidden beyond this world raises questions about what is real or authentic, especially when even within the subterranean world there exist different levels of the visible: for example, the child-ghosts can only be seen through the magic stone; Coraline's parents are seen behind a mirror. What of this is real, and what is a dream? As Marilyn Brahen points out, Gaiman's work abounds with:

> dualistic transmutations. Concurrently everything is real and everything is an illusion, and somehow the world is, if not always better for it, at least more meaningful because of that union.[65]

While the novella implies that divisions between dreams and the waking world are unstable, the animated visuality of the film extends this instability. The alternate reality that Coraline encounters instantiates Jean Baudrillard's principle of the simulacrum, and the notion of hyper-reality created by an increasing tendency to construct artificial realities

[64] It is interesting therefore that Freud (1919) links a fear of losing one's eyes with the morbid anxiety associated with the uncanny in his analysis of Hoffman's story of the eyeless doll that finally drives Nathanial to suicide.

[65] Brahen 2007: 145.

through technology, theories which have influenced postmodern theory and culture.[66] To watch the film is to enter a different world that has notional similarities with our own, but which makes no effort to simulate reality perfectly: Coraline has blue hair, for example. Yet theater audiences who put on their 3D glasses (the equivalent of the magic stone that grants Coraline sight), enter a kind of dream world in which these anomalies are temporarily real.

For Coraline, an encounter with the simulacrum of home is a movement towards wisdom and heightened perception that gives meaning to her everyday world. Gaiman's text makes this abundantly clear because once the danger is over and she is safely in her real home, Coraline notices that now, "The sky had never seemed so sky; the world had never seemed so world" (168). Her time in the netherworld is thus a variation on the wisdom tradition of catabatic narratives, and a Platonic anabasis from a phantom world to one that only the enlightened can apprehend. Only one other being has the ability to move freely between the two worlds with an awareness of this dualism and the ability to name it. The nameless black cat, which she had earlier pushed away for being "mangy," turns out to be a mentor in that other realm, and helps Coraline understand both the powers and frailties of Other Mother. *Coraline* is in this respect typical of catabasis tales that narrate a learning process leading to maturation or fulfillment through the agency of a mentor figure, although he (and in the film the cat is male, voiced by Keith David) is not fixed in Hades, nor is he central to it.

This is a story of transition and enlightenment, as catabatic tales often are, but the admixture of the male heroic descent with the myth of Persephone gives it a special applicability for a young girl. Like Odysseus Coraline has a happy homecoming, and unlike Persephone she will not be shared between her mother and the underworld. Odysseus resists dangerous, confining females, and Coraline defeats the repressive Other Mother, not so that she can become a mother or bride herself (or at least not in the near future), but so that she can continue her childhood and restore her parents to their roles as care-givers. In other words she achieves a happy *nostos* (homecoming), although to do so she must

[66] When the double materializes, writes Baudrillard, "it signifies immanent death" (1994: 95).

visit and do battle in a wonderland in order to understand the value of home.

Gaiman-Selick's *Coraline* taps into the same conceptual wellspring as Byatt's "Morpho Eugenia" to exploit the insect motif as a metaphor for transformation within the context of children's underworld culture, although their uses of these themes are diametrically opposite. At the center of both underworlds is a web-spinning, riddle-posing, creative, arachnid, female: the Fairy-beyond-the-wall is a power of release and enlightenment, whose spinning symbolizes narrative creation, while *Coraline's* matrix is controlled by Other Mother, a force of confinement, whose creativity cannot empower the visitor, and whose riddles are designed to keep Coraline bound in her web. In both stories the underworld is imagined as a creative female space visited, in the first instance by a male voyager, Seth, and in the second by a girl whose autonomy is associated with the male heroic tradition. The remainder of this chapter is devoted to the works of Elena Ferrante, who similarly connects the subterranean with female creativity and power, but whose association of the ascent from Hades with women's literature represents a provocative revision of an ancient idea.

The Doll's Descent: Searching for Persephone in the Novels of Elena Ferrante

As Coraline learns, the underworld can be a place of alternative realities and insubstantial doppelgängers. The site of phantoms and dreams, the subterranean realm has become in our cultural imagination a mirror in which other possible lives and selves exist. Hence the passage between the world of the living and that of the dead can denote the creation, or dissolution, of boundaries between identities, including the personal, social, or even literary. We now turn to the Italian writer whose authorial doppelgänger is Elena Ferrante, creator of vividly realized female characters confined by, and sometimes ascending from, a social netherworld maintained by the traditionally patriarchal culture of contemporary Italy. *Smarginatura* ("dissolving margins"), the dissociative disorder that afflicts Lila, a character in Ferrante's Neapolitan Quartet, is her unique affliction, but the condition is also symbolic of the complex relationship that she shares with her childhood friend Lena, narrator of the tetralogy. The word is a book-binding metaphor that refers to cutting the margins of a page, or pages, but Lila extends its meaning to encompass a temporary state of indeterminacy, of not comprehending the bounds between her own physicality and that of the world around her. It is, we assume, Lila's subconscious way of coping with the brutality that she witnesses and experiences. Her father, in one appalling instance, throws her out a window, breaking her arm, when the child insists on continuing her education. And the porous margins of Lila's psyche also dissolve into those of her closest friend, Lena, who narrates the novels; the girls' lifelong attachment is a poignant example of the Aristotelian dictum that a "friend is another self." Psychoanalyst Alison Lee explores how the depiction of the two women's intense lifelong relationship, forged by a shared childhood exposure to violence and poverty, produces a mutual identification. They "blur" into each other at times, merging selves as their similar names suggest. The "fantasy of a shared personality," according to Lee, allows each girl "to look to the other as in a mirror to find her identity affirmed (or undermined)."[67]

Extending the metaphor, we can apply the concept of dissolving margins to the literary persona that the writer, whose identity has not been publically disclosed, has created for herself, and even further to understand how she effaces the boundaries between her separate literary productions.[68] For whoever the "real" Elena Ferrante may be, she has assumed a consistent authorial identity that seems to inhabit the borderland between factual and fictional truths. And certain names (including her own) and situations (such as lost dolls) travel between the pages of separate novels. In a collection of interviews and letters entitled *Frantumaglia*, "fragments," (reflecting another theme running through the Ferrante oeuvre), the author answers questions about her "self", or the self that she has constructed for her readers. While *Frantumaglia* is not necessarily a biography of a "real" person—we do better to regard it as postmodern metafiction—it does nonetheless illuminate a writer well acquainted with classical literature. She cites a degree in Classics combined with an interest in feminist psychoanalytic theory, influences

[67] Lee 2016: 493–4.

[68] Into this composite we should include the American translator of all Ferrante's work, Ann Goldstein, whose voice melds with that of the author. All references to Ferrante's work are to the publication of Goldstein's English translations.

apparent throughout her work, and such details replicate those of the narrator of the Neapolitan Quartet so that author and character blend into each other.

My Brilliant Friend and its sequels are narrated by Elena Greco, a fictional novelist who rises from an impoverished background in postwar Naples to study Greek and Latin at the prestigious Scuola Normale in Pisa during the 1960s, but is thwarted of an academic career due to her class and gender, while her husband Pietro, a rather plodding philologist, and her lover Nino, a charismatic but unscrupulous opportunist, find their places in the academy. The novels explore how women intellectuals, entrepreneurs, and political activists experience motherhood, female friendship, sexuality, and careers in contemporary Italy against a backdrop of the post-World War II "economic miracle," student uprisings, political factionalism, the Camorra crime syndicate, and the rise of feminism within this intensely macho culture.[69] As a student Elena Greco writes a thesis on Dido and Aeneas, and eventually, like Dido, is betrayed by the man she loves. Forsaken women are a staple of Ferrante's fiction, a theme that she attributes (in *Frantumaglia*) to reading about "many abandoned women, from Ariadne to Medea, from Dido to de Beauvoir's *Woman Destroyed*."[70] Yet the important relationships in the Quartet, as in most of Ferrante's fiction, are between women: contentious mother/daughter dynamics and difficult intimacies between female friends. Here again Ferrante suggests classical influences: she cites Apollodorus' variant myth of Helen and her mother Leda, for example, as the inspiration for her novel about a conflicted scholar, *The Lost Daughter* (2008), although she concedes that her story eventually went in a different direction.[71] Our interest of course lies in how the author has deployed that enduring motif of classical literature, the *descensus ad infernos*, enhanced by the setting of most of her novels.

Naples, set between Lake Averno, where Aeneas made his descent to Dis, on one side, and the necropolis of Pompeii on the other, easily lends itself to the catabatic fantasy.[72] The city is steeped in myth and folklore

[69] Bullaro (2016: 24–6) provides a useful survey of the social backdrop of Ferrante's Italy.

[70] Ferrante 2016a: 210.

[71] Ferrante 2016a: 218.

[72] Ferrante's representation of Naples fits well with the association of urban centers with Hades beginning in the nineteenth century as identified by Pike (2007), and also with the ancient idea of the underworld as a vast city.

that support its identification with the underworld, an association that Margaret Drabble exploits in *The Seven Sisters* (2002), and that fascinates the adult Lila in *The Story of the Lost Child*. Correspondingly, Ferrante's Neapolitan novels are among her works that call into play the *Homeric Hymn to Demeter*, not only to explore the theme of loss and abandonment, but also as a means of bringing issues of women's education, careers, familial attachments, and friendship to the surface. In her analysis of Ferrante's early novel, *Troubling Love* (2006), Tiziana de Rogatis hypothesizes that the author was inspired by the Demeter and Persephone myth in her story of a daughter's attempt to recuperate her deceased mother's past as she travels throughout Naples. According to de Rogatis, the novel draws on the rites of the Thesmophoria to articulate a feminine identity that links antiquity with the present.[73] This is a good beginning, but we can go further by reading Demeter's loss of her daughter as the foundation beneath several of Ferrante's other novels. With this analogy in mind, before approaching the Quartet's extensive chthonic themes I survey two earlier related works, which share the theme of a lost doll, an object that signifies both another self and a maternal relationship. As the subsequent analysis argues, these dolls are Persephone figures, which can guide our understanding of the catabatic themes that pervade *My Brilliant Friend* and its sequels.

The Lost Daughter

Ferrante develops her Demetrian motif in *The Lost Daughter* (2008), narrated by Leda, a middle-aged, divorced professor, originally from Naples, whose visit to a coastal Italian town for her summer vacation brings her problematic maternity to the surface. The narrative compresses issues of abandonment with fantasies of abduction, while situating Leda in a psychic underworld where she adopts a demonic role as the child-snatching bogey-woman of myth and folklore. Her adult daughters have now set off on their own lives, but rather than relaxing in her untethered state Leda becomes fixated on a young woman, Nina, and her daughter, part of a raucous extended family that dominates the beach. When the little girl, Elena, wanders off in search of her lost doll, it is Leda who finds her and returns the child to her family. The event triggers

[73] de Rogatis 2016: 185–206.

memories of Leda's own mother who threatened to desert her children, and also of a time when Leda's daughter went missing. The restoration of the lost daughter, Elena, to her mother, however, is only notionally parallel to Leda's history, and it soon becomes obvious that the title of the novel applies more appropriately to the lost doll. When Leda finds Elena's doll partially buried in the sand, rather than returning it she perversely keeps it for herself, recalling a quarrel over her old childhood doll that her daughter had refused to relinquish. That an educated, professional woman would choose to keep a distraught child's toy, a doll that little Elena believes is pregnant, is a perplexing act of cruelty. The girl is devastated, a Demeter in miniature, but Leda ignores her distress, and persists in her fetishistic attachment to the doll, buying it new clothing, and treating it as her own child. Disturbingly, she compares her possession of the toy to the abduction of a child (70). At the same time the doll represents a distortion of maternity when Leda subjects it to a type of excavation/abortion that yields sea-water (a kind of amniotic fluid?), and then results in the doll disgorging a disgusting worm.

Although Leda does eventually return the doll to the girl's mother, she has seemingly become another iteration of the child-snatching bogey-woman of the underworld, a Mormo figure akin to Other Mother who threatened to destroy Coraline. Elena's mother, enraged when she discovers that Leda has kept the doll, and knowing how deeply Elena grieved its loss, stabs Leda with a hairpin, causing a minor injury. Leda's final line in the novel is to her daughters over the phone, "I am dead, but fine," suggesting a symbolic underworld in which Leda exists. This tightly bound tale operates within a system of intersecting correspondences and oppositions to imprison Leda in a remembered past. Her neurotic attachment to the doll releases a cascade of associated memories: from childhood, of her mother threatening to abandon her; during her marriage, of her own temporary abandonment of her daughters while she pursued her education and a lover; and her fractious relationship with them as they grew up. On the other hand the roles of characters in the story are often ambiguous. The title of the novel, *The Lost Daughter*, has multiple referents, including the doll, Elena the child, Leda's daughters, and even Leda herself. Simultaneously daughters are also mothers: Elena is the doll's mother; the doll is "pregnant"; and Leda's conflicted feelings towards her own mother and daughters are projected onto her ambiguous connection with Nina, the little girl's mother, who is involved in an adulterous affair with a beach attendant. The worm that the doll "aborts" seems symbolic of Leda's own abhorrence of maternity, and yet she also desires a mother-like relationship with Nina, an impulse that has disappointing consequences. Suffice to say, boundaries between roles and identities are unstable in this acutely realized story of a woman's psychic descent.

The Beach at Night

What can we make of the setting of *The Lost Daughter* at the seashore, a place where borders are physically indeterminate, always shifting with the waves and tides? Beaches figure prominently as a site of danger, transgression, and desire in much of Ferrante's fiction: child molestation, seduction, adultery, and precocious sexuality are enacted in the liminal spaces between the elements of earth and water.[74] Even boundaries between genres begin to dissolve when the land meets the sea. *The Beach at Night* (2016), ostensibly a children's picture-story book, offers a coda to the tale of Leda's descent into neurosis, and presages the chthonic symbolism of dolls in the Neapolitan Quartet. While *The Lost Daughter* recounts the abduction of a doll from the perspective of a child-snatching bogey, *The Beach at Night* is in the voice of a doll victim, named Celina, lost at a similar beach. Accidentally left behind by her child-mother, Mati, Celina is snatched by a vile, mustachioed, beach-cleaner, who threatens to steal the words that the doll has shared with Mati. The doll becomes a paradigm of feminist resistance to the masculine control of language as she resolutely clings to those precious maternal words, trying to hide them in "my chest and my stomach" (32). Celina exerts her most determined efforts to escaping the fire that would consume her along with other beach detritus, and ends up sinking "down, down, down" to the bottom of the ocean, whose comforting movements remind her of Mati. Mara Cerri's illustration represents the doll lying at the bottom of the ocean amidst "Fish, Tin Cans, broken Bottles, two Crabs, a Starfish" (30–1), as if she is enacting Adrienne

[74] Elena Greco is molested by Nino's father while on vacation at Ischia, and then later seduced by him on the beach in *The Story of a New Name*. Lila begins her adulterous affair with Nino at the same beach; her son Rino exposes himself to Elena's daughters at another beach. In *The Lost Daughter*, the child Elena's mother, Nina, conducts an adulterous affair.

Figure 3.2 Celina at the bottom of the ocean. Elena Ferrante, *The Beach at Night* (2016).

Rich's "Diving into the wreck" (Figure 3.2). Celina's watery catabasis, although comforting, is happily reversed. The uterine sea protects the doll and her words from the beach-cleaner's fire; her ascent through the salty water into the dawn is like a birth:

> I've barely got time to clamp my mouth around the last remaining word: mamma. With my teeth clenched around mamma, I go up, up, up.
>
> (*The Beach at Night* 36)

Celina is carried home by the "Dark Animal," Mati's new kitten, reminiscent of the boundary-crossing cat that befriended Coraline. Perhaps we assume that Celina is a "mama doll" with a voice box giving her that single bleating utterance, but she has a story to tell like other survivors of the descent, and she tells it to Mati, who has been sobbing disconsolately all night. Mother and daughter are joyfully reunited after Celina's abduction by a male predator and her subsequent descent into a womb-like place, a charming re-enactment of the Demeter and Persephone reunion after a terrifying, nocturnal adventure.

Chthonic dolls

Both *The Lost Daughter* and *The Beach at Night* feature dolls seized by predators who are in some way reminiscent of underworld figures. The beach-cleaner who snatches Celina is suggestive of Hades abducting Persephone. When she steals Elena's doll, Leda takes on the characteristics of Mormo and other demons of ancient folklore, such as the Lamia and Gello, held responsible for killing children, pregnant women, and unborn babies.[75] Leda's operation on the "pregnant" doll is consistent with the miscarriages caused by the demonic Gello, while her "abduction" of the toy is symbolic of the death of a child. The ancient imagination situated these female bogeys in the "ghostly or demonic realm;" one ancient scholar describes Mormo as the "nurse of Acheron" (Sophron frg. 9 Kaibel)—whether in reference to the underworld river or its personification, the infernal qualities of the monster are unambiguous.[76]

Since lost dolls are an important thematic and structural element of the Neapolitan Quartet, where their associations with the underworld are even more pronounced, it is worth contemplating their significance in more detail. As a miniature model of a human being, a doll is a symbol, one that presumably invites girls to practice and negotiate their anticipated adult roles, although doll play often goes beyond this simplistic analysis.[77] When dolls are featured in literature they are, as Trinna Frever puts it, "a sort of representation-cubed (a representation of a representation of a representation)" that can act as "a pivot-point through which all other cultural representations of womanhood are revised."[78] In *Frantumaglia* Ferrante puts it this way: "Dolls can be stand-ins for women, in all the roles that patriarchy has assigned us."[79] Dolls figure prominently in her fiction, where they help to articulate the complex and often tragic dynamics of women's relationships with each other and their daughters, although they are also polyvalent signifiers that do not submit to straightforward analyses. Animated by girls' imaginations, dolls are alive and evoke maternal relationships with their child owners, yet they are also representative of girls themselves. The little girl Mati knows her doll's story even before she tells it; her fantasies are projected onto Celina so thoroughly that she seems to share her thoughts. Like Celina, these dolls come to life most vividly when they are lost, thereby accentuating Ferrante's recurring themes of separation and abandonment. Like *The Lost Daughter* and *The Beach at Night*, the Neapolitan Quartet hinges on the narrative of loss and reunion between child and doll. Because dolls

[75] A character in Theocritus (*Id.* 15.40) threatens her child with the Mormo, for example. See Johnston (1995: 361 n. 2 and 366 n. 12) for further references to children's fear of Mormo, and to Gello's role in terminating pregnancies.

[76] Johnston 1995: 366–7, n. 13.

[77] Dolansky (2012: 278–82) imaginatively applies the scholarship on doll play to Roman girls' interactions with their dolls.

[78] Frever 2009: 124–5.

[79] Ferrante 2016a: 205.

are lost and grieved by their child-mothers, and then returned to them, they invite comparisons with the *Homeric Hymn to Demeter*. Significantly the dolls lost at the beach are submerged in sand, water, or both, in a kind of burial; in *My Brilliant Friend* two dolls are thrown into an underground chamber. These performances of a subterrestrial voyage, inherent in the Demeter/Persephone narrative, imbue Ferrante's dolls, or daughter-substitutes, with an intense symbolism, conveying the emotions of anger and sorrow that contribute to the psychological potency of her fiction.

The suggestion that a doll can experience a catabasis similar to that of Persephone is most pronounced in *My Brilliant Friend*, the first installment of the Neapolitan Quartet, but I want to linger for a moment more on dolls' association with Persephone, bride of Hades, before approaching those novels. It could be argued that all dolls have a morbid aspect—Other Mother's first contact with Coraline was through a doll that resembled Coraline. Dolls' most salient feature is their stiff and lifeless—let us say corpse-like—quality, until they come to life in the fantasy world of the girls who play with them. Like Persephone they exist between the margins of life and death. Thinking of dolls, however, in the context of classical antiquity (and bearing in mind the education that Ferrante cites for herself and her character Elena Greco) we find more support for this homology. The ancient Greek word for "doll" is *korē*, which helps to establish this connection with Korē/Persephone, and also *nymphē*, which can mean "bride," one of Persephone's roles.[80] Many of the ancient dolls that have survived up to the present were buried with girls and adult women as grave offerings, thus accentuating their association with the underworld and the afterlife. For example, a mummified eight-year girl, who probably died in the third century CE, is displayed in Rome at the Palazzo Massimo alle Terme along with her grave goods, which include a beautifully rendered, ivory, jointed doll, a model perhaps of the wife of the emperor Marcus Aurelius.[81] Such artifacts can be seen in museums throughout Italy, and are no doubt familiar to Ferrante. A finely carved grave relief, commemorating the death of a little Athenian girl in the fourth century BCE, shows the child gazing fondly at the doll that she holds. Affective relationships between girls and their dolls

[80] Elderkin 1930: 455–6. The term *kora* is used in the *Palantine Anthology* 6. 280.
[81] Discussed in Dolansky 2012: 256–7.

were just as characteristic in antiquity as they are today. The survival of dolls from the ancient world is largely in the context of the death of girls (victims of Mormo and her kindred demons), although there is one related exception to which we shall shortly return.

These symbolic associations inform the mythic qualities of dolls in Ferrante's fiction, in particular the lost doll's identity as a Persephone figure, and her role in the recurring Demetrian intertexts. The gynocentricism of Ferrante's fiction, and especially her interest in women's relationships with each other, is consonant with the focus on the female experience in the *Hymn to Demeter*. Isobel Hurst has aptly described the myth of Demeter and Persephone as "an archetypal narrative of women's experience" that epitomizes Adrienne Rich's definition of "the essential female tragedy."[82] In other words the poem offers a template not only for the emotional lives of ancient women, but also of women throughout history. This rare woman-focused narrative is also a story about anger, the wrath of Demeter when Zeus and Hades arrange the marriage of her daughter without consulting her. It is this element of anger that seems most consonant with Ferrante's work, which is animated by the rage and ferocity of her female characters, who like their mythic counterparts find that they must exist within a society that would deny them subjectivity, and views them as prizes to be won or objects to be abused and discarded. This ferocity is one of the most striking features of the Neapolitan novels, which also incorporates the figure of the female child-snatching demon. On an emotional level then the loss of the dolls adumbrates women's frustration and struggle for self-determination within the parameters of a traditional culture that represses women's abilities and forces them to navigate their precarious positions within a male-dominated society. The loss of a doll is thus a loss of the self projected onto it, and a loss of maternal language that a rapacious beach attendant, in all his many forms, threatens to devour.

The dolls' descent

Dolls are intense affective figures in the Neapolitan Quartet, which manipulates their chthonic symbolism from the early moments of the first novel (*My Brilliant Friend*) to the conclusion of the last

[82] Hurst (2012: 176) cites Adrienne Rich (1976: 196) *Of Woman Born*. Cf. Foley 1993: 80.

(*The Story of the Lost Child*). *My Brilliant Friend*, set in the postwar slums of Naples, recounts the childhood friendship, up to the age of sixteen, of two women, the narrator Elena Greco, known as Lena, and her friend Lila (Raffaella Cerullo). The similarity of their names contributes to the fluctuating symbolic system of substitutions and slippages that develops throughout the tetralogy. Both are girls of talent, determination, and ambition whose lives diverge, converge, and diverge again over a period of fifty years. The origins of this dynamic flux are traced to the girls' early years in school. A fierce, precociously intelligent child, Lila prevails over older boys in arithmetic contests, defends herself by throwing rocks at her disgruntled male rivals, and causes her teacher to collapse in the classroom. Lena is in awe of her. Their attachment to each other begins when the eight-year old Lila pushes Lena's doll through a grate into a cellar:

> We showed off our dolls to each other but without appearing to, one in the other's vicinity, as if each of us were alone. At some point we let the dolls meet, as a test, to see if they got along. And so came the day when we sat next to the cellar window with the curled grating and exchanged our dolls, she holding mine and I hers, and Lila abruptly pushed Tina through the opening and grating and dropped her. (*My Brilliant Friend* 54)

Lena matches this shocking act, less in vengeance than imitation, pushing Lila's doll Nu through the same grate. Her recollection of the event, unleashed like a traumatic memory in disordered fragments over twenty-five pages, punctuates her account of the girls' early years. The dolls' symbolic descent to the underworld is an important programmatic event that lends a mythic quality to the account of Lena and Lila's relationship as it oscillates between separation and reunion throughout the next five decades. When the two friends subsequently descend into the dark cellar to retrieve their toys, a terrifying and also futile quest, they do not find their lost daughters, but see a murky figure scuttling off into the dark, presumably with their dolls. They believe that the abductor is Don Achille, a local loan shark and proprietor of the cellar, whom Lena describes as "the ogre of fairy tales," and imagines as "a huge man, covered in boils . . . a being created out of some unidentifiable material, iron glass, nettles" (27–8). He is, in their imagination, a creature of myth, and Lena's reaction after the loss of her doll has a mythic timbre. The child is inconsolable; falling ill, she is like Demeter, enduring "unbearable sorrow."

For me the doll was alive, to know that she was on the floor of the cellar, amid the thousand beasts that lived there, threw me into despair. (55)

On the other hand, the doll-tossing marks a transition in the girls' lives and thus suggests a rite of passage. Ferrante has expanded the symbolism of the doll in yet another way that suggests an influence from the ancient world. As a form of sacrifice the expelled dolls are reminiscent of ancient Greek girls' dedication of their toys as they approach puberty. An anonymous epigram in the *Palatine Anthology* commemorates the offering by Timareta to Artemis before her marriage: "a girl (*kora*) dedicates her girls (*tas koras*) to a girl (*korai*)" (*Anth. Pal.* 6. 280. 3–4). Hundreds of jointed dolls have been excavated from sanctuaries of Demeter, for example in Corinth, where they are the most common form of dedication from the Archaic Greek to the Hellenistic period (*c.*600 to 100 BCE).[83] While the purpose of these dedications may vary, Timareta's epigram strongly suggests a sacrificial offering to mark a status transition. Considered in this context, Lena and Lila's reciprocal doll-tossing accentuates the initiatory significance of the girls' descent to the cellar "and the thousand beasts that lived there." An underworld descent is often associated with puberty rites, but the most relevant evidence here comes from Locri, an ancient Greek settlement in Western Italy, where young girls apparently simulated a catabasis by descending underground as a rite of passage at the shrine of Persephone at the Grotto Caruso, a site where dozens of votive dolls have been excavated.[84] Ferrante's depiction of the doll sacrifice and subsequent virgin catabasis by Lena and Lila resonates profoundly with this ancient cult.

The girls' descent and the birth of the author

But what exactly is the transition effected by Lila and Lena's descent and ascent from the cellar? Although they do not retrieve their dolls, they will not accept their loss passively either. After bravely descending to the dark subterranean space, Lena follows Lila's lead again, this time to the apartment of its proprietor, Don Achille, whom the girls believe they saw "running through underground tunnels" (57) with the dolls. This involves another ascent up the stairs of a dark passage to confront Don Achille. Seen in mythic terms, the event corresponds to an initiatory trial

[83] Merker 2000, passim.

[84] See MacLachlan (2004) for further details.

in which the hero must defy the monster at the center of the labyrinth, or brave an audience with Hades, or another male figure at the center of Hell. Notice, however, that the girls are now enacting a *male* initiation myth, in which they assume some agency. As Lena recalls the event, she represents it a kind of trial, and comments: "we went to expose ourselves to fear and interrogate it" (29). Her childish worldview has been infused with death from the beginning of the memory, including a macabre catalogue of deceased acquaintances and a list of possible ways of dying, both of which establish the chthonic tone of the episode. But the confrontation with the monstrous owner of the cellar is a turning point, and a syncopation of the Demeter and Persephone story pattern. The inevitable resolution of the myth is intercepted by the rhythm of the traditional necromantic encounter of an author with traditions of the past.

As Grace Russo Bullaro rightly notes, the girls enter a "hellish underworld" when they descend to the cellar. Her analysis is concerned with how the tetralogy refracts the economic zeitgeist of postwar Italy by delineating a sense of before and after:

> The images of dark cellars and hidden spaces evoke an underworld where all is mysterious and frightening: Italy's dark past of fixed social classes, poverty, lack of opportunity, and abuse of power.[85]

This observation is consonant with David Pike's suggestion, in his survey of the underworld motif from the medieval to the modern period, that the descent has "a fundamentally allegorical form: the core fact of death is imbued with the hero's individual past, the past of his society, and the past of the motif itself."[86] For Ferrante the cellar serves as a metaphor for a past that includes traditional gender roles and class distinctions.[87] It is a past that is in binary opposition to the progress and social mobility offered through the schools and libraries utilized by both girls.[88] Ultimately education and progress involve leaving the neighborhood; the cellar

[85] Bullaro 2016: 20. [86] Pike 1997: 2.

[87] The tetralogy activates a dichotomy between before and after, as Gallippi notes (2016: 101).

[88] Love (2016) identifies a series of oppositions working throughout the tetralogy, all of which are encompassed within the opposition between school and neighborhood that conditions how characters engage with the world. The school promises progress, while the neighborhood is associated with the past. This binary is metonymic of four other salient oppositions associated with Italy's modernity: North/South, standard/dialect, teacher/mother, and self/other. Love, however, sees Lena and Lila as disrupting these oppositions,

qua underworld is a highly concentrated symbol for the traditions perpetuated by the *rione*, and thus to descend into it and then ascend becomes a movement from the past into the future. The motif, however, expands and takes on related meanings: the cellar image is strongly associated with history, and thus presumably with death and the underworld, but the children's catabasis is also the precursor of literary production, a by-product of education when educating girls was a new way of doing things. Consequently the descent becomes a version of the "birth of the author" idiom, familiar from Dante, Pound, and Barth discussed in the previous chapter ("the past of the motif itself," in Pike's words), although in this case the prototype of the *Nekyia* has become entwined with the Demeter–Persephone myth.

That the descent is a precursor to the fashioning of a woman's authorial identity is intimated when the girls agree to accept financial compensation for the lost dolls from Don Achille, whose motives for doing so we can only surmise—perhaps to get rid of the annoying children, or even to cover up his son Alfonso's theft of the dolls. The confrontation with the "ogre" is a critical moment nonetheless, and it bears an ironic resemblance to Odysseus' necromantic consultation with Tiresias, or that of Aeneas with his father. Ironic, because the loan shark Don Achille is an embodiment of criminal patriarchal power, yet he will facilitate a woman's rise to literary celebrity. The girls use the money to buy a book, *Little Women*, and agree that they will become writers themselves. The dolls, little women of a sort, are thus replaced by fiction that recounts the story of a girl, Jo March, becoming a novelist. To be more accurate, however, Lila is the child who orchestrates the entire sequence of events, but her literary aspirations are thwarted, or at least occluded by the narrator. Lila produces a short story, "The Blue Fairy," but its contents are never disclosed to the reader. Her future literary output is never published, and mentioned with jealousy, anxiety, and suspicion by Lena, who even suspects that her first successful novel is a version of her friend's childish story. To suppress the humiliating possibility that she is but a pallid imitation of her brilliant friend, Lena destroys a manuscript that Lila gives her for safekeeping when they are adults, teasing the reader with the possibility of a text beyond our

and suggests that the series narrates "the dramatic tensions that emerge in the in-between spaces where the school and neighborhood intersect."

apprehension, one that remains hidden in another library of books never written, that tells a different version of this tale. On the other hand, the descent to the cellar, the loss of her doll, and the substitute for the doll, the shared book, ultimately lead to a rich intellectual life for Lena. Through talent, determination, the support of her parents, and Lila's encouragement, she is able to ascend from the poverty, corruption, and violence of her neighborhood to attain a place in middle school, a university scholarship to study Classics, and a literary career. She is, because of her education, upwardly mobile, achieving security, respect and middle-class status as a professor's wife, and as a successful writer. Tellingly, Lena thinks of her acquisition of education, and her social mobility as an ascent that allows her to "pull out of the neighborhood" (*The Story of a New Name*, 315).

Lila: the chthonic woman

Lila, on the other hand, denied further education, applies her considerable abilities to developing her father's shoemaking business, and is fixed in the subterranean realm from which Lena escapes. Her biography belongs to an alternative subterranean world that recalls the summation of Gaiman's Lucifer, who imagines Hell as a shadow or reflection of Heaven, yet one that is necessary to give meaning to it. Lila, the chthonic counterpart of Lena, serves as a "dark reflection" of her more fortunate friend's successes. An uncommonly beautiful girl, she is wooed by a local Cammorista, Marcello Solara, whose links with tradition and the past are suggested by his boast about his family's successful pastry shop, which began in his grandfather's cellar: "You begin with a cellar and from generation to generation you can go far" (*MBF* 201). Bullaro comments on his historical perspective:

> As in every case where the cellar is mentioned, it functions as a recall of the various associations to the dark, both literal and metaphorical.[89]

Although Lila rejects Solara as a suitor, she remains tied to these dark spaces by her early marriage to the abusive Stephano Carracci, son of another cellar-owner Don Achille, a Hades to her Persephone, so to

[89] Bullaro 2016: 29.

speak. Notably, until she vanishes forever, she never ventures beyond the neighborhood with all its violence and venality, although her marriage is short-lived. When Lena tries to rescue her friend from the hellish sausage factory owned by the Fascist Bruno in *Those Who Leave and Those Who Stay*, the third novel in the quartet, it is as if Lila is caught in an underworld of proletariat exploitation. This is the alternative trajectory for a girl of talent in mid-century Naples, a narrative that Lena escapes by means of education. Their experiences in the cellar thus have different outcomes for each girl: one remains in the metaphoric Hades; the other ascends from it. Although they remain in each other's orbits for many decades, and are even in a sense each other's shadow selves, they are also distinctly different. Education is the great divider, giving one girl advantages, and leaving the other to make her way in life on a different path. In a world whose boundaries are established and penetrated by books and words it is significant that the social divide is frequently signified linguistically. Lila speaks the Neapolitan dialect that signals her ties to the neighborhood and its values, while Lena's use of Italian (and her acquisition of Greek and Latin) are appropriate to her new social status.[90] Nonetheless, like Persephone, Lila acquires wealth and standing in the *rione* as she maneuvers her career through the economic surge and technological revolution of mid-century Italy.

Lila's chthonic persona is emphasized at various points and by different means throughout the tetralogy, perhaps nowhere more evocatively than at the beginning of the fourth novel when the two friends, both pregnant with their daughters, find each other during an earthquake: Lila appears as if "directly from the churning guts of the earth" (*The Story of the Lost Child,* 51). The image emphasizes Lila as a subterranean force, especially in the context of the close bond between the two women. The catabatic moment that initiated Lena's ascent—the loss of the girls' "daughters" to Hades—also implicated her in a Demeter/Persephone relationship with Lila. This formative event creates the lifelong bond between the two friends, which fluctuates between adoration and enmity; at times the two friends seem almost to merge into one, a reunion akin to that of Demeter and her daughter, and at other times break apart.

[90] Ferrante's metalinguistic comments indicate when Lila speaks the Neapolitan dialect. See Cavanagh's elucidation (2016: 66) of how the distinction between the two friends' social status is emphasized by language.

Relatedly, and in a way that enhances the impression of their symbiotic relationship, the friends exchange roles at times. Lena's ascent from Naples and return to it suggest an infinite cycling between the upper and the lower realm, while her periodic reunions with Lena in Naples both reinforce the Demetrian analogy but disturb its equations; Lena too becomes a Persephone. Throughout the series Ferrante articulates a sense of a shared persona, although Lena wavers between either seeing herself as an inferior version of her brilliant friend, or as a socially superior woman of accomplishments in contrast to the "uneducated" Lila. At times, repulsed by Lila's politics and overbearing control, Lena withdraws, but she eventually rejoins her friend in the same Neapolitan neighborhood of their youth, pulled back by her childhood love, Nino Sarratore, also Lila's former lover and another dark force, in the final novel. The pulse of this withdrawal/reunion/withdrawal is the heartbeat of the four novels; their rhythm, suggesting the death and rebirth of the beloved daughter, is corroborated by Lee's comparison: "[a]s though Elena's struggle with Lila involves some remainder of the little girl's fused identification with her mother."[91] Still it would be too simplistic to suggest that Lena and Lila share a quasi-mother/daughter bond, nor is this what Lee hypothesizes. Rather the connection between the two begins as "a hiding place from trauma and a defence against annihilation."[92] The loss of their dolls creates an inextinguishable connection between the girls, as if each were replacing the other's lost toy; one girl is Persephone to the other's Demeter, alternating between loss and consolation.

Persephone redux

The Demeter/Persephone subtext entangling the personae of the two women is corroborated by the tragic disappearance of Lila's daughter in the final novel. As a grieving mother she now melds with Lena when she lost her doll, Tina, and it is significant that Lila's daughter has the same name as Lena's lost doll—a dramatic example of the fluidity between the two women's identities. When Tina, now in human form, is pulled into the underworld, Lila takes on a more complex mythic dimension. At the same time, the city around her develops an increasingly Hadean quality, as if in response to her sorrow. Naples from her perspective is saturated with

[91] Lee 2016: 496. [92] Lee 2016: 500.

subterranean imagery as Lila dwells on how its once beautiful palaces and gardens have fallen into decay and are haunted by spirits of the dead. She takes it upon herself to instruct Imma, Lena's daughter, about how:

> sometimes nymphs, dryads, satyrs, and fauns inhabited them, sometimes the souls of the dead, sometimes demons whom God sent to the castles.
>
> (*SLC* 441)

Lila entrenches these ghost stories within a broader cultural context that extends to language; for her, "words are full of ghosts," and so is art (441). As her imagination populates Naples with phantoms and devils, Lila speculates about the violent subterranean history of the church of San Giovanni a Carbonara built over a charnel pit filled with the mutilated corpses from vengeful public killings—"all that filth, all that chaos of broken limbs, and dug-out eyes, and split heads" (447)—covered by a valuable monastic library. She vividly constructs a Hell beneath the surface of culture and learning, and imagines it extruding into the library, an extraordinarily violent variation on the concept of the underworld as a literary space. It is not that she would deny culture and literature's association with the infernal realm however, but rather that she understands an even deeper chasm beneath the stratum that they occupy.

As Lila grows increasingly more agitated, Lena makes her final ascent from Naples, relocating with her daughter Imma, who, she fears, is too much under the sway of Lila. She sees her friend for the last time as a menopausal woman struck by hot flashes and turning "fiery red," (451) a demonic figure in an underworld of grief. Lila becomes a fixture of Hell, and her interest in Imma makes her too uncomfortably similar to those child-snatching monsters whose fiendish power arose from their own maternal losses. Lena's awe and fear of her friend were enough to remind her, at a much earlier point in their lives, of another woman's superstitious suggestion that: "Lila had a tremendous power, that she could cast an evil spell by fire, that she smothered the creatures in her belly" (64 *Those Who Leave*). In the dark Neapolitan spaces that Lena constructs for her reader, Lila becomes a variation of the "Terrifying-Female-Apparition-in-the-Underworld" that drives Odysseus away from Hades, and frightens other male catabants.[93] Ferrante's contribution to the tradition is to give the female fiend a story and a soul.

[93] The hyphenated term is from Clark (2009) who reviews the motif.

The author redux

Lena, however, is able to transmute loss into literary production once again: just as her literary success was ultimately a substitute for her lost doll, so too the grief for her friend's lost child leads her to write her final masterpiece. As the quartet reaches its conclusion Lena turns her thoughts to the dolls, now understood as a proleptic symbol of Lila's tragic loss, as well as Lena's career as a novelist. Lena, approaching old age with her literary career in decline, brings fame and fortune back to life by writing *Friendship*, "the story of our lives from the loss of our dolls to the loss of Tina." The parallels with the frame narrative are too obvious to ignore, especially since in Italian all four novels are grouped as *L'amica geniale*. Lena's new novel, her most successful, recounting the relationship between Lena and Lila, and the loss of the daughters, becomes a self-reflexive story within a story, a *mise-en-abyme*. Psychological trauma and literary output become homologous in the crucible of the abyss. Her ascent from Hell again turns her into a writer. Ferrante's unique variation on the convention of the catabatic hero becoming a storyteller is to graft it onto a version of Persephone's fecundating return to earth.

While Lena is able to recuperate her career, the publication of the novel severs what remains of her connections with Lila, who disappears after erasing all evidence of her existence down to the last photograph. As she deals with her loss, Lena speculates about why she wrote *Friendship*:

> I intended to capture her, to have her beside me again, and I will die without knowing if I succeeded. Sometimes I wonder where she vanished. At the bottom of the sea. Through a fissure, or down some subterranean tunnel whose existence she alone knows. In one of the many dimensions that we don't know yet but Lila does, and now she's there with her daughter. (441)

From Lena's point of view, and it is the only one we are allowed throughout the tetralogy, if Lila disappears it can only be to an even deeper chthonic place. As she has been throughout the quartet, Lila is associated with the infernal realm, even when she vanishes from Naples. But for the woman author, that encounter with the subterranean has resulted in literary production and reaffirms her intellectual fertility. As Lena's meditation reveals, her final novel was a replacement for her friend, a way "to capture her, to have her beside me again." Instead, what she will retrieve is her lost doll, for which a book became a substitute, and which now becomes a substitute for a friend. The novel closes its circle with the reunion of the daughter-doll and its child-mother, now a lonely old woman who finds a mysterious package in her mailbox, which contains: "the dolls we had never found, although we had descended underground to look for them" (473).

The Story of the Lost Child ends with a mother and child reunion that raises questions never to be answered. There is no doubt that the dolls are from Lila, but what is their history? How long has Lila possessed Lena's Tina? How did she come into her possession? By keeping Lena's doll she seems to fit the role of the child-snatcher Mormo, a parallel that has been implied by Lena's fantasy that her friend occupies some unknown subterranean dimension. The quartet began at the moment when Lila's son Rino reported her missing, which provoked Lena's memoir of their friendship beginning with the lost dolls. It ends with a message as if from some uncharted subterranean space. At least that is the way the story is told. The motif of descent and ascent is Lena's way of ordering reality along the grid of mythology; Lila's account would probably have been different, for as she realizes "Each of us narrates our lives as it suits us" (*TWL*, 64).

Female underworlds

In his study of how the concept of the underworld shapes modern urban culture, Pike observes that, "Like all spaces, but in an instructively self-evident way, an underground space is filled with conflicting definitions."[94] Although he refers here to physical spaces, the observation is pertinent to those imaginary or metaphorical spaces of postmodern narrative that we have just examined. Byatt and Ferrante deploy two different descent myths—those of Odysseus and Persephone—in ways that appropriate the motif of the underworld as a literary space to accommodate the anomaly of the female narrator. Both leave their marks on a symbolic topography that does double duty—as female space and cultural archive—in the gendered dichotomy of Western culture. As Coraline's confrontation with Other Mother confirmed, it is easy to configure the subterranean as a feminine space, a womb. According to a dominant cultural fantasy, the subterranean is a place from

[94] Pike 2007: 16.

which the male catabant must ascend, after which he enters the Symbolic Order by telling stories or founding an imperial dynasty. Byatt and Ferrante are inspired to intervene in this tradition, but they simultaneously embrace the equivalence of the underworld and the feminine. They accomplish this by adroitly employing elements of children's culture so that they can insert women authors into the narrative. Using the vehicle of the fairytale, Byatt replaces the familiar male mentor of the underworld with a powerful female spinner who seems to be the dynamic force of both the embedded and the frame tale. She is the creation and the analogue of a female narrator, whose power and significance incarnate a cross-cultural myth of a spider goddess, who spins the material universe into being. Coraline's encounter with the arachnid Other Mother gives insights into the darker side of this creative female force, who has parallels with more sinister shape-shifters of folklore, for instance, the "Earth Spider" of Japanese tales.[95] Other Mother also embodies the traditional role of the demonic child-snatcher, a figure brought to life by Ferrante, whose contribution to the catabatic tradition is to meld an ancient coming-of-age ritual, a doll sacrifice, with the necromantic encounter that authenticates an author or poet. Ferrante recuperates an ideological construction for feminist fiction by grafting the Persephone story and the notion of the underworld as a womb onto the recurring motif of an author's investiture in the crucible of Hades.

[95] The Earth Spider was a shape-shifter who could turn herself into a beautiful woman, and who lived in a haunted house according to medieval Japanese folktales; see Reider (2013). Amditis (2009) traces the image of the spider in nineteenth-century Russian Symbolist poetry back to the Upanishads' metaphor of the spider spinning a web of creation.

4

The Wanderer's Descent

The Underworlds of Diaspora

ἄλλον δ' ἂν ἄλλᾳ προσίδοις ἅπερ εὔπτερον ὄρνιν
κρεῖσσον ἀμαιμακέτου πυρὸς ὄρμενον
ἀκτὰν πρὸς ἑσπέρου θεοῦ.

And you can see one soul after another fly away
like a fleet-winged bird, faster than irresistible fire,
to the shore of the western god.

(Sophocles *Oedipus Tyrannos* 175–7)

The fantasy of a visit to the kingdom of Hades addresses a sense of loss, not just of loved ones, but also of homelands. As the most distant point on the mythic traveler's itinerary, a sojourn in the netherworld offers an evocative metaphor for the social or cultural displacement of transient populations, immigrants, exiles, refugees, and enslaved peoples who find themselves, as Iain Chambers puts it, "living between worlds, caught on a frontier that runs through your tongue, religion, music, dress, appearance and life."[1] Migrancy writes Shailja Sharma, "can be called the reigning trope of the twentieth century," and evidence of her assertion can be found in abundance in recent fiction.[2] This chapter explores how four novelists use the descent paradigm to convey the experience of protagonists who grasp for an insubstantial world populated by ghosts and dreams of past homelands. Toni Morrison (*Song of Solomon*), Amy Bloom (*Away*), Salman Rushdie (*The Ground Beneath Her Feet*), and Ann Patchett (*State of Wonder*) evoke myths of Odysseus, Persephone, Orpheus, and Aeneas in their stories of men and women who are haunted by evanescent memories of lost families and homes. The

[1] Chambers 1994: 6. [2] Sharma 2001: 594.

metaphor fits several categories of loss. From the perspective of those left behind, an emigrant may seem to have "vanished, as if the earth had swallowed him," the words of an early twentieth-century Russian whose kinsman left for America never to be seen or heard from again.[3] On the other side of the Atlantic, the immigrant narrator of Rushdie's *The Ground Beneath Her Feet* contemplates a "now unavailable home," "breathing under the earth . . . like a lover gone down to Hell" (492). For other transplanted peoples life in a new country may be a form of Hell where they endure isolation, discrimination, privation, and hardship. And while the conceptually flexible underworld can signify loss and nostalgia felt on both sides of the ocean, the ascent from Hades betokens the possibilities of new life in a new land.

The following analyses explore how fiction deploys the *descensus ad infernos* to symbolize the lives of diasporic populations whose displacement is imagined as the death of one identity and the rebirth of another, or who struggle to assimilate to their new environment while they mourn and mythologize a lost past. Such an association is already implicit in Vergil's account of Aeneas' descent, which results in his transformation from Trojan refugee to proto-Roman conqueror after he learns of his destiny in the underworld. The narrative of *Aeneid* 6, ending with the parade of notable Romans, progresses from myth to historical reality as the hero prepares to take his place as a settler in a new land. Admittedly, the imperialistic agenda of Vergil's epic is antithetical to the narratives of dispersed peoples in today's world, but like them Aeneas endures the loss of family—his wife Creusa when he makes his flight from Troy, his father en route—and like refugees and immigrants of all times his journey is fraught with uncertainty and hardship. The visit to Hades is a timeless metaphor that encapsulates the bewildering process of moving from one society to another, of leaving behind a life of familiar places, sounds, food, and faces to become a stranger in a strange land. It must have resonated in Vergil's time, an era of shifting populations and new borders, much as it does in our own.

The condition of diaspora, the scattering of populations from their original homelands, means, to quote Chambers again, "to live at the

[3] The phrase is attributed to a neighbor who lost contact with a relative who emigrated to America at the turn of the twentieth century in Mary Antin's autobiographical (1912) *The Promised Land.*

intersections of histories and memories."[4] As William Safran writes, the term "diaspora" is increasingly used for several categories of people: "expatriates, expellees, political refugees, alien residents, immigrants, and ethnic and racial minorities *tout court*."[5] They are represented in the four novels discussed below by protagonists who share a common background as members of different expatriate minority communities; either they or their ancestors made the trip across the Atlantic to America, a common (but not unique) destination in immigrant fiction. All are members of the "eighth continent," to use a term coined by Alba Ambert to describe "an emotional and psychic limbo teeming with people who do not belong where they are and can no longer return to the place where they came from."[6] Ambert's metaphor, "limbo," reveals how well the language of the afterlife fits the immigrant experience.

To ameliorate the present and reconcile the past these scattered populations, as Safran observes, tend to engage in a shared "mythification" process, using collective memories of their place of origin.[7] Gillian Bouras, a transplanted Australian writer living in Greece, exemplifies this tendency when she describes how dislocation affected her own identity in a way that made the past into a form of myth, in contrast to a present reality: "[W]e are suspended between the myth and the reality, not quite sure who we are or where we fit."[8] A shared inheritance of myth also contains and universalizes memory in narratives of migrant peoples, juxtaposing the past with a more prosaic present to fashion what Stuart Hall describes as "an imaginary coherence on the experience of dispersal and fragmentation."[9] Of course this mythologizing process does not necessarily mean that diasporic populations understand their past as versions of Greco-Roman narratives, but it helps to explain why authors let their characters use myth as a way of mitigating the trauma of displacement.

The previous two chapters outlined how contemporary culture leverages the traditional association between the underworld and creativity to work through and (re)enact the poetics of the past. This chapter extends the association between narrativity and the subterrestrial to explore how stories of a visit to Hades function as a paradigm for a related endeavor: the attempt to impose meaning on an otherwise chaotic situation by

[4] Chambers 1994: 6. [5] Safran 1991: 83. [6] Ambert 2001: 9.
[7] Safran 1991: 88. [8] Bouras 2001: 18. [9] Hall 1990: 224.

relating it to a story-tradition. In all but one of the four novels, the protagonists focalize their experience through the lens of underworld myth; in the fourth, *Song of Solomon*, the narrator leads us to make that connection ourselves. In the same way that the myth of the trip to the netherworld corresponds to a transition between childhood and adulthood in coming-of-age stories, or the demarcation of a new ritual status in mystery cults, it can also represent the psychic rupture of relocation, cultural transplantation, and the transformative assimilation of a migrant into a new homeland.

The body of immigrant fiction is immense and continually growing, for its appeal is far-ranging. A rich vein of postcolonial theory has analyzed the different forms of immigrant and diasporic narrative in recent novels as a reflection of the lived reality of shifting populations and their effects on global politics and economies. Accounts of the ordeals of dislocation and the pangs of nostalgia are specific to migratory populations, but also resonate with readers who can identify their own sense of disorientation in the rapidly changing globalized world of late capitalism. In *Imaginary Homelands* Rushdie, whose oeuvre is permeated with these themes, observes that: "We all cross frontiers; in that sense, we are all migrant peoples" (279). The passage between life and death, a border that every living soul must cross at least once, not only serves as a potent and widely applicable metaphor for the migratory voyage, but also invites us to interrogate the fundamental notion of home, whatever our history and ancestry may be.

The novels treated in this chapter are linked by their deployment of the infernal descent to reflect the lives and emotions of transplanted peoples in the United States, people whose origins (or those of their forebears) are Africa, Russia, and India. Two of the most celebrated authors of our time, Nobel laureate Toni Morrison and "Best of the Booker" winner Salman Rushdie, themselves members of diasporic communities, apply the metaphor to represent protagonists who must come to terms with a cultural displacement that can extend back several generations. Morrison and Rushdie have established their position in the canon of "literary fiction," as evidenced by the sheer volume of scholarship devoted to their work. Their adaptations of underworld narratives tap into a deeply resonant metaphor, and thus engage on multiple levels with classical antecedents. The other two novelists have been less the focus of academic inquiry, although history may change that. Amy Bloom and Ann Patchett are not explicit about their debt to Greek and Roman literature, referring instead to later adaptations of the mythic descent. Yet like Morrison and Rushdie they draw on the descent motif to represent the trauma of expatriation and deracination. Each of the four novels includes an explicit signal that puts it in dialogue with at least one catabatic predecessor, although the allusions are always more complex than a single straightforward source text. And although they share the motif, these authors use the descent in different ways, illustrating the flexibility and wide applicability of this ancient story pattern. By examining how the descent plot works as a structuring device and symbolic touchstone for novels of dislocation, migrancy, and exile, we can also identify how the catabasis is intrinsically associated with the memory of and desire for home, but also how America is imagined as an afterlife for its immigrants.

The discussion begins with Toni Morrison's *Song of Solomon*, the story of an African-American man whose loss of history and culture manifests as form of living death. The explicit allusions to the *Odyssey* invite us to recognize an adaptation of the Homeric *Nekyia*, but the narrative also problematizes the European tradition that valorizes the myth. Amy Bloom's *Away*, the shortest of the four novels, treats the story of a Russian-Jewish refugee, whose arrival in America is likewise constructed as a version of an underworld journey. *Away* makes self-conscious references to the Demeter and Persephone story that provides a mythic template for a woman's traumatic background, but also lets the catabatic intertext illuminate themes of integration and assimilation. The most densely intertextual of the four novels is Salman Rushdie's *The Ground Beneath Her Feet*, which announces itself as a revision of Vergil's Orpheus story, and constructs the narrator's exile from India as the loss of Eurydice. The last of this quartet is Ann Patchett's *State of Wonder*, which likewise makes an explicit comparison between its protagonist and the figure of Orpheus to engage with issues of deracination and her longing for a sense of place. The common element of these novels is their application of the catabasis paradigm in narratives of transnational displacement, especially in an American context. The most recognizable descent narratives—those of Odysseus, Persephone, Aeneas and Orpheus—leave their literary footprints in these chronicles of diasporic populations, cultural transplantation and attempts at, or resistance to, assimilation. However, the adaptations of the mythic source texts are neither celebratory nor consistent. These migratory themes are activated by the readers' knowledge of their catabatic intertexts, yet complicated by provocative intersections between different ancient versions and their descendants. They demonstrate the eclecticism of underworld stories, both ancient and postmodern, identified in previous chapters. The potential for bricolage that already exists in ancient narratives of the trip to Hades facilitates a postcolonial critique of hegemonic narratives, such as that of Aeneas, in which the migrant is successfully assimilated into his or her new context.

Ascending from Oblivion in Toni Morrison's *Song of Solomon*

The central character of Toni Morrison's *Song of Solomon* (1977) is Macon "Milkman" Dead III, a young African-American man surviving in a form of Hades ruled by his slumlord father, son of an illiterate ex-slave. Set in an unnamed Michigan city during the 1930s, the novel charts Milkman's voyage from the oblivion of a death-like existence to a social and psychological rebirth that restores him to his community and their common past. It is a journey from selfish individualism and cultural amnesia to an awareness of a collective identity, an awakening stimulated by his interaction with the Gullah people of Virginia, conservators of a unique West African culture, who share his history and provide Milkman with an understanding of his diasporic heritage. This transition is staged as a mythological adventure that casts Milkman in the role of a young hero whose rite of passage includes a visit to the underworld and a series of trials in which he proves his manhood, wins a woman, and acquires knowledge. It is a pattern familiar to any student of Greek mythology.

Morrison's education at Howard University included Classical Studies, a background that she has cited as an influence on her craft, and one evident in *Song of Solomon*.[10] While it may well be true, as Tessa Roynon suggests, that she structures the novel based on the *Oresteia's* dynamics

[10] See Mobley 1991: 41, 119. In a 1981 interview with Thomas LeClair Morrison suggested that her inclination toward the tragic could be due to her "classics minor" at Howard (Taylor-Guthrie 1994: 124); cf. Roynon (2013: 13–16) who notes that classicist Frank Snowden was a professor at Howard during Morrison's years as a student.

between the individual and the chorus, there is good reason to believe that Morrison is deliberately framing *Song of Solomon* as an adaptation of Homer's *Odyssey*.[11] The figure of Circe, the ex-slave midwife who sends Milkman on his *Nekyia*, as the Homeric Circe did for Odysseus, obviously refers to *Odyssey* 10, specifically Odysseus' interlude with his companions on Circe's island. An important impact on Morrison's engagement with classical literature is Martin Bernal's theory that Greek culture was influenced by Africa, which might account for her rendition of a black Circe.[12] She uses the Odyssean source text, however, not to make any claims about the African origins of its characters, but rather to put it in tension with a folktale about a man who could fly back to Africa.[13] All these ingredients contribute to *Song of Solomon*'s arrangement as a cultural mélange fusing together different traditions of African-American storytelling and classical Greek epic poetry. This hybridity has a postcolonial inflection summed up by Hall's observation that African diasporic culture can be "'framed' by two axes or vectors, simultaneously operative: the vector of similarity and continuity; and the vector of difference and rupture."[14] In other words, we can look at *Song of Solomon* as a citation and hybridization of its Homeric predecessor, but also as a contestation of the source texts that it adapts.

The mythic structure of *Song of Solomon* has been widely acknowledged since the novel's debut. For example, A. Leslie Harris identified Milkman as a traditional hero whose early life story resonates "with symbolic and archetypal significance."[15] He undergoes a period of alienation from his family, and isolation (a common element of coming-of-age stories) that leads to a quest ostensibly for gold hidden by a prospector in a cave, but one that sets him on a path to discovering his genealogy. Other characters in the novel can be slotted onto this mythic grid, notably women such as his aunt Pilate and the midwife Circe, who correspond to female helpers in quest narratives. Such approaches understand Milkman's life story as an exponent of a formalist mythic pattern, which valorizes the male initiation narrative.

[11] Roynon (2013: 135–8) also draws parallels between the trilogy's focus on justice, and the retributive justice of Guitar and the Seven Days.

[12] See Roynon (2013: 18) for Morrison's engagement with Bernal.

[13] For the myth as part of the Gullah tradition, see Walters 1997.

[14] Hall (1990: 226) in reference to Caribbean literature, although his remarks apply here as well.

[15] Harris 1980: 69–76, 70.

And while this mythic reading is to a certain extent valid, it does not accommodate the novel's critical confrontations with race and gender. Other scholarship suggests that Morrison manipulates the male initiation theme in order to complicate it, a more nuanced approach. Gerry Brenner and Michael Awkward, for example, both identify how Morrison deploys the archetype to critique an androcentric narrative in which women function only as a supplement in the hero's quest.[16] Noting the numerous attempts of scholars to draw parallels with Greek mythology—Jason's search for gold, Odysseus' voyage home—Trudier Harris goes further to contend that such methodologies cannot accommodate how the novel exemplifies the dualistic African-American storytelling tradition.[17] Although Harris oversimplifies the heroic figure of Greek myth, which also allows for some moral ambiguity, she is right to make us wary of simplistic mythic equations. In the final analysis, it is most effective to approach *Song of Solomon* as a hybridized text that manipulates and subverts the catabatic component of a coming-of-age narrative by positioning it within a wish fulfillment fantasy about flight. The direction of Milkman's voyage is of crucial importance in interpreting the novel: how does its catabatic intertext relate to the theme of flight? The novel begins and ends with a man leaping into the air. Will he descend or ascend?

Living with the Dead

With these considerations in mind we turn to a closer analysis of the mythic journey of Milkman Dead. His moniker, "Milkman," which stays with him since childhood, was bestowed at an early age. His neurotic mother Ruth, neglected and abused by his father, breast-fed her son long into his early boyhood, an act witnessed by a neighbor who bestowed the nickname. This designation, which suggests a prolonged maternal attachment, contributes to the initiatory theme by suggesting that Milkman is fixed in a female world from which he must break free, a common element in coming-of-age myths. But before he reaches any form of equilibrium and maturity, Milkman veers sharply towards misogyny, accepting his father's callous view of women most disturbingly in

[16] Brenner 1987: 13–24; Awkward 1990: 482–98.

[17] Harris 2009: 5–34.

his treatment of his lover (and cousin), Hagar, whom he exploits and cruelly discards. The quest for his true name and that of his forebears is his story. It becomes a process that requires considerable stripping away of his hyper-masculine identity, and a renunciation of his father's solipsism and materialism, leading to a different kind of relationship with women.

As his family name signifies, Milkman is born into a living death that also enshrouds his lineage. The second Macon Dead, Milkman's father, recounts that when his father (Jake Solomon) registered with the Freedman's Bureau, the man behind the desk was drunk:

> He asked Papa where he was born. Papa said Macon. Then he asked him who his father was. Papa said, "He's dead." Asked him who owned him, Papa said, "I'm free." Well, the Yankee wrote it all down, but in the wrong spaces . . . and in the space for his name the fool wrote, "Dead" comma "Macon." (53)

Death displaces and thus conceals the name of Milkman's forefather, who kept this misnomer because his wife "[l]iked the name. Said it was new and would wipe out the past"(54). It does indeed wipe out his history, not only of slavery and subjugation, but also of what came before. It also becomes a prediction of the violent demise of Macon Dead, murdered in front of his two young children, Milkman's father and his sister Pilate, by a wealthy white neighbor who covets his land. The Dead name is significant in other ways, not only because it represents the cultural annihilation and oblivion in which Milkman exists, but also the loss of identity suffered by all the generations of displaced Africans throughout the Americas. J. Brookes Bouson identifies the novel's addressees as African-Americans, "who have a kind of amnesia about their cultural history—about the shame and trauma of family histories rooted in slavery."[18] Milkman finally apprehends this wider meaning when, upon learning the story of his ancestors, he asks:

> How many more dead lives and fading memories were buried in and beneath names and places in this country? Under the recorded names were other names, just as "Macon Dead," recorded for all in some dusty file, hid from view the real names of people, places, and things. Names that had meaning . . . when you

[18] Bouson 2009: 58. In her conversation with LeClair Morrison expands on how the theme of naming in *Song of Solomon* reflects how African-Americans lost their connection with Africa when they lost their names (Taylor-Guthrie 1994: 126). The significance of naming in *Song of Solomon* is also discussed at length by Mobley (1991: 102–8).

know your name, you should hang on to it, for unless it is noted down and remembered, it will die when you do. (333)

Milkman's history, like his real family name, has been buried, but this other name, Dead, casts a pall on all those around him.

The death motif is enhanced in the first half of the novel by tales of ghosts and corpses. The story begins with a man plunging to his demise in the belief that he could fly. Milkman's father claims to have seen his wife Ruth naked, sucking the fingers of her dead father. Ruth obsessively visits her father's grave at night. Freddie, Macon's assistant, sees ghosts; so does Pilate who saw her father's ghost and (unknowingly) keeps his bones in a sack. The most toxic figure in Milkman's life, his father, drives a funereal Packard, referred to by the rest of the community as "Macon Dead's hearse." The repressive Macon Dead II stifles the vitality of his wife and daughters with debilitating control:

Macon kept each member of his family awkward with fear. His hatred for his wife glittered and sparked in every word he spoke to her. The disappointment he felt in his daughters sifted down on them like ash, dulling their buttery complexions and choking the lilt out of what should have been girlish voices. (10)

Milkman's father is motivated by the same greed and materialism that drove a white man to kill his father for his farm. Like his father's murderer, the second Macon Dead craves more land and commodities. As he tells Milkman, there is only "one important thing you'll ever need to know. Own things. And let the things you own own other things. Then you'll own yourself and other people too" (55). His ideals are the antithesis of being owned, and of the slavery of his ancestors, but they negate the vibrant cultural heritage that connects him with his ancestors' pre-diasporic world. The result of this debased version of the American dream is a form of Hades that emphasizes a mythical propinquity of wealth and death, and recalls that Hades or Pluto is often represented as the richest of the gods. As Patrick Bryce Bjork writes:

For Macon Dead, late capitalism and its socializing effects have replaced the rural, Southern past and he has therefore made it inaccessible to his children.[19]

By contrast his sister Pilate, who lives only on the margins of the Dead family life, embodies this past and transmits it by means of songs that

[19] Bjork 2009: 42.

contain clues to the lost history of the Dead family and name. She is one of several women who provide links to Milkman's past and his African heritage.

Milkman's Nekyia

Like Pilate, the figure of Circe functions as a conduit to this history, but she also helps to situate Milkman within the context of ancient Greek myth. Milkman begins his encounter with the past by visiting her in Danville, Pennsylvania, site of his grandfather's murder. His father's recollections of Circe are the motivation for his visit. She is the only character in *Song of Solomon* to bear a Homeric name, an important consideration for a novel in which names weigh so heavily.[20] As the most explicit signpost of the source text, Odysseus' visit to the land of the dead, Circe is a referent that mythologizes Milkman's narrative as a heroic quest. By thus engaging with the Homeric *Odyssey*, the novel suggestively puts its theme of naming in an ancient heroic context, since names and naming are also an important component of the epic that contributes to the sense of its hero's changing identity.[21] Like Milkman's forefather, Odysseus gives up his name, becoming "Nobody" in the Cyclops' cave and returning home as a nameless beggar. His encounter at the gates of Hades represents the ultimate negation of his former self, since he sees the ghosts of his Iliadic comrades, and thus his own warrior identity is in flux. We have already noted how John Barth alludes to the *Nekyia* as a symbol of a different kind of social change in which a youth becomes an author in "Lost in the Funhouse." Morrison is similarly aware of the symbolic potential of this mythic episode, but she puts additional weight on the transformative abilities of Circe. The "dread goddess" plays an important role in Odysseus' visit to the underworld because it is she who informs him that he must make the trip to Hades, and gives directions on how to get there. An integral part of the *Nekyia*, she frames it with her presence both before and after Odysseus' visit.[22]

[20] See Marinatos (1995) for a discussion of Circe in the *Odyssey*; Fletcher (2006) for further discussion of the significance of Circe in *Song of Solomon*. More broadly, Yarnall (1994) surveys Circe in the classical tradition.

[21] The significance of names in the *Odyssey* has been much discussed, for example Peradotto (1990).

[22] See Ogden 2001: 139–41. Ogden records Circe as being the first of a line of female necromancers in literature. He argues that her knowledge of Odysseus' consultation with

Yet her new incarnation, and her association with transformation, should not be thought of as a mere borrowing from the classical source. Emphasis on her extreme old age hints that she might even *be* the Homeric Circe, the incarnation of an African-looking Circe preserved on several fourth-century BCE ceramic vessels.[23] But her connection with Milkman's family history is unequivocal: she connects past to present by presiding over a reenactment of a formative event in Milkman's history, the visit to a cave that symbolizes death and rebirth. Morrison's Circe performs important narrative and intertextual functions: she sets Milkman on his quest for knowledge of his cultural background and fixes him in a Homeric story pattern, which gives deeper shades of meaning to his experience. The first mention of her name, well in advance of Milkman's visit, already suggests that she will play her Homeric role. When Milkman's father, remembering his childhood, recounts how Circe hid and succored him and his sister Pilate as children to protect them after the murder of their father, he recalls smoke from a cook stove, the same signal that revealed Circe's home to Odysseus and his companions (*Od.* 10.196–7). She is for Macon and Pilate a nurturing and protective figure, reminiscent of a fertility goddess, as her role as midwife suggests. Macon recalls the pigs that she kept and cooked, for example one named General Lee, an unmistakable allusion to the Homeric sorceress and her sty of transformed men. When Milkman finally finds the ancient woman she is now living with a pack of Weimaraners. The dogs with human-like eyes, we suspect, are the former owners of the decaying mansion, home of the first Macon Dead's killer, that she now occupies and is in the process of ripping apart. These creatures bring to life the Homeric simile describing Odysseus' companions, who greet him "like dogs fawn on their masters," when restored to their original forms (*Od.* 10.215–16). Whether they are in fact her former masters is never specified. If so, they secure Circe even more tightly to the Dead family past as a force of vengeance. Reverend Cooper had advised Milkman that "any evening up left to do, Circe took care of" (233); readers are left to make their own conclusions about the full details of her retribution.

Tiresias in the underworld suggests that she accompanied him unseen. For further folktale parallels, discussion and bibliography see Heubeck and Hoekstra (1989: 50–2).

[23] Jennings (2008: 160–2) refers to these vases and speculates on what might have influenced Morrison's version of Circe.

Among her daemonic powers Circe is a threshold figure associated with the cave that Milkman and his father visit on separate occasions, and which functions as a transformative space for both men. After several weeks under Circe's care, the children take refuge in the cave where young Macon, surprised and frightened by an old prospector, stabs him in the back. Macon wants to take the old man's gold; but his sister Pilate intervenes. It is here that Macon's character is imprinted with the values of the man who killed his father only weeks before. As an adult, Macon Dead still lusts for the prospector's gold, instilling the same greed in his son and setting Milkman on his voyage with hopes that the gold will bring him independence from his family. Instead the quest for treasure becomes a different kind of journey, set in motion by Circe, towards self-knowledge and a renewed sense of identity. It bears mentioning that just as Circe bookends Odysseus' *Nekyia* (both sending him to Hades in Book 10 and greeting him when he returns in Book 12), she similarly brackets the underworld of the Dead family first by tending Macon and then by greeting his son Milkman (whom she first mistakes for his father). The implication is that Macon Dead and his family have been in Hades for a very long time.

As Morrison explains in an interview with Thomas Leclair, Milkman has to go into the earth: "that is his coming of age, the beginning of his ability to connect with the past and perceive the world as alive."[24] The cave in Danville, where his father killed the old prospector (or at least thought he did), is a place of death, and also strongly connected to Milkman's past; this is the familiar symbolism that aligns chthonic spaces with memory, tradition, and the past, for example the cellars in *My Brilliant Friend*. Circe's reference to Milkman's grandfather's corpse, improperly buried in a shallow grave in the cave, confirms the underworld theme and provides Milkman with an excuse for his investigation.[25] Circe, like her Homeric namesake, gives him directions; his motivation to visit the cave at this point is still to find gold, although he claims that he wants to give his grandfather a decent burial. Milkman Dead's visit to a cave reverberates with ancient traditions associated with the acquisition of knowledge, and he follows a well-established

[24] Taylor-Guthrie 1994: 126.

[25] The unburied corpse, and the hero's obligation to bury it, is parallel to the corpse of Elpenor in the Odyssey (10:552–5 and 11.72–8).

route.[26] Like Odysseus and other underworld travelers, he must cross water to arrive at his destination, slipping completely into the stream at one point. The topography that he traverses en route is redolent of mythic predecessors, but then things start to go askew for the reader anticipating a hero's descent.

> Then he saw, some fifteen to twenty feet above him, a black hole in the rock which he could get to by a difficult, but not dangerous, climb, made more difficult by the thin soles of his shoes. (252–3)

Contrary to our expectations Milkman must go *up*, not down. His climb to the cave's entrance is arduous; he rips his clothes and exhausts himself scrambling up the rocky slope. Although the Homeric allusions and the burial motif suggest a descent, it seems instead to be an *anabasis*, a "going up." The destination, a cave so dark that he is blinded by the absence of light, is a (by now) familiar womb-like chthonic space. He has embarked on the hero's journey away from his mother, but now after a difficult passage through the stream, he crawls back symbolically into the maternal body—a striking variation of the traditional catabasis, and a decided temporal inversion that will begin to reverse his grandfather's erasure of the past. Once inside the cave he manages to find the pit as expected, but it contains neither gold nor his grandfather's bones. Frustrated and exhausted Milkman emerges from this cavern with a damaged watch (a gift from his mother), its hands twisted, as if time has somehow become distorted. The subterranean, as it does for John Barth's author-in-training, Ambrose Mensch, not only evokes the past, but also distorts time.

Indeed time has folded in on itself for Milkman who experiences a symbolic reversal of the birth process, and then moves towards his rebirth, midwifed by a Homeric enchantress. If Milkman's damaged watch signifies a departure from linear chronology, it also announces his release from quotidian temporality. He has been sent forth from a mundane existence as his father's minion into an epic landscape where he will be transformed by connecting with his past. When she dispatches Milkman to the cave, Circe effectively sends him into that narrative matrix which heroes, from Odysseus onwards, visit; Milkman is thus also positioned in a mythic history, and all that it entails. Chapter 10, the beginning of the second part of the novel makes its Odyssean intertexts

[26] See Ustinova (2009) discussed in the Introduction.

manifest and potent, contextualizing Milkman's journey in the tradition of Odyssean descendants such as Aeneas' catabasis (also through a cave, *Aeneid* 6.237–42), and those of subsequent catabants.[27] Milkman will emerge from the cave to move toward a different world than the one he left behind; he will enter a mythic continuum in which his view of life and of himself will be drastically changed. The encounter with Circe has emphasized a different sense of time, that exemplifies what Julia Kristeva has called "Women's Time," circular and eternal, a temporality which suffuses a landscape strongly inflected as feminine, and which is also deeply resonant of an established mythology that is constantly being recycled.[28] In her revisionist catabasis Morrison has emphasized the strong connection between the midwife Circe and the womblike earth, and set aside the wise old man Tiresias whom Odysseus had to consult.[29]

But for all the maternal imagery and lack of a male mentor, the hero of this tale is still a *man* on his voyage to maturity and knowledge, and despite the missing necromancer at its chthonic center, his story follows the Homeric pattern. Like Odysseus, who is divested of possessions and clothing, Milkman loses his luggage in Danville, obviously symbolizing the shedding of an earlier identity. The ancient Circe has set him on course for Shalimar, Virginia, his grandparents' original home, a Gullah settlement that maintains the traditions of his African ancestors. Trudier Harris notes that Milkman inverts the ideal journey of African-American narratives in which the protagonist travels northward to wealth and freedom. Just as the climb into the cave was both a reversal of a catabasis and a birth, Milkman upends the typical journey by leaving his prosperous roots in Detroit to travel south in a quest to discover his history and reconnect with his ancestors.[30] As Mobley recognizes, the cave has been "a turning point in Milkman's journey because it begins his series of encounters with life-threatening situations."[31] Milkman's experience in Shalimar, the home and name of his great-grandparents, is a continued citation of the *Odyssey*. Hades and home are dialectally linked—from

[27] See Ogden (2001: 62–9) on the necromantic associations of the cave at Avernus; and more generally on the association of caves and wisdom, Ustinova (2009), discussed in Chapter 1.

[28] Kristeva 1993: 443–62, 445.

[29] The Reverend Cooper, with whom Milkman stays before visiting Circe, could be read as a Tiresias figure.

[30] T. Harris 2009: 14.

[31] Mobley 1991: 121.

Odysseus, who descends to learn of his *nostos* (11.479–80), to Coraline who rejects its replication for the real thing. Milkman's *nostos*, set in motion by his underground seclusion, is of a different order, a return to the home of his ancestors. Nonetheless the parallels with the *Odyssey* are clear. He arrives in Shalimar without recognizing it, as Odysseus does in Ithaca. He encounters hostile males (Penelope's suitors for Odysseus, the men in Solomon's store for Milkman) who insult, assault, and challenge him. After his trials are successfully completed, now fulfilled by the knowledge of his forefather that has been his true quest, Milkman has a romantic affair with a Penelope-like woman named Sweet in a mutually satisfying intimacy, much different from his previous exploitative relationship with Hagar.

Gender and tradition

This refashioning of the epic poem accentuates the initiatory aspects of Milkman's experience: most significantly the nighttime hunting expedition with the elders of the town.[32] Milkman comes to understand the value of his cultural heritage to his selfhood. By undertaking his trek to Shalimar, he comes into contact with the unique culture of his ancestors, which retains elements of pre-diasporic West African society. It is a form of homecoming organized as a *Bildungsroman*, which continues the Odyssean allusions with its *telos* of domestic integration. His new sense of belonging inspires him to bring his aunt Pilate back to Shalimar to give her father's bones a proper burial. Furthermore he has traveled into the past, which the South often represents in Morrison's fiction, in a variation of the "mythification" process identified by Safran. His experience is charted along a narrative axis that corresponds to a male coming-of-age narrative—all well and good—but there is a tragic twist, when Milkman confronts figures from his present life in Michigan, who undermine the heroic connotations of his journey to selfhood.

[32] See Page (1995: 103), who synthesizes approaches which interpret the men's collective skinning of the bobcat, i.e. Milkman's initiation into the black male community, as an induction into "his racial identity and past." The hunting, flaying, and evisceration of the animal are reminiscent of the atrocities performed on black men. Milkman receives the heart of the bobcat, a symbol of his "new heart in communion with the natural world of the bobcat, and implying his rebirth as a new man and his penetration to the heart of himself, his ancestry, his community, and his universe." Cf. Harris 2009: 20.

Milkman's mythic trajectory is completed within the compass of Chapter 11 (the Shalimar episode), which is in its own way a *Nekyia*, a conversation with ghosts, a visit to the past, and an immersion in a cultural archive, the songs and stories of his heritage, but the remainder of the novel contests this apparently heroic resolution. The mythic tale is interleaved with and subverted by the narratives of Hagar, his former lover, and Guitar, his childhood friend, rival, psychic shadow, and hitman for the Seven Days, a group committed to avenging the murders of black people. As Milkman is putting the pieces of his family story together, his rejected lover Hagar dies. Her narrative is also associated with a darker version of the homecoming that comprises an important facet of Milkman's genealogy. In Shalimar Milkman hears the popular folktale of the slave who was able to fly back home to Africa, a feat attributed to his great-grandfather, Solomon. The wish-fulfillment fantasy of escape from slavery is deeply rooted in African-American storytelling, especially in the Gullah culture; at least two dozen variants have been recorded by ethnographers.[33] But critically retold by Susan Byrd, a wise woman in Shalimar, the tale devalorizes Solomon's flight by focusing on his wife Ryna whom Milkman's great-grandfather left behind with twenty-one children.

Two versions of homecoming collide at this point: the Homeric *nostos* associated with a descent, which optimistically offers a reunion between male and female, clashes with the folktale of flight told by a woman who recounts the tragic separation of a wife from her husband. In the context of Milkman's life story these spatial polarities, the descent to Hades in search of a *nostos* and the flight homewards to Africa, become especially meaningful when he returns to Michigan to tell Pilate his discovery about their lineage. Angered at the death of her granddaughter Hagar, which Pilate attributes to Milkman's humiliating rejection, she knocks her nephew unconscious and then imprisons him in a cellar. It is essentially a second catabasis for Milkman during which he is able to make a connection between his desertion of Hagar and Solomon's flight from Ryna, and the subsequent deaths of both women. The knowledge of the devastating consequences of his great-grandfather's flight hits Milkman

[33] Walters 1997: 4.

with full force while he is underground, thus merging the two mythic traditions of flight and descent in a moment of catabatic knowledge.

In his optimistic reading of *Song of Solomon* Philip Page suggests that Milkman "reaches the womb of his family (the cave) by embracing the terrifying but guiding Circe who models Milkman's quest by fusing Western and African-American cultural traditions, life and death, and present and past."[34] From Page's perspective Milkman is able to integrate his fragmented family, his position in the diaspora, and the two cultural traditions, African and European, which are in harmony at the end of the tale. But this analysis, attractive as it may be, does not fully reconcile the cross currents of gender and tradition within the novel. Acknowledging the trajectory of initiation and learning, Trudier Harris turns to all the female sacrifices that allow Milkman to situate himself in his family history—those of his mother, his sisters, Hagar, and finally Pilate. Her critique is in accord with Mar Gallego Durán's resistance to the notion that diasporic identities and narratives are formed regardless of gender. As Durán points out Morrison's is "a gendered model that both interrogates and complicates any univocal interpretation of the black diasporic experience." Consonant with this approach, Wendy Walters observes that *Song of Solomon* deliberately shifts the emphasis from the male story of flight from freedom to the female experience of desertion.

The heroic resolution and Homeric citations that connect his story to European literary history are further compromised when Guitar's bullet misses Milkman (mistakenly believing that he was not sharing the gold that he discovered), and kills Pilate as they are burying Jake's remains. The novel ends with Milkman leaping off a cliff in a reenactment of his great grandfather's escape. The linear tale of a young man's quest with its promise of closure is now circumscribed by a ring composition, suggesting eternal repetitions of flight. We can choose to think that Milkman has plunged to his death, like Robert Smith, whose suicide flight opened the novel, or that he has flown away like his great-grandfather. However our imagination completes the tale, two related structural qualities are obvious: first, the story is circular, coming back to where it began with a man leaping into the air; second, the story ends in mid-air, that is to say it

[34] P. Page 1995: 100.

does not end. This circularity is identified by Cedric Gael Bryant as a "trope of resistance . . . that informs Morrison's method of interconnecting narrative elements by reversing causality."[35] While the catabatic myth is repeated again and again in literature, it is skewed here by a circular tale from a different tradition.

Up to this point my analysis has identified postmodern authors, both male and female, who engage with the Judeo-Christian or European canon of descent narratives. Morrison's intervention, however, is an exceptional version of postmodernism's program of "complicity and critique," because she sets the trip to the underworld in opposition to a folk tale from a different culture, one that has been nearly erased from its people's memory. In addition Morrison's treatment of the descent narrative within African-American literature is extraordinary. While *Song of Solomon*, with its assimilation of Circe, engages explicitly with the Homeric *Odyssey*, its catabatic motif also puts it in dialogue with other African-American and Afro-Caribbean adaptations of the *descensus ad infernos*. Milkman's brief descent into Pilate's cellar is suggestive of Ralph Ellison's *Invisible Man* (1952), although the protagonist of that novel remains nameless, unlike Milkman who discovers his true name. *The System of Dante's Hell* (1965), an imagistic, experimental novel by Amiri Baraka (Le Roi Jones), correlates a young black man's psychological hell with Dante's *Inferno*, and features a coming-of-age theme that has similarities with Milkman's experience. Acknowledging a resurgence of underworld themes in twentieth-century modernist fiction, Michael Cooke argues that Hades has a special significance for black writers such as Ellison and Baraka, while Justine McConnell identifies underworld themes in Afro-Caribbean poet Aimé Césaire's *Cahier d'un retour au pays natal* (1939), Derek Walcott's *Omeros* (1990), and other postcolonial adaptations of the *Odyssey*.[36] Of specific relevance to the themes discussed in the previous two chapters is Walcott's, "Hotel Normandie Pool," which stages what Thurston has called "the

[35] Bryant 1999: 98–9.

[36] Cooke 1974; McConnell 2013: 53, 120–1. See also McConnell's discussion of Walcott's *Omeros* in which the Caribbean fisherman, Achille, returns to Africa to encounter people of the tribe from which he is descended. She observes that the visit to Africa is not a *nostos* (homecoming), but a catabasis, because Achille thinks of St. Lucia as his home. His trip to Africa resembles a catabasis because he acquires knowledge.

necromantic encounter," in this case between the poet and the shade of Ovid, envisioned at a Caribbean hotel's poolside.[37]

Although these and other examples from African diasporic literature share the underworld theme with *Song of Solomon*, it is important take into account the intersection of race and gender in Morrison's use of the trope. In all four novels discussed in this chapter the catabatic intertexts are often problematic in how they confront other narrative traditions, and how a sense of direction implicit in the descent story becomes confused, creating a subtle critique of the master narrative. Specifically, Morrison has utilized this narrative strategy to undermine the heroic implications of Milkman's catabasis by setting it against women's experiences. Roynon has pointed out how the female characters in the novel are marginalized with regard to the retributive justice as propounded and enacted by Guitar and the Seven Days, a comment on the position of black women within the early American civil rights movement.[38] Most significantly Pilate is sacrificed at the end of the novel when she takes the bullet intended for Milkman. Her life story has not been the major focus of the novel, but nonetheless it suggests catabatic elements that lend further ambiguity to the implied heroics of Milkman's journey. She too spends time in the cave in Danville after her brother Macon stabs the prospector, although the reader is not privy to her thoughts, emotions, or actions during this period. Like Milkman she journeys south to Virginia, wandering like Demeter, and like the goddess suffers grief and anger at the death of her granddaughter Hagar, although there is no palliative reunion in store for them. Pilate has played her role in this story of a young man's ascent from oblivion, and she is among the women who preserve and circulate the stories that give it meaning, but unlike their story, hers remains in the margins. It is this intertextual overlap created by the faint shadow of another story of descent, a woman's story, with a traditional heroic quest that gives an even deeper resonance to the more obvious Homeric source text. The next section of this chapter turns to another conflation of these two different mythic prototypes, the Odyssean and the Demetrian, although the effect of the combination is more optimistic.

[37] Thurston 2009: 99–103. Cf. Greenwood (2009: 255) on the "intertextual intervention of shades/ghosts of specific poets" in Walcott's oeuvre.

[38] Roynon 2013: 152.

Amy Bloom's *Away*: Dreams of Hell

The Russian-Jewish immigrant Mary Antin begins her much-acclaimed 1912 autobiography, *The Promised Land*, with this reflection:

> I was born, I have lived, and I have been made over. Is it not time to write my life's story? I am just as much out of the way as if I were dead, for I am absolutely other than the person whose story I have to tell. (1)

Like that of the Trojan refugee Aeneas, Antin's passage to a new identity involves a form of resurrection. Remembering her childhood, she describes playing corpse in a game of funerals, after which she felt as a ghost among Gentiles, a subtle prelude to the theme of her memoir. Her rebirth as an American woman, as Jolie Sheffer observes, is characteristic of a trope in which immigration is conceived as "an experience akin to death and resurrection."[39] While still a young girl Antin and her family fled the persecutions that had sent nearly one-third of the Jewish population of Eastern Europe to America by the 1920s. The journey to New York via Poland that Antin recounts is precarious and confusing, a rite of passage followed by assimilation into a new life with more liberal opportunities for young women. Her biography is typical of immigrant tales in that it is structured around "the losses and psychological ruptures" that mark "the end of her old life and beginning of her new life."[40] Growing up in New York Mary Antin goes to school, learns Greek and Latin, and eventually marries a Gentile—a radical departure from the parochial expectations of her culture. She views this process as a rebirth that incorporates her identity as a Russian Jew and her new life as an American woman:

> Now I am the spiritual offspring of the marriage within my conscious experience of the Past and the Present. My second birth was no less a birth because there was no distinct incarnation. (xi)

Amy Bloom's *Away* (2007) melds *The Promised Land* with the biography of Lillian Alling, a European immigrant who attempted to return home via Siberia after trekking across North America, and was last heard of trying to rent a boat in the Aleutian Islands in 1927.[41] Evoking

[39] Sheffer 2010: 141; cf. Boelhower 1982: 15–16.
[40] Sheffer 2010: 141.
[41] Lillian Alling's story is reconstructed by Smith-Josephy (2011).

Greco-Roman mythological paradigms, specifically the Demeter and Persephone tale and the story of Odysseus' *nostos*, *Away* incorporates the metaphor of death and rebirth in its final resolution, although it initially resists the conventions of immigrant narratives exemplified by *The Promised Land.* The central character is Lillian Leyb, a Jewish woman escaping the Russian pogroms, who arrives in New York in the 1920s, and attempts a return like that of her historical namesake. Bloom fashions a tragic history for her protagonist that accounts for her driving need to return to Russia: the little daughter that she left behind. Lillian is thus caught between worlds as she goes through the motions of assimilation, but yearns for her child and a return to Russia.

Typical of immigrant narratives is the sense of a double self: "It is painful to be consciously of two worlds" (xiv), writes Mary Antin, a sentiment that Chambers, in reference to diasporic identities, describes:

> To come from elsewhere, from "there" and not "here," and hence to be simultaneously "inside" and "outside" the situation at hand, is to live at the intersections of histories and memories, experiencing both their preliminary dispersal and their subsequent translation into new, more extensive, arrangements along emerging routes.[42]

This duality shapes the inner life of Lillian Leyb, who exists between the trauma of her past and the promise of her new life. While she manages to adapt quite well to New York, she cannot fully integrate into American life as long as she is pulled back by the past through her dreams, a descent into trauma with flashing visions of the slaughter of her family and, most painfully, the loss of her little girl, Sophie. The imagery of death predominates. In the earliest of her recurring nightmares she herself is dead with blood dripping over her face and body. Blind at first, she suddenly sees her dead husband, parents, her broken possessions, and most terrifying of all, her four-year old daughter's empty bed. Bloom's training as a clinical social worker and psychotherapist is evident in her ability to delineate a credible portrait of a woman coping with trauma, and replaying events in her dreams until she can come to terms with her loss. Her dream of death is significant because Lillian is psychically dead and bereft of what matters most deeply. The Jewish émigré Yaakov

[42] Chambers 1994: 6. As Boelhower (1982: 18–19) recognizes, immigrant narratives often feature a rebirth, "but it is a doubling, not an erasing process."

describes the morbid affect that they both share: "'Now I am the beautiful corpse. I am a waltzing cadaver. You know.' And she does." (42)

The landscape of Demeter

It is not difficult to map this grieving mother's trauma onto the myth of Demeter's search for Persephone, a paradigm cited explicitly later in the novel, and affirmed by persistent underworld imagery. Lillian does eventually recover and assimilates into American society through marriage and a new family, a resolution that invites a retrospective remapping of her tale onto a different myth, that of Odysseus the wily wanderer whose underworld visit precedes his homecoming. Lillian lives by her wits, like Odysseus, stealing food at first, insinuating herself into a job for which she is under-qualified, and cleverly gaining two influential lovers in New York, as she maneuvers her way through and around a cast of exotic characters and places—a Yiddish impresario, prostitutes, and prison inmates. Alerted by a relative that Sophie may still be alive, she manages to cross the continent by stealing, hiding, conniving, and even assisting in the murder of her friend Gumdrop's pimp. Along the way dreams of her dead family continue, although now they feature at least a glimpse of her daughter. The ghosts of the past and the longing for her lost child are so strong that throughout much of the novel Lillian refuses any possibility of remaining in North America. In this important respect *Away* subverts the momentum toward assimilation that structures immigrant narratives such as *The Promised Land*; the sense of loss seems too profound for Lillian to adapt.

Like many immigrant narratives, Lillian's is peripatetic, involving a trek west, then north through Canada and Alaska. It is not a voyage to a new home that she attempts, however, but a return home. She would reverse her immigration and de-immigrate, as it were, like Lillian Alling. And as long as she retains this hope she remains in an underworld of grief and denial that shapes the world around her. The frozen landscape of the North corresponds in her mind to the "circles of hell" (193), while Lillian's situation and surroundings maintain a Hadean quality. It is as if she projects her internal suffering onto the sterile ground, like the drought Demeter inflicts on the earth. Death is everywhere in this landscape, it seems. She comes across a household of small children in Alaska whose mother has died, and helps to "wrap the stinking corpse of Mrs. Mason in canvas and bury her on the slope to the left of the privy" (201). As Mr. Mason recites Psalm 23, Lillian reflects that "she walks through the valley of the shadow of death every day and she fears everything" (202).

An important shift starts to happen in the Prince Rupert prison where Lillian spends the winter (incarcerated for her own safety, as Lillian Alling was). Here Bloom shows some therapeutic techniques in action. Research into trauma resolution has demonstrated that survivors of horrific events will replay the experience in their minds until they can create a coherent narrative of the trauma.[43] After Lillian tells a friend about her nightmares in a version of the talking cure, the dreams cease, but there is also another recuperative process at work. During her prison winter Lillian begins to read a copy of *Bullfinch's Mythology* which she uses as a paradigm for her own environment and experience, comparing the omnipotent librarian to Zeus and Hera, for example. But it is the myth of Ceres and Proserpine, adapted from Ovid's version of the story, that has the most meaning for her when she resumes her journey north.

Mythic paradeigmata

Until Lillian is able to read her own life through the lens of myth, the narrative threatens to overturn the conventions of immigrant fiction. When she finally meets the man with whom she will settle, John Bishop, the myth of Proserpine's descent becomes both a way of working through Lillian's traumatic experience retroactively and of projecting it onto a narrative of assimilation. In a moment of self-awareness she recognizes her own version of the Ceres and Proserpine story:

> Surely somewhere in the back of Bullfinch, in a part Lillian had not gotten to, there is an obscure, (abstruse, arcane, shadowy and even hidden) version of Proserpine in the Underworld in which a tired Jewish Ceres schleps through the outskirts of Tartarus, an ugly village of tired whores who must double as laundresses and barbers, a couple of saloons, a nearly empty five-and-dime, and people too poor to pull up stakes. (212)

Lillian adapts the myth to reflect her own biographical details, but also to accommodate another possible outcome for her lost child.[44] Although the Ceres–Lillian figure is searching everywhere for her daughter,

[43] Sheffer 2010: 149.

[44] The Demeter–Persephone myth has also been used, as Hurst (2012: 179) shows, as a symbol for the displacement felt by Greek-American or Italian-American women writers.

Proserpine has eloped with Pluto, having crossed the river Cyane, and is contentedly settled in her new surroundings in the underworld. When Ceres does eventually reach her, Proserpine refuses to leave Pluto, her new husband, and deliberately eats the pomegranate seeds in order to stay with him. In this version Proserpine never comes back to her mother.

The revision and application of the myth to Lillian's situation is double-coded, however, since she corresponds to both Ceres and Proserpine. In Lillian's adaptation Ceres has been in the underworld herself, if only on the outskirts. She obviously resembles Lillian, a "tired Jewish Ceres," trudging through what sounds like a northern American frontier settlement. Ceres is in Tartarus because Lillian has been in a form of Hades throughout much of the novel. Her retelling of the myth reshapes its source text in order to reflect circumstances of her particular situation, which is how mythic *paradeigmata* operate in Homeric epic.[45] The various embedded myths of the *Iliad* incorporate elements of the external narrative by drawing parallels between situations and characters in both the inner and the outer text. In order to create these alignments, the internal narrator of a mythic *paradeigma* will often make unique variations that accommodate the specific situation of characters in the frame narrative. For example, in order to make Priam, grief-stricken for the death of Hector, eat when he crosses enemy lines to retrieve his son's corpse, Achilles tells a version of the Niobe story in which the bereaved mother partakes of food (*Il.* 24. 599–613). Lillian makes her own adjustment to Bullfinch's version of the Ceres and Proserpine story that will help her accept the loss of her daughter. The narrator, who is both omniscient and prescient, helps the reader apply this new version of the myth to the eventual fate of Sophie, who is adopted by a Russian Jewish family and lives a happy and fulfilling life. Like Lillian's Proserpine, she is never reunited with her birth mother whom she forgets entirely.

Yet viewed from a different perspective, Proserpine is also the immigrant who adapts to her new home, and for whom nostalgia has no power to draw her back to her former life.

[45] The literature on Homeric *paradeigmata* (myths used as models for situations in the Homeric narrative) is extensive, but the reference here is to the proposition suggested by Willcock (1964: 141–51).

'We have to get home,' Ceres says.
'I am home,' her daughter says. (213)

Lillian like Proserpine has travelled over water to a new home where she is about to find a husband and another life: by the end of the novel she is reconciled to staying in Alaska with John. This reading of Lillian's variant myth accommodates the duality of immigrant identities. She exists as two mythic analogues, the bereaved mother, Ceres, whose gaze is still fixed on her home of origin, and the daughter-wife, Proserpine, who has accepted her new home, which sounds much like an idealized version of America, with picnics in pleasing meadows and "wide benches like the ones in Central Park" (212). Of course this is a proleptic application of the myth, since at this point Lillian has yet to accept life with John Bishop in America. And although her acceptance of these changed circumstances echoes the myth of Proserpine, it still aligns her new home with the underworld, however charming and verdant it may be.

Lillian's symbolic catabasis and anabasis, the psychic death of her Russian identity and resurrection as an American woman, is achieved through a mythic paradigm shift that reinforces the parallels with Odysseus. She hires a boat and sets off for Siberia, but is shipwrecked and loses all her belongings. Although he is washed shore and loses his possessions at several points in the epic poem, Odysseus is not shipwrecked when he finally reunites with Penelope. But Homer uses the image of the shipwrecked man in the famous simile that describes their reunion, which we have already seen applied in Byatt's "Conjugial Angel," discussed in the previous chapter:

> He wept as he held his beloved wife, steadfast of mind, as when the land appears welcome to men swimming because their sturdy boat has been smashed in Poseidon's sea . . . (*Od.* 23: 233–5)

The application of the Odyssean paradigm is reinforced when Lillian returns to Alaska after losing her boat and sees her lover John in a crowd; it is a moment of recognition and homecoming that again recalls the Homeric prototype. She lives the rest of her life with John, has children, and becomes integrated into her new homeland. By evoking an Odyssean reunion, the text also brings Lillian above ground, so to speak, and suggests that her sojourn in the underworld has brought about her rebirth and new identity, just as it did for the Homeric hero.

Thus the common element of immigrant narratives, an ascent from the dead, is presented as the imbrication of two mythic *paradeigmata*: the separation of Proserpine and Ceres, and the homecoming of Odysseus.

Democratizing the immigrant's descent

Although *Away* is less literary and provocative than *Song of Solomon*, Bloom's novel demonstrates the broad applicability of the descent motif in the context of diaspora. The two novels share Odyssean and Demetrian intertexts, although each uses them in different ways. Morrison is in a direct dialogue with Homer's *Odyssey*, which includes careful citations of the Circe episode, so that Milkman's journey to connect with his past juxtaposes the modalities of homecoming and descent implicit in the Odyssean intertext. The power of these citations, however, is diminished by the oblique suggestion that Pilate is a Demeter figure.

Bloom's program is less ambivalent and also less critical. She refers to a popularized collection of myth, meant for the general reader, as a tool to aid her character's reconciliation with her new home, and acculturation into American life. Bullfinch's collection befits the circumstances of Lillian Leyb, an uneducated immigrant woman of the early twentieth century, who would be unlikely to read a Greek or Latin author in a Canadian prison. Regardless of the prestige of the source text, however, Lillian and Milkman share a remarkable condition: as a result of trauma related to their diasporic identities, America is a form of Hell from which they must ascend. Like Odysseus both are immersed in water and lose their luggage along the way, events that suggest a death and rebirth of their identities.

The next two sections of this chapter turn to a different descent myth, that of Orpheus, to explore how its theme of mourning the irretrievable can be translated into the loss of a homeland and racial identity.

On the Outside Looking In: Salman Rushdie's *The Ground Beneath Her Feet*

The Ground Beneath Her Feet (1999) opens with the death of rock diva Vina Apsara, pulled into a chasm during an earthquake in Mexico on February 14, 1989, the date of the Ayatollah Khomeini's *fatwa* condemning Salman Rushdie for blasphemy. Rushdie's subsequent exile and underground existence for the next nine years (during which he wrote this novel) have parallels with the losses felt by his characters, who cope with Vina's death and their own expatriation in this adaptation of the Orpheus myth. The novel is certainly much more than auto-fiction, however. Its celebration of a syncretic transnational culture, which encompasses yet goes far beyond Rushdie's life story and career, suggests that art comes most alive when it crosses boundaries. Nostalgia for a lost nation is mitigated by the recognition that leaving home can be a productive journey to a new type of citizenship and a contribution to a globalized culture, in this case the world music that Ormus and Vina create with their group VTO. While it is possible to project the author's exile onto this ambitious and heterogeneous work whose central characters find themselves, like their creator, "living between worlds," we must also recognize how Rushdie's novel implicates its readers in its construction of alternate worlds. We find ourselves on the outside looking in, inevitably part of a world external to the reality of the novel. At times, the text positions different worlds, the "elsewhere" of a former home, and the "here" of a new country, as an underworld and an upper world, although we should be cautious about our directional terminology. There is a disorienting ambiguity about whether the characters ascend or descend to their new home. This ambiguity is intensified by the sci-fi plot element of two parallel universes about to collide. But there is no uncertainty about the effects of passing between these different worlds. For the central characters the transit between the East and the West, the old and the new, is seismic, emotionally and psychically disruptive, but also produces a rich cultural blending, although it is not immune from the corruption of the capitalistic music industry.

Correspondingly, the novel itself is another form of syncretism that combines classical literature and popular culture. *The Ground Beneath Her Feet* announces its palimpsestic condition in its first chapters with conspicuous references to the Aristaeus epyllion (and the story of Orpheus) in Vergil's *Fourth Georgic*. Cultural border crossings are at the heart of the novel: Orpheus's power to cross the threshold between life and death is homologous with the novel's power to transition between high and low art, and its characters' transits between East and West. The imprint of the Orphic descent is also discernible in the struggles and adventures of each of the three wandering characters: Rai the exile forced out of India, his friend Ormus the immigrant who chooses to leave, and their object of desire, Vina, a nomadic character who seems the most mobile, travelling back and forth between continents and hemispheres, east, west, south, and finally down beneath the ground. While it is Vina who endures an actual physical descent, her two lovers, Ormus and Rai, undergo symbolic passages to and from Hades. The metaphor of rebirth or resurrection, implicit in the infernal voyage, and a common symbol for the immigrant's experience (for example that of Mary Antin), applies to each of the three central characters. And although the self-conscious references to the myth of Orpheus and Eurydice seem best to fit the relationship between the two rock stars, Ormus and Vina, there is often ambiguity about which character in the novel matches up with which Vergilian prototype. Each of the three central characters corresponds to Orpheus at one time or another and for various reasons. All cross geo-political borders that are symbolized by an Orphic passage into or out of the underworld, and all are involved with cultural production. Art and culture issue from the subterranean realm in this narrative: literature, music, photography are aspects of cultural afterlives, as the reincarnation of Vergil's ancient text suggests.

Migration, the afterlife, and the arts are thematically linked throughout the novel. Wrapped up with this parcel of ideas is the concept of a cultural mash-up, especially music, and in particular rock and roll, a mongrel genre that cuts and pastes, assimilates, and reinvents different elements of a diverse selection of musical cultures—it gains power by effacing borders. Rock music is arguably the most globalized form of culture of the present day. Having spread throughout the world, it is what Rushdie has described as the "mythology of our times," and Chambers as "the sound score" of modern life.[46] While it is true that the narrator, Rai Merchant, claims a South Asian origin for rock music—"This is the story of Ormus Cama who heard the music first" (99)—he

[46] Shortly after the publication of *The Ground Beneath Her Feet* Rushdie gave an interview in which he identified rock music as the "mythology of our time" and the unifying "language of cultural reference" (cited in Mendes 2013: 135–6). See Chambers (1994: 77–8) on the hybridization of rock music. He acknowledges the genre's origins as a product of "an established, largely Anglo-American hegemony," but traces the growth and influence of world music as "a representative of a cultural, economic, and historical shift that disputes the very nature of the centre-periphery distinction."

acknowledges a form of music, created and disseminated by Ormus and Vina, that produces a transnational polyphony:

> the sexiness of Cuban horns, the mind-bending patterns of the Brazilian drums, the Chilean woodwinds moaning like the winds of oppression, the African male voice . . . the grand old ladies of Algerian music with their yearning squawks and ululations, the holy passion of the Pakastani qawwals. (379)

It is not only international boundaries that music dissolves; rock music seeps across the border between non-being and being to issue from the underworld, which eventually claims Vina, its most renowned performer, as its victim.

The alignment of art and culture with the underworld is explicitly advertised when Rai, whose tale begins in the India of his youth, establishes his role as a catabatic traveller in a literary genealogy that extends back to Orpheus:

> at the gate of the Inferno of language, there's a barking dog and a ferry man waiting and a coin under my tongue for the fare. (21)

This acknowledgement of his own role and his story's place in the literary space of the netherworld initiates a consistent and familiar message throughout the novel: the afterlife is both a product and a producer of culture. This includes photography, Rai's chosen medium and one easily associated with death and the spirit world. It is not only that Rai takes photographs of his dead parents, other people's funerals, and the disappearance of Vina into the earth, but also that the camera's images are conceived as ghosts, which Rai records to document the existence of an otherwise unseen parallel world. As he learns from his mentor, the French photographer Herlot, films are like phantoms, and postcards are the "souls of things." But photographs, like written texts, can also dissimulate. In the first chapter Rai describes his narrative as "an underworld of ink and lies" (21), a self-undermining gesture that portends his own dishonesty as a photojournalist. Rai is forced into exile after his pictorial exposé of the fraudulent Bombay businessman, Piloo, perpetrator of a lucrative scam based on a fictitious goat-milk industry. But the damning photographs of the non-existent goats (and empty pastures) are in fact another man's, a dead man whose work, images of absence and nothingness, Rai fortuitously stumbles upon.

Alternate worlds

If artistic production, be it music, photography, or writing arises from the underworld, as the novel suggests—a formulation that much of the fiction discussed in the preceding chapters embraces—it is also a form of deceit that like a ghost provokes questions about reality and authenticity. Nonetheless to speak of lies is to claim an immutable truth, a claim that this text challenges. One of the questions that Rushdie implicitly poses concerns the relationship between the reader's own world and the fictional world that his novel represents, another variant of the elision of narrative levels that McHale identifies as the defining feature of postmodernist fiction.[47] The suspension of disbelief required to enjoy the novel requires us to accept that our own reality is a fiction, the ultimate postmodern paradox. The theme of twin worlds, so frequently emphasized, is a playful metafictional flourish in this work of magic realism: there is a parallel universe in which the Watergate scandal, for example, is an event in a novel, while Kilgore Trout (Vonnegut's fictional character) is a real author. The external world of the reader becomes a fiction, while what we believe to be fiction is reality. The theme of alterity extends to the collision of parallel universes, causing a series of earthquakes along borders, which are eventually explained by an alien contact from that other universe. Rai has access to this alternate world through his photographs and a video camera that records its message. Ormus sees it through one damaged eye, which he usually covers with an eye-patch. Vina vanishes into it during one of the earthquakes caused by the collisions. The proposition of a double reality recalls the Other World that Coraline visits, similar to the quotidian household that she shares with her parents, both idealized and threatening. Yet while Coraline keeps those worlds separate, *The Ground Beneath Her Feet* posits a ghost world that haunts and penetrates the world of the living.

The unsettling effect of this preoccupation with double vision goes beyond a metapoetic reflection on the relationship between reader and text, or another version of the postmodern "heterocosm" (to use McHale's term), to subtly align our constructed outsiderness with the conditions of diasporic peoples. As readers we are led into a state of

[47] McHale (1987: 31–3) uses the term "heterocosm" to denote the alternative realities of fiction. Cf. Hutcheon 1984: 50.

disorientation, and must accept that *we* are the others, members of that alternate, fictional universe in which the Watergate scandal happened. "Disorientation," states Rushdie's narrator, means "loss of the east" (5), and is a condition experienced by the immigrant in a new homeland, but it is also an affect that this novel imposes on its readers by setting us up as "outsiders" who are never quite sure which direction we face. This instability, caused by our relegation to a world outside the reality of the novel, puts into literary form the experience of the migrant who must apprehend society through a double consciousness. In her essay on Rushdie's deployment of the tension between real and imaginary worlds in *The Ground Beneath Her Feet*, Nilufer Bharucha theorizes its duality as a metaphor for a diasporic worldview that has its source in a confusion of identity (and recalls Chambers' descriptor, "living between worlds"):

> Living in diaspora entails existing on at least two different planes. The diasporic person lives simultaneously in the past and in the present. S/he is a member of the new host community and at the same time hasn't severed ties with the old/originating community.[48]

The motif of the underworld, or the otherworld, has set up a complex system of dualities that reflect this double consciousness.[49] Readers live in both our homeland of external realities, and the world of the novel. Reading becomes a passage that can fracture our sense of self in a way that makes us accept that external reality as another world that, we are told, is "an underworld of lies."

This interplay between phantoms and duplicity extends to music, the art most obviously associated with Orpheus. But just as Rai's photographs reveal an alternate world, there is again a division between the "here" populated by the novel's characters, and the "elsewhere" of musical inspiration. The rock god, Orphic counterpart to Vina's Eurydice, is Ormus, a musical genius born playing air guitar with his tiny fingers, who hears Ur-versions of the hit parade before they manifest via

[48] Bharucha 2001: 59. See her further comments (2001: 51–2) for a brief history of the Indian diaspora, which encompasses the displacement of peoples due to British colonization, and the voluntary diaspora of later generations of Indians to Britain and America.

[49] Linguanti (2006: 107–23) surveys the different versions of other worlds in the novel in the context of theories of parallel universes. She adds the interesting analysis that the interpenetration of worlds in *The Ground Beneath Her Feet* is a comment on the incursion of Western culture into the East.

Western superstars. He is a "musical sorcerer" and "golden troubadour whose lyrics could unlock the very gates of Hell" (89). His preternatural talent is explained by his access to a spectral realm inhabited by the ghost of his stillborn twin Gayomart. His misheard lyrics (e.g. "the ganga my friend is growing in the tin") originate from "that Las Vegas of the subterranean world" (145). The authenticity and proprietorship of Ormus's creations are paradoxically both validated and undermined by their infernal source. The producer Yul Singh threatens legal action for what seems to be a pirated rendition of the (ironically) yet to be released "Yesterday," one of many songs attributed to the West that Ormus learns from his brother in the underworld. Rai compares this relationship to that of Castor and Pollux; his twin exists in Hades, while he lives in the temporal realm.[50] Like Rai's photographs his creations are not his own, but second-hand products of his ghost twin: "in his brother he found the Other into which he dreamed of metamorphosing, the dark self that first fueled his art" (99).

This suggestion of an alter ego or a ghost Other advances the theme of the unstable identity of the artist who exists between two cultures. The South Asian culture that produced Rushdie and his characters is a complex blend of British colonialism, which left its imprint on Indian culture, and a pre-existing culture that may have shared an Indo-European origin with the Raj. This is the intellectual project of Ormus' father, Cyrus, who seeks to align Greek gods with Hindu/Parsi myth. Cultural blending began long before this novel, suggests Rushdie, whose own identity is a product of this shared heritage, although any blend of British imperialism and Indian myth is not the globalized culture that he champions. The novel sets up a dialectic between the ridiculous anglophile, Cyrus Cama, who identifies with the British classical tradition (and its troubling association with Aryanism), and his son, Ormus, who strives to move beyond this antediluvian colonialism.[51] Paradoxically

[50] "After the death by spearing of mortal Castor, Polydeuces the son of Zeus spent alternate days below the earth with his dead brother, at a place named Therapne; and in return the dead twin was allowed to spend alternate days with his brother on the surface, with the ground beneath his feet instead of over his head" (*GBHF* 54).

[51] In his study of the influence and use of classicism in colonial India, Vasunia (2013: 240) observes that while classical literature was associated with the British imperialism, Indian culture was able to exploit some of its motifs for their own nationalistic agenda. The preferred texts were Homeric. Vergil's *Aeneid*, the definitive text of imperial expansion, was less useful. Falconer (2005: 208) also notes that the message of foreign invaders taking over

Ormus is nonetheless constructed as a figure from Greek myth.[52] On the other hand Rushdie, by articulating the possibility of an alter ego or ghost Other that produces the popular music of Western culture, may be responding to the Eurocentric concept of an Eastern "underground self," identified by Edward Saïd, whose work Rushdie has seen as complementing his own.[53] In his seminal work *Orientalism*, Saïd theorizes that European culture has constructed the Orientalized Other "as a sort of surrogate and even underground self" that stabilizes Western identities.[54] In his non-fiction writings Rushdie has emphasized a concern for the West's problematic cooption of Eastern culture, and its representation of this Orientalized Other. By locating the matrix of popular music in "an underground self" that is the doppelgänger of a South Asian composer, Rushdie decenters the Western subject position, identified by Saïd as dependent on this Asian Other. No longer a projection of a Eurocentric hegemony, the Other becomes the source of culture rather than its distorted reflection.[55]

The exile and the emigré

The emphasis on the subterranean associations of artistic endeavors that cross borders between the metaphysical and the temporal—the wraith-like reproductions of photography and the music flowing from Hades—correspondingly implicates this ghost culture in themes of exile and relocation. But is the migrant artist's transit an ascent or a descent?

a pre-existing culture was less salutary for Rushdie's text, and thus he uses not the descent of *Aeneid* 6, but rather the earlier version of the *Georgics*.

[52] Mondal (2007: 169–83) remarks that the strategy of ascribing hegemonic Western myths to Eastern origins is on the one hand a postcolonial gesture that decenters the West, but at the same time requires the reader to know what is being displaced. The juxtaposition of high and low culture—Vergil's *Georgic* 4 and rock and roll—only works to the extent that readers are familiar with both.

[53] See for example Rushdie's "On Palestinian Identity: a conversation with Edward Said," in *Imaginary Homelands* (1992). On the changing nature of the relationship see Waheed (2013).

[54] Saïd 1978: 3.

[55] As Ormus and Vina will discover, their contribution to music forces them to confront some corrupt producers and managers. "This reversing of the origins of rock-and-roll goes against an assimilationist understanding of globalization and instead posits its diversification potentialities. This shift allows for a nuanced critique in the novel of globalising forces in such a way that the cracks and contradictions within power structures are exposed and explored through Rushdie's rendering of the workings of the music industry" (Mendes 2013: 138).

Both young men leave India for reasons associated with their creative talents, and both find fame in another continent because of their role as culture makers. Each responds differently to his departure: one goes voluntarily with high expectations, while the other's departure is enforced. Ormus achieves fame and fortune as a musician/composer, and is reunited romantically and professionally with Vina, his Eurydice, who sings the songs that he creates. Rai enjoys success as a photojournalist, and occasionally substitutes as Vina's lover. As the primary focalizer of the narrative his perspective on leaving India shades the text with the deepest sense of nostalgia. On the one hand, Rai is the self-identified Aristaeus of this self-proclaimed adaptation of Vergil's *Fourth Georgic*, creating a new art form from the carcass of an ancient poem, as Aristaeus created his new colony of bees (an ancient symbol for poetry) from the ritual bugonia performed on the hide of a dead heifer.

The first chapter, which begins with Vina's death in the earthquake and is titled "Keeper of Bees," makes this equation explicit. In the source text Aristaeus the bee-keeper crosses the boundary between land and sea (the ocean being another ancient symbol for poetry) in a watery catabasis that leads to an encounter with the shape-shifting Proteus who tells him the story of Orpheus. For Rai this mythical baptism is the template for his youthful desire to leave India: "My dream ocean led to America, my private, my unfound land" (59). The central chapters are devoted to the long-awaited transition between continents. Rai, eventually driven out of the country in fear for his life, ends the India section with a retrospective lament for his expatriation:

> I am writing here about the end of something not just the end of a phase of my life the end of my connection with the country, my country of origin as we say now, my home country I was brought up to say, India. I am trying to say goodbye, goodbye again, goodbye a quarter of a century after I physically left it. (203)

Thus the India-half of the novel draws to a conclusion with Rai's sorrowful farewell to his country, now personified as a lost wife. In the mutating symbolism of the novel another shift occurs and now Rai corresponds not to Aristaeus but to Orpheus. His lost homeland is the most poignant version of Eurydice possible in this novel of displacement and exile:

> [T]he moment comes when you have to turn away from your wife, from the unbearably beautiful memory of the way you were, and turn towards the rest of your life . . . and so farewell, my country. (248)

His friend (and Ormus's rejected fiancée) Persis, one of several threshold figures in the tale, arranges his ticket, just as she helped Vina leave India earlier. Rai's exilic departure is framed as a crossing from one life to the next:

> Persis gentle gate keeper of our lives. Who stood by the river that separates the worlds and helped us to cross, but could not do so herself. (247)

The metaphor suggests that Rai is dying as he gives up his national identity and citizenship. Thus categories are blurred: India is the lost wife, whom Rai lets go, while he himself submits to death when he leaves India. This ambiguity about the location of the underworld and its ghosts contributes to the disorienting quality of the narrative, which only increases as its characters move westward.

The subterranean theme links art and expatriation in different ways for both the exile and the émigré. For Rai the connection between cultural production and exile is a relatively straightforward causal relationship. Because of the inflammatory content of his photojournalism he is forced into exile, an experience that now positions him as an Orpheus figure, saying goodbye to his wife for the last time. The transition for Ormus is also configured as an Orphic passage between two realms of existence. His migration, occurring a decade before Rai's departure, is treated in detail, and occurs in several stages. In one of the transitional central chapters, "Membrane," Ormus has a vivid sensation of passing through an invisible boundary into the West. For him, unlike Rai, there is no sense of loss, "he is leaving for good, without regret, without a backward glance" (252). While Rai's departure from India was like losing a beloved wife, for Ormus it is emphatically unlike the loss of Eurydice. He has only anticipation of new possibilities as he follows Vina westward. With absolutely no intention of remaining with his mother and her new husband in England, he takes his leave of her as soon as he lands, also "without a backward glance" (268), although the separation is not as clean-cut as he expected. It is Rai who feels the exile's sense of loss, while Ormus anticipates only opportunity. He feels but a brief sensation of nostalgia on his touchdown in England, and "jerks himself free of it" (269).

Ormus' final destination (he hopes) is a multi-cultural America, whose inhabitants (he believes) are more like him in that they all come from somewhere else. His migration is a transformative experience, as it is for all immigrants, but his spectacularly so. On the flight to England, amidst other passengers of varying stripes (excited children, a terrified bride, fellow countrymen in lumpy Western clothing), he is irradiated and mutated by a divine force pulsing through a rip in the sky as he begins his apotheosis into a rock god.[56]

The chapter entitled "The Season of the Witch," part of the transition section of the novel, has Ormus existing in limbo. His time in Britain is represented as his first assimilation into Western culture, symbolized by his craving for white bread. During his metamorphosis, not only into his identity as a rock superstar but as a new member of the Western world, Ormus experiences racist taunts, the patronizing sexual interest of women who exoticize him, and a general sense of invisibility. All around him he sees examples of his own culture coopted by the West, such as Antoinette Corinth's pseudo-mysticism, exemplifying a "descent into an inferno of privilege" (287).[57] He is disgusted, but he likes the bread, and does not give "a backward glance to the fabled breads of home" (289).

The nomad

Rock diva Vina corresponds to Eurydice in many overt and significant ways, although she scarcely resembles the silent poetic symbol of thwarted desire. In her childhood, after reading Jules Verne's *Journey to the Center of the Earth*, she imagined her descent. She yearned for an Icelandic entrance to Hades, "an Arctic Taenarus Gate" (128), suggesting that she is hardly a passive victim of subterranean forces. This Eurydice has agency and subjectivity; she is a rescuer, not only a victim. Rushdie is by no means the only postmodern writer to subvert her tradition. In "Eurydice", included in her collection of poems, *The World's Wife* (1999), Carol Ann Duffy represents Eurydice's perspective from a pleasant underworld where she is glad to be rid of the annoying poet, and resents having to go back to life with him. She appeals to his vanity to get him to turn around and read his tedious poem to her again so that

[56] His journey on the plane is marked by other mythical experiences that make parallels between coming-of-age narratives and catabatic tales, a common conflation, as we know. Ormus regards his migration as a passage into adulthood. Like other mythological Greek heroes in such tales, he rejects his mother, Spenta Cama, although his break is not as easy as leaving her in the airport. Mull Standish, a mentor-guide figure, offers him a place on his version of the Argo, an offshore radio station where he will begin his initiatory ordeal.

[57] The condescending appropriation of Eastern culture is an idea that Rushdie repeatedly exposes, for example in his critique of Attenborough's *Ghandi*, in *Imaginary Homelands*.

she can return to her comfortable existence free from the annoying stalker-poet. But Vina is a much more enthusiastic boundary-crosser than Duffy's Eurydice, and willingly participates in the culture industry that develops around her.

Vina is a multi-ethnic (Greek-American-Indian) nomad, going back and forth between continents. In a reversal of her usual role as the one who follows Orpheus out of Hades, she rescues Ormus from a coma, summoned by his music to his bedside. It is a feat that she compares to that of the Hindu goddess Rati who brought back Kama, the god of love, from the underworld. Nonetheless her departure from India back to North America into "that immense underworld made up of all the things and places and people we did not know" (178) is explicitly compared to the loss of Eurydice—although Ormus does not immediately follow her "into this inferno, the underworld of doubt" (178). Like the music that he hears, she belongs to the infernal realm. At one point, thinking of the historical development of the Eurydice myth, Rai wonders: "did she actually bubble up from the underworld to capture Orpheus' heart; was she an avatar of the queen of darkness herself?" When he wonders if "in being swallowed by the earth, was she merely going home" (399), he only repeats the age-old gendering of the underworld as female, which we encountered in *Coraline*, for example.

Disorientation

All three of the central characters of this novel—Rai, Ormus, and Vina—correspond at some point to Orpheus, while Ormus and Vina exchange the role of Eurydice. The novel constructs an intricate web of surrogates and doubles that emphasizes the theme of alterity. Even before Vina disappears, a double named Maria appears from a parallel world in an attempt to seduce Ormus, and another will eventually take over the persona of Vina. After her death, there is a spate of Vina impersonators. The existence of Ormus's twin brother, and the implication that Rai is an alter ego of Ormus also contribute to the blurring of identities. Boundaries around selves, it would seem, are permeable, as are boundaries between nations, cultures, and between the land of the living and the land of the dead. Caught between cultures, the characters in this novel are also caught between worlds and identities. Their dilemma symbolizes not only how an immigrant-self can be split between his or her former citizenship and new sense of self, but also how this fractured self can be reflected spatially. In her discussion of the literature of exile, Christina Dascălu comments that geographical displacement can result in an indeterminacy of identity:

> For while accepting that the subject is not a stable and static being (it is the construction of its surroundings), the subject can also deform and destabilize those surroundings from which it emanates.[58]

This phenomenon is writ large in the physically indeterminate landscapes that confuse the location of the otherworld and the upper world in *The Ground Beneath Her Feet.*

For all its catabatic imagery—and in this novel it is overdetermined—there is a confusion about the direction of Hades.[59] Where is the underworld? Is it India? Ormus regards himself and other Indians as "underworlders." Is it England, where Ormus will lie in a coma for years until Vina leads him back to life in America? Is it America, "that immense underworld made up of all the things and places and people we did not know"? Or is it Mexico, where Vina disappears forever?[60] The intradiegetic seismic shifts and alternate realities that we encounter within the novel are mirrored extradiegetically by the interpretive ground beneath our feet. We are "unhomed," to use Homi Bhabha's terminology, like the characters in the novel as we are destabilized by the world that Rushdie has imagined for us.[61]

The Ghost of the Father in Ann Patchett's *State of Wonder*

"The news of Anders Eckman's death came by Aerogram," reads the opening line of Ann Patchett's *State of Wonder* (2011). From the corporate sterility of a Minnesota winter Marina Singh, a medical researcher

[58] Dascălu 2007: 18.

[59] As well as the multiple allusions to the story told by Vergil, there are other kinds underworlds, for example the one which Rai's father tries to find by digging, or the imprisoned serial killer-brother of Ormus, a psychopath who possesses his seductive charms (not with music but with words he uses to captivate his victims), but who also exists at times in a "cavernous underworld of self-loathing" (137).

[60] Falconer (2005: 202–3) is less uncertain about the location of the underworld in the novel. She reads a three stage journey from the "paradise" of Bombay to the inferno of New York City and finally to the lower reaches of Hell, Mexico.

[61] Bhabha 1994: 141.

for the Vogel pharmaceutical company, journeys in search of the truth of this announcement to the Brazilian rainforest research colony where her colleague reportedly died, and her fellow employee and former professor, Dr. Annick Swenson, has worked incommunicado as a rogue scientist for several years. The text proclaims itself as a version of the Orpheus and Eurydice story, but also calls other iterations of the descent narrative into play, complicating its explicit reference to a romantic Orphic paradigm. The Orphic theme frames the disorientation and deracination shaping the inner life of its protagonist, but beneath the narrative's surface await deeper catabatic allusions adumbrating ethical concerns about corporate capitalism boring into the center of the jungle.

It is notable that Patchett's novel, like others discussed in this chapter, imposes a directional readjustment, a 180-degree turn that upends its catabatic metaphor. The narrative situates its underworld ostensibly in South America, although any sense of up or down must be radically recalibrated in the final stages of Marina's journey. A deliberate symmetry between Brazil and the literary space that we have come to know as Hades is emphasized almost as soon as Marina steps off the plane in Manaus where she is greeted by her driver and psychopomp Milton, who will take Marina into the dark heart of the literary landscape. She meets an American woman who explains, as she offers a concoction to mitigate the transition to South America, that: "This is what we do down here in hell" (129). It is a gesture, no doubt, towards the transformative potions that Alice drinks before entering Wonderland, one of several substances that Marina ingests in this state of Wonder. The catabatic theme is finally most conspicuously and self-reflexively announced when she attends a performance of Gluck's eighteenth-century baroque opera *Orfeo ed Euridice*. The mezzo-soprano role of Orfeo (originally written for a castrato) is performed by a woman, allowing Marina to recognize it as her own story.

> She knew the story of Orpheus, but it wasn't until the singing began that she realized it was the story of her life. She was Orfeo, and there was no question that Anders was Euridice, dead from a snake bite. Marina had been sent into hell to bring him back. Had Karen [Ander's wife] been able to leave the boys, she would have been Orfeo. (124)

Nevertheless, the equivalence is not as simple as Marina lets herself believe. *State of Wonder* sets the happy operatic adaptation of Orpheus' descent against more disturbing variants of the catabatic story-pattern, some more recent and others traceable to antiquity. The overt references to an eclectic assortment of literary predecessors—*Paradise Lost*, *Alice's Adventures in Wonderland*, to begin with—conjure up a company of literary ghosts who extend the margins of this adventure story. If Patchett's novel takes its shape from preceding members of its sequence, it has organized this series as a chain of confrontations between romance, horror, and grief that encompass the melancholia of its central character and the world of transnational capitalism in which she participates as an employee of the Vogel corporation.

On the surface Marina's self-conscious reference to Gluck's *Orfeo*, with its joyful finale in which the lovers are reunited a second time after the fatal backward gaze, is the most overt catabatic signpost of the text. The opera features an optimistic ending that Rushdie parodies in the opening chapter of *The Ground Beneath Her Feet*, although the pre-Vergilian version of the story probably ended with a single reunion of the couple. But as we know, there is no stable closure to the Orpheus story, which can end happily or sadly; its open-endedness and the generic hybridity of other catabatic intertexts complicates any expectation of a fairytale conclusion to Marina's story. The Brazilian setting, for instance, might recall Camus's classic film *Orfeu Negro* (1959) set during the Carnival of Rio, in which characters, just as Marina does, realize they are playing a part in the story, and which ends on a note of tragedy even though Orpheus, the Brazilian guitarist, believes that he can save Eurydice from Death. More disturbingly, however, *State of Wonder* reaches back to a different descent narrative: Joseph Conrad's *Heart of Darkness* (1899), and its filmic offspring, Francis Ford Coppola's *Apocalypse Now* (1979).[62] All three cultural products are versions of the infernal descent configured as a river trip through a tropical jungle to meet with a mentor figure, whose ancient literary prototypes include Aeneas' encounter with the ghost of his father Anchises.

The intertextual landscape

The natural world depicted in descent narratives often possesses mystical qualities, its topographies charged with, or standing in for, the supernatural kingdom beneath the earth. Like Milkman and Lillian

[62] Falconer (2005: 196–7) analyzes *Apocalypse Now* as a "descent of a Western, imperial hero into a demonic Southern/Eastern underworld" which ultimately demonstrates that the demonic "lies in the heart of the West, not the East."

Leyb, Marina (whose name suggests a nautical voyage) traverses a landscape infused with chthonic symbolism. Her excursion down the Rio Negro into the forest primeval and her encounter with its occupants draw upon several recursively layered source texts. There is, to begin with, Marlow's voyage into the thick jungles of the Congo, which recalls the forests of Dis observed by Aeneas, a feature of other underworld topographies; again we are aware that trees can serve as a metonymy for the literary tradition. Marina's journey through the rainforest thus implicates the narrative in a deeper, more complex intertextual level than Gluck's operatic version, and these allusions produce an intricate symbolic template. The water passage goes back to the earliest representations of infernal voyages: Odysseus must travel to the gates of Hades by Ocean; Aeneas and Orpheus cross the Styx; and the migrant characters of all the novels discussed above make passages by water. Rivers are a consistent feature of Hades, often demarcating boundaries between the living and the dead, or even different categories of the dead. This essential feature of underworld topography recurs in the Brazilian rivers that Marina traverses, populated with "water snakes whose heads rode the surface of the river like tiny periscopes" (213). While these reptiles may refer tangentially to the snake that bit Eurydice, they have other literary antecedents. Classical underworlds are replete with snakes or snake-like monsters.[63] Vergil's image of the Cocytus slithering around the forests of Dis captures the serpentine aspect of Hades that manifests in the *drakontes* that inhabit it. Its rivers are appropriately sinuous and ophidian:

tenent media omnia silva, Cocytusque sinu labens circumvenit atro. Aen. 6.131–32.

Forests lie in all the middle spaces which the gliding Cocytus encircles with its dark coil.

When the Vergilian metaphor reappears in Conrad's image of the Congo, it contributes to the Hadean quality of his landscape. His central character and narrator, Marlow, recalls:

I was going into the yellow. Dead in the center. And the river was there—fascinating—deadly—like a snake. (*HOD* 15)[64]

[63] Ogden (2013: 247–8) demonstrates that serpents are a fundamental feature of the Greco-Roman underworld.

[64] All citations from *Heart of Darkness* are from the 2012 edition featuring an introduction by A. Hochschild, with apparatus and notes by T.S. Hayes.

Correspondingly *State of Wonder* embeds its version of the underworld in a fecund landscape accessible only by a river passage; the snake imagery becomes part of the material reality of the novel, but imparts the same sinister quality to the setting.

Conrad's image of the snake-like river, which he repeats several times, is one of many ways that he aligns his story with the tradition of *Aeneid* 6.[65] Vergil—not to simplify an often ambiguous portrayal of his hero—celebrates an imperialistic hegemony; Conrad appears to problematize that agenda. Scholarship is far from unanimous on his own colonialist worldview, but *Heart of Darkness* offers a discernable critique of the depredations of late nineteenth-century Belgian ivory merchants in the Congo. By referring to the imperialistic tradition represented by the *Aeneid*, Conrad creates a new version of Hades that prefigures the ethical and environmental concerns informing *State of Wonder*. He compromises the heroic tradition of colonialism by mimicking its narratives and showing the invidious consequences of its international expansion, trade, and commerce. Coppola's *Apocalypse Now* (an adaptation of Conrad's novel) replaces the commercial with the militaristic, but creates a similar vision of a tropical Hell produced by Western imperialism.[66] Conrad appropriates features of Vergil's landscape—the river and the forest—but suggests that the Belgian ivory trade has turned the jungle into a form of Hell. The infernal landscape is occupied by tormented African men and women enslaved by the Belgians, or their battered corpses strewn throughout the jungle that is "Dead in the centre" (*HOD* 38). In her analysis of Marlow's relationship with the African landscape, Ann McClintock observes that: "The mystical journey is figured in this way as darkly infused by colonial trade, as corrupted, and thereby secularized."[67]

Conrad's jungle river and subsequently those of Coppola and Patchett provide much more than a recognizable *mise-en-scène*. Marlow's nautical voyage, while evoking literary predecessors, is also an inner journey, although one that disassembles the long history of European humanism

[65] Feder (1955: 280–92) makes a straightforward comparison between Conrad's novel and Vergil's description of Hades in *Aeneid* 6.

[66] Although as Falconer (2005:196–200) observes, the film has been used as a training tool for American marines to enculturate them in the American military.

[67] McClintock 1984: 40. McClintock offers a nuanced reading of the problematic relationship between Marlowe and the African landscape within the colonialist narrative tradition, which situates Conrad within his historical context.

associated with the quest story pattern. The river trip is correlative with a catabasis that often symbolizes or encompasses a search for knowledge and truth: Anchises' prophecy of Aeneas' role in founding Rome, or Milkman Dead's search for his history. *Heart of Darkness*, however, capsizes that paradigm. McClintock contextualizes Marlow's river passage within a philosophical tradition that represents "truth" as a goal of such an interior journey. He does not encounter any version of the truth that he can recognize in this corrupted forest, only an inchoate horror. Conrad thus recreates the underworld topography of the *Aeneid*, but eviscerates the tradition leaving only a narrative husk to emphasize the emptiness of his protagonist's quest.

The mentor at the center of a lie

Marina's expedition on the Rio Negro is also an attempt to reach the truth, although, as she realizes very soon, that as it does for Marlow, such a mission can only lead her to the center of a lie. On the surface level of the narrative she finds what she is looking for, her missing colleague, but the trip down the river, which exposes her doubts about her own racial and national identity, has a less secure outcome. Patchett adapts the format of *Heart of Darkness*, itself an adaptation of Vergil's *Aeneid*, as a river voyage through a dark forest, but (although the structure of the story implies as much) the seeker does not ultimately achieve knowledge imparted by a mentor figure, as in the classical prototype. According to the syntax of the heroic descent, after passing through a forest, taking a river trip, and fulfilling various trials, the traveler will encounter this mentor. We have already seen disturbances and variations of that idiom in the works of John Barth and Elena Ferrante. Not every descent narrative features this tutelary element, but since *State of Wonder* makes strong references to that tradition, we can consider how the novel has reworked this ancient prototype by alluding to *Heart of Darkness* in which the wise mentor is replaced by the more disturbing figure of Kurtz, whose insanity confounds the truth rather than expounding it. In keeping with the Orphic gender inversion in *State of Wonder*, the father/mentor/Kurtz figure is recast as a woman, Annick Swenson, Marina's professor in medical school, who resumes her tutelary role in the Amazonian research camp. Indeed just as Kurtz hopes to name Marlow as his successor, Swenson proposes that Marina could carry on her legacy and complete her research project. Like

Kurtz (both versions) Annick Swenson, however, is a distortion of the mentor role; she does not reveal the truth that Marina searches for, but instead obfuscates it with her lies by claiming that Eckman was buried, in addition to other untruths.

Among the most significant of these lies is her dissimulation about her relationship with a child named Easter. Swenson has kept Easter, a boy from the nearby Hummocca tribe, in her power for many years, presenting him to Marina as her foster child, although he seems more like a slave performing menial tasks at her bidding. Although Swenson maintains that Easter's parents abandoned him, Marina eventually learns that she essentially abducted the boy eight years earlier, claiming he had died while under her care. Easter is an important figure in this narrative, corresponding on one level to the African woman that Kurtz keeps as his slave-concubine in Conrad's novel, but he has more significance than this: as we shall presently see, he serves as a narrative fulcrum that shifts the interpretive axis of the text. A prelude to this pivotal moment occurs when Marina has to grapple with a giant water snake that nearly strangles the boy during a trip down river, another manifestation of the serpentine imagery of Hades. By hacking away at the deadly anaconda and cutting it to pieces to release its hold on the child, Marina performs a heroic trial that will give her special status among the Lakashi (the local indigenous tribe). When the unconscious Easter is brought back to life, he seems to fulfill the meaning of his name (and suggests his association with the Orphic themes), although his true resurrection has yet to be completed. The suffocating snake is symbolic of the woman at the center of this underworld, which brings us back to Annick Swenson.

While she corresponds to Conrad's Kurtz (whose African captive woman is Persephone to his Hades), Swenson is a creature of a different order; she is the mythopoetic tradition cut into bits, and reassembled. A marvelous amalgamation of the megalomaniacal Kurtz with such infernal females as the Red Queen in *Wonderland*, her composite persona extends even more remotely to the terrifying Sumerian Queen of the Dead, Erishkegal, who keeps Inanna's lover Dumuzi in Irkalla. And since Easter was only a small child when Swenson took him for herself, it is possible to read Marina's mentor as a version of the child-snatching demons discussed earlier, for example Mormo or, to give a more recent example, Other Mother in *Coraline*, who occupy the underworld. In the figure of Annick Swenson, the bogey-woman is melded with other infernal female monsters, with Hades himself, and finally with the conventional mentor figure. As an intertextual creation she thus reaches much deeper than the mentors of *Heart of Darkness* or the *Aeneid* to the most ancient descent stories.

Goddesses of the underworld, if that is how we choose to read Swenson, are often associated with fertility, for example Persephone; the tomb/womb analogy prevails in several mythologies including Greco-Roman and Vedic, and we have seen this manifestation in previous chapters, as well as in *Song of Solomon*.[68] Swenson fits this category in a grotesque and troubling manner. She is investigating an antimalarial drug found in a particular tree bark on behalf of Vogel, but is also concealing its fecundating powers from her employer.[69] The women of the Lakashi tribe, under the control of Swenson's research colony, chew the bark to keep themselves fertile. In fact Swenson is pregnant herself at the astonishing age of over seventy. Reigning over the Lakashi, whom she imperiously describes (along with all indigenous people) as "intractable" (168), Swenson has no qualms about using them as human guinea pigs. Her research team has been conducting experiments on these tribal people, drawing blood samples, training the women to conduct their own cervical swabs, while infecting the men in her control group to test the antimalarial properties of the tree bark.

Ghosts

At the same time that Patchett represents Swenson as an agent of a capitalistic corporation who feels entitled to exploit indigenous people as experimental commodities, the author herself seems unable to avoid stereotyping her fictitious tribal peoples. In her *Chicago Tribune* review of the novel (2011-07-08) Laura Ciolkowski writes:

> Patchett's natives are only semi-human; they don't possess civilized language, but make sounds "less like words and more like the call and answer of birds." They swim in the river in packs with "their long throats stretched up like turtles" and they swarm in a beam of light like massive schools of oversized fish. Doomed to a life outside of the grand narratives of Western progress, left behind by the

[68] Bodewitz (2002: 213–23) identifies the tomb/womb equation in Vedic myth; Rigoglioso (2005: 5–29) speculates about a similar phenomenon in the ancient cult of Persephone in Sicily.

[69] The tree grows symbiotically with a hallucinogenic mushroom, so Swenson's ostensible reason for keeping it is a secret is that the forest would be overrun with drug dealers.

forward march of modernity, the Lakashi coexist with archaic creatures, like the "freakish brand of great white bird with a wing span of a pterodactyl" and are seemingly impervious to evolutionary change.

Criticisms of the one-dimensional quality of the Lakashi have justification, but Patchett's creations have their predecessors in other descent stories, for example Conrad's depiction of the anonymous African natives, or Coppola's South Asian people in the thrall of a different Kurtz. In *Apocalypse Now* (Figure 4.1), the viewer sees a throng of ghostly white-painted tribal people coming to greet Willard as his ship approaches the shore. A corpse hanging from a nearby tree helps to set the tone, while several hellish looking fires burn in the background. A parallel moment in *State of Wonder* occurs when Marina first encounters the Lakashi in Swenson's encampment after her trip down the Rio Negro:

> There were people on the banks of the river... The boat crept towards the waving, spinning flames until they were close enough that Marina could just make out the shape of heads behind each of the fires, every man and woman waving a burning stick... (185–6)

In other words, the Lakashi have their place in the anonymous populations of ghosts that inhabit earlier versions of Hell. Conrad and Coppola's natives are descendants of the Vergilian crowds of unburied

Figure 4.1 Arrival at Kurtz's compound and the "souls on the shore." *Apocalypse Now*, dir. Francis Ford Coppola (1979).

dead waiting on the banks of the Styx. The same phrase describes them in both *Georgic* 4, and *Aeneid* 6: *turba ad ripas ruebat*, "a throng kept rushing to the shores" (*G.* 4.475 and *Aen.* 6.305). A similar multitude of anonymous souls appear, for example, in both of T.S. Eliot's catabatic poems (*The Waste Land* 63–4; *The Hollow Men* 57–60).[70]

While Patchett's Lakashi may be one of many ghostly populations whose origins stretch back to ancient texts, they also provide an entry point into concerns of diaspora and nostalgia at the heart of this novel. Their monolithic anonymity notwithstanding, the Lakashi are a catalyst for our recognition of Marina Singh's own fissured state. Like other wanderers, Odysseus, Milkman, and Lillian Leyb, she loses her luggage, a familiar symbol for an identity in flux. When she adopts the Lakashi garb, joins with them eating the tree bark, and is even mistaken for one of them by a group of tourists, she recapitulates the uncompleted processes of immigration and assimilation that lie in her background and haunt her dreams. Although she retains her role as an American researcher, Marina exists between two cultures as a racially hybrid figure occupying this hybrid text. The child of a Minnesotan mother and Indian father, who left the family and returned to his country of origin, Marina found herself having to explain her darker complexion throughout her youth, and eventually claimed to be from India, disavowing her American birth. Her racial ambiguity is deeply implicated in her psychic makeup, and her sense of lack of place in the world. As a child, nostalgia for her absent parent became conflated with a yearning for India, where she would visit periodically:

> what she was longing for was not only her father but an entire country, that place where no one would turn around and look at her. (35–6)

Childhood memories of visits to her father in India filter her experience in the Amazon, continuing in her dreams as she makes her way deeper into the rainforest. She is already, in a sense then, a displaced person even before she takes her journey to Brazil. The trip reveals her fractured sense of selfhood, instead of securing a heroic identity as it does for Aeneas or other catabatic heroes.

While various ghost texts haunt the narrative and invert the traditional gendered dynamics of the Orphic quest, her father's ghost

[70] Dick (1975: 41) draws this and other comparisons with *Aeneid* 6.

haunts her dreams, resonating with the surface story, accounting for its gendered inversions (since he becomes a Eurydice figure), and reflecting the problematic colonialism of its depiction of anonymous crowds of indigenous peoples. Shortly after she had agreed to take the trip to the jungle, and induced by her ingestion of the anti-malarial Lariam, Marina is awoken by a frightening dream, the first of several, which causes her to recall her visits to her now deceased father in India. As a child and after the separation of her parents, she had also taken Lariam, her "India pills" (34) to prepare for her trip: in her childhood dream she lets go of her father's hand and is swept up in a sea of people in Calcutta, an anonymous crowd of ghosts, as it were. The first mention of these dreams and the child Marina's mourning for her still living, but absent, father gives the novel's Orphic theme a very personal significance:

> Marina did not forget her father in his absence, nor did she learn to accept the situation over time. She longed for him. (35)

The loss of a loved one, who is between life and death, is therefore specifically relevant to Marina, and connects these embedded narratives, her dreams, within the larger adventure of her life.

Dreams signify the psychic dimension of Marina's underworld, just as they did for Lillian Leyb in *Away*, and Coraline; Gaiman's Morpheus makes explicit connections between the realms of death and dreams. As in the most ancient versions, dreams are associated with the underworld. Homer situates the "land of dreams" (δῆμον ὀνείρων, *Od.* 24.12) at the entrance to Hades, and has ghosts speaking to the living through their dreams. The association is understandable: both exist beyond the temporal and material level. For Marina dreams connect her with the past, not just in terms of their content, but also as a repetition of her childhood experience of dreaming before she left for her visits to India. Dreams of her father, long since deceased, persist throughout the trip to Brazil, linking Marina's yearning for India with her voyage to the Amazon. The running theme of these dreams is loss: various permutations of the separation from her father that are a subconscious recognition of her grief, both in the past and the present. In her adult dream immediately before her departure for Brazil she is conversing with her father in her office, but again crowds of people swarm around them, a version of the souls on the banks of the Styx. In these repetitive dreams the inverted

Orphic myth reveals Marina's special connection with the source text, a symbol of her own loss.

Certainly these dreams of her father resonate more deeply with the Orphic paradigm than does the disappearance of her married colleague, Anders Eckman. Marina's declared identification with Orpheus brings the grief and trauma of separation from a cherished parent and imaginary homeland more closely to the surface. Thus Marina's indeterminate status within the Lakashi colony, a people whose home has become a scientific laboratory, parallels her own lack of a sense of place, a disorientation closely associated with mourning her father, and dreams of his absorption into crowds of anonymous souls. The overlap between Anders and her father, her two Eurydices, however, leads to a third level of correspondence. When another American woman claims to have seen the ghost of her own father among the hostile Hummocca, Marina puts it all together and understands that it is Anders Eckman, Eurydice to her Orpheus, and stand-in for her father.

The underworld inverted

Deciding that, "There was in fact a circle of hell beneath this one," Marina mounts a river expedition to the Hummocca, which the boy Easter insists on joining. As suspected she does see Anders among them; he is not dead as she had been told, but lives in captivity among the Hummocca. The retrieval of Anders, however, involves another loss, that of Easter, the third Eurydice figure in this complex. At the unexpected sight of their long lost son his parents react in surprise: they had brought the boy to Swenson to be treated for an illness eight years earlier, but believed her when she told them that he had died. It is a life-changing moment of exchange that turns the story upside down:

> The man with the yellow forehead stood there waist deep in the water, his chest against the pontoon, and the look on his face was the same look that had been on her own face a moment before when she first saw Anders, a cross of joy and disbelief, a look that was willing to accept that which was not possible . . . [Easter] stretched out his hands to her and Marina closed her eyes. She left him there. She let him go. (341–2)

In a transaction that operates beyond the world of corporatized trade, one abductee moves into the position of another, both apparently rising from the dead—depending on which side of the river we stand. The story seems to do a 180-degree turnaround in a moment of disorientation that recalls Rushdie's disruptive universes. Easter is another version of the lost Eurydice, not only from Marina's perspective, but also from that of his parents, who believed their child was dead and now have him back. In their story, which we must create for ourselves, that child was snatched into the land of the dead.

Easter (whose name prefigured his death and resurrection from the grips of the anaconda and corresponding release from Annick Swenson) is the interpretive nexus of this catabatic tale. He is the immigrant/refugee/slave par excellence, a subaltern male Persephone/Eurydice hybrid, whose reunion with his tribe and family functions as a point of rupture in the persistent allusions to Marina's heroic quest. The readers' recognition of the Orphic prototypes of Marina's story are thus confounded when we must reconcile the text's invitations to recall that prototype with the suggestion of a different vision of Hell suggested by the structural and thematic similarities with *Heart of Darkness*. On one level we can say that the story has followed the operatic version of Orpheus' descent with its happy ending, and that the Eurydice figure is returned to life, or what passes for life in this world of pharmaceutical engineering and corporate hierarchies. But the darker stories of imperialism and colonialist horror invite us to question just exactly where Hell is in this tale. Marina was right when she decided (in reference to Easter's original home) that there was "a circle of hell beneath this one," although she was not aware which direction "beneath" lay. Easter's catabasis and anabasis skew the story of Marina and Anders by intimating that their return to North America is actually a descent. Easter has existed in the liminal space of the American research colony where he has learned table manners, how to read, and other cultural mannerisms, but despite his partial assimilation into North American society (and Anders' desire to send him to America), he returns to his place of birth. But is this his home? His narrative complicates and troubles the Orphic paradigm, and raises questions about the fragile configuration of home in this novel.

The Catabatic Diaspora

Six characters in search of a home make their ways through these novels. Their identities imprinted by migration, or its aftershocks, Milkman, Lillian, Rai, Ormus, Vina, and Marina find or return to a home in

America, many of them yearning for a lost or imaginary place of origin, for loved ones left behind, or both; another, Easter, returns to a different, perhaps forgotten, home. They are all, at some point in their lives, "unhomed," using Bhabha's coinage, which is to say they are in a position of having to renegotiate their place in the world, "when the border between home and world becomes confused."[71] Their chronicles encompass traumatic, disorienting, melancholy, and dangerous encounters that construe the notion of home within a mythic dimension. Nostalgia—a word of Greek origin that combines "homecoming" with "ache"—suffuses these novels in which the desire to return to or find a home is coincident with a descent to the land of the dead. It is a most ancient conflation that first occurs in the *Odyssey* when the hero, dispatched to "learn of my *nostos*," speaks with the shades at the mouth of Hades,and again when Aeneas, fleeing his ravaged city, traverses the now fully delineated landscape of Dis to hear of the new homeland that he will reach. The overlap between *nostos* and catabasis is so firmly established that other descent stories, those of Orpheus and Demeter, have the potential to infuse diasporic narratives with a sense of memory and desire; the yearned for lost wife or daughter becomes the embodiment of nostalgia, as *Away*, *The Ground Beneath Her Feet*, and *State of Wonder* make evident. At the same time, mythic paradigms shift, mutate, and bifurcate within these stories. A commonality shared by the four novels is how they skew the catabatic story structure with confrontations between multiplicities of literary ghosts. Their convergences impose new meanings in a form of hybridization that recapitulates a transnational world culture.

Three novelists, Morrison, Bloom, and Rushdie, are members of the displaced populations about which they write, but Ann Patchett makes no such obvious claim. That *State of Wonder* is able to channel the mythological turn of diasporic fiction testifies to the broad applicability of the descent motif in this context. With its themes of nostalgia, transformation, and regeneration, the catabatic myth lends itself to narratives of diaspora, but it is a flexible, polyvalent, and at times ambiguous device that will often decenter and destabilize the text in which it is embedded. The frequent blending of different myths, and the

[71] Bhabha 1994: 141.

upending of classical source texts in these novels of displacement, exile, and deracination provide powerful ways of expressing the experience of transplanted peoples whose lives have been turned upside down, and yet who must keep their heads above ground. In their introduction to a collection of essays by authors of immigrant fiction, Anne Luyat and Francine Tolron write about "a flight from certainty and timeless truths erasing centuries-old landmarks of national and linguistic consciousness, transforming irrevocably both cultural and literary landscapes." In their diverse adaptations of the ancient myths of the underworld, these four authors give a sense of what it is like to be in "flight from certainty."

Epilogue

The viewer of Anish Kapoor's "Descent into Limbo" (1992) enters a cubical structure (6 × 6 × 6 m.) with a black hole in the middle. Using a deep blue pigment, the artist has created what appears to be a bottomless abyss. Believing it to be a flat surface, a visitor in the summer of 2018 fell into the two-and-half-meter chasm, suffering minor injuries.[1] It is unlikely that the hapless catabant learned much more than to heed warning signs posted in museums when he was in the bottom of the pit (no wise mentor awaited him), but perhaps his accident was the necessary fulfillment of the piece's imminent meanings. Kapoor's installation—simultaneously an apparently infinite chasm and a one-dimensional flat surface (although it is neither)—gives physicality to the dynamics that encompass descent narratives discussed in the preceding chapters, all of which operate through contrapuntal systems of surface texts and deeper traditions. Arguably the man who fell into Kapoor's void embodies the combination of curiosity and disbelief that exerts its force on those lovers of wisdom drawn to the underworld. But it is a certainty that his intervention in a static piece of art created a narrative.

Descents are movements through space and time, in other words they have the basic elements of a story. The catabatic narrative beckons to us with promises of concealed significances that will make the mundane world more meaningful. It gives shape to the formless. In her discussion of Oliver Sacks' memoir *Awakenings* (1973) about patients emerging from a deep coma, Wendy Lesser observes: "like other voyagers to the underground—like Odysseus and Dante, for instance—they bring back

[1] The incident occurred on August 13, 2018, during a retrospective of Kapoor's work at Fundação de Serralves, Museum of Contemporary Art in Porto, Portugal. Source: https://news.artnet.com/art-world/man-injured-falling-into-anish-kapoor-hole-1335176. Accessed September 2, 2018.

this experience in the form of literature." Her point here is that their descent into deep unconsciousness, which she fits into the readily available template of the catabasis, gains meaning through narrative. The preceding pages have outlined this impulse in an array of genres and media testifying to the broad applicability of the underworld tale, but it is striking how they often have something to tell us about the connection between Hades and the manufacture of culture. This alliance, I believe, is more pronounced than ever in contemporary culture, and my selection of nine analyses is by no means exhaustive.

Take, for instance, Andrew Sean Greer's Pulitzer Prize winning novel *Less* (2017), a picaresque comedy whose protagonist travels around the world, losing his luggage along the way. Art Less, author of *Kalipso*, a novel about a gay Odysseus, has a Skype session with his former lover, a distinguished poet now hospitalized and surrounded by medical personnel: "A procession of shades, as with Odysseus, and here before him: Tiresias. The seer" (241). It is to be expected that this Odysseus figure, an author, would have a *Nekyia* in which he encounters Tiresias. And since this metafictional tale, with its *mise-en-abyme*, *Kalipso*, inscribes the act of writing as a comment on mimesis, it is appropriate that the shade of the prophet appears as a simulacrum by means of technology. The digital transmission of texts and images available to contemporary consumers makes the consanguinity between ghosts and cultural production ever more apparent.

The tale will keep being told in endless variations and by unforeseeable means. The heroic catabasis, a veritable Möbius strip, an autochtonous knot, is a narrative with no beginning or end. It thus lends itself to postmodern interrogations of authenticity, history, and authorial proprietorship. If there is no Ur-text, only different permutations that are endlessly variable, who can claim that any version is the most authoritative? Adding to this indeterminacy are the multiple retellings of the story that suggest a polyphonous text. Most of the narratives discussed in the previous chapters reveal a layered recursivity that contributes to this effect. Barth sets Joyce over Homer; Gaiman juxtaposes Milton and Vergil; Byatt entwines Tennyson's *Ad Memoriam* with the Odyssean *Nekyia*; Patchett offers Gluck's Orphic tale in a novel that intimates other darker intertexts including those of Conrad and Vergil. Rushdie's cultural syncretism imagines links between South Asian antiquity and Greek myth that produce rock musicians. These various forms of eclecticism are not only diachronic but also include strategic synchronic blends of ancient versions of the tale—those of Odysseus and Persephone blend in *Coraline* and *Away*, for example.

While these submerged texts insinuate that the underworld is populated by ghosts of itself, Hades is often simultaneously a place occupied by doubles or replicas of the terrestrial realm, further dissolving the notion of authenticity. The poet Louise Glück conveys this concept well in *Averno* (2007), her cycle of poems about Persephone. In "A Myth of Devotion" the god Hades creates a duplicate of earth and everything familiar to his intended bride to help her adjust to life among the dead. When Gaiman's Lucifer describes Hell as the "dark reflection" of Heaven he poeticizes a concept intrinsic to all the underworlds that we make for ourselves. The kingdom of Hades contains and propagates doppelgängers of the mortal world, which is what fiction does as well. Although his situation is exceptional, the fact that Heracles can exist in two places after his death—one version of him in the underworld, the other on Olympus—exemplifies the pervasive idea that Hades is a world of shadowy duplicates. So too, the twins Castor and Pollux, who exchange life above and below ground on a daily basis, convey the duality implicit in the cultural constructions of Hades since antiquity. The idea persists in several of the works we have just surveyed. Coraline finds a replica of her own home with simulacra of her parents in the Other World. Ferrante's Elena Greco engages with her alter ego, Lila, and their symbolic selves, the dolls Tina and Nu, in the Hadean landscapes of Naples. Rushdie creates a ghostly twin for his Orphic hero, Ormus Cama, but also expands and complicates the notion of a twin universe with colliding parallel worlds.

Frequently these ghostly others are aligned with dreams, a homology that goes back to the earliest texts, and is another form of mimesis. In the Assyrian story of Prince Kummay, the tour of Hades and its prophecies occur in a dream, and Homeric ghosts speak to the living through the medium of dreams. Indeed as Homer has it, Sleep is the twin brother of Death (*Il.* 16, 672); dreams will be found at the entrance to the underworld (*Od.* 24.12); and Aeneas leaves through the gate of "false dreams."[2] The association is a natural one and carries over, for example, into the

[2] Albinus (2000: 23–96) provides a thorough discussion of the association of dreams and Hades.

dreams of Patchett's Marina Singh whose father reaches her in her sleep. Bloom shapes Lillian's nightmares as a form of Hell, and Rushdie lets Ormus encounter his twin in dreams. Gaiman makes especially good use of the association: not only does Coraline dream her Other World, but his most famous creation, Morpheus, a frequent visitor to Hell, shapes dreams into stories. All of these alignments between dreams and the afterlife provide a rich tradition from which to launch a postmodern challenge to the notion of reality and history.[3] Like death, dreams suspend time, and the narratives of descent often stop or distort time, although this is only another illusion. Odysseus and Aeneas find themselves at the junction of past and future where the dead exist as static versions of their former selves; they encounter the past, but also learn of the future. Ambrose Mensch connects with a Homeric bard but moves into the future with a new form of fiction. The dark subterranean spaces of Naples come to represent the past from which Lena Greco ascends. Milkman Dead's broken watch signifies his submersion into a different temporal modality, a more circular matrifocal time. Gaiman's Orpheus story distorts linear history, folding the present back onto the past, but also playing with the notion of historical continuity. The disturbance or interruption of the regular flow of history's rhythm allows the possibility of an alternate world, and also of parallel narratives.

Especially provocative is the notion of the unwritten or unseen text conjured within the hidden spaces of the ghostly realm, a suggestion that there is always something outside the frame that the reader cannot access—the unwritten books of famous authors in the vast library of Morpheus, Lila's mysterious journals which seem to threaten Lena's authorial prestige, Lilias Papagay's unfinished novels, the unwritten Demetrian tale of Pilate Dead in Morrison's transcoded *Odyssey*, or the alternative fictions produced in Rushdie's parallel universe. These incorporeal texts conform to the consistent association of the underworld with cultural production and imply an infinite, timeless archive of tales waiting to be brought to life.

[3] According to the dystopic views of the theorists such as Frederic Jameson (e.g. *Postmodernism, or, the Cultural Logic of Late Capitalism*, 1991), the postmodern condition produces a simulated condition of reality that leads to a flattening out of reality.

Bibliography

Albinus, L. (2000) *The House of Hades: Studies in Ancient Greek Eschatology*. Aarhus.

Alfer, A. and A.J. Edwards de Campos (2010) *A.S. Byatt: Critical Storytelling*. Manchester.

Almond, P.C. (2016) *Afterlife: A History of Life after Death*. London and New York.

Al-Tabaa, N. (2012) "Hell can be good for you," in *Neil Gaiman and Philosophy: Gods Gone Wild*, eds. T. L. Bealer, R. Luria, W. Yuen. Chicago and La Salle: 127–44.

Ambert, A. (2001) "The eighth continent or living on the edge," in *Flight from Certainty: The Dilemma of Identity and Exile*, ed. A. Layat and F. Tolron. Amsterdam and New York: 9–16.

Amditis, E.K. (2009) "The Maya Spider in Russian Symbolism," *The Slavic and East European Journal* 53: 219–39.

Amory, A. (1963) "The reunion of Odysseus and Penelope," in *Essays on the Odyssey: Selected Modern Criticism*, ed. C. H. Taylor, Jr. Bloomington: 100–21.

Anderson, W. S. (1982) "The Orpheus of Virgil and Ovid: *flebile nescio quid*," in *Orpheus: The Metamorphosis of a Myth*, ed. J. Warden. Toronto: 25–50.

Antin, M. (1912) *The Promised Land, by Mary Antin; with illustrations from photographs*. Boston and Cambridge, MA.

Armstrong, N. (2006) "What feminism did to Novel Studies," in *The Cambridge Companion to Feminist Literary Theory*, ed. E. Rooney. Cambridge: 99–118.

Atwood, M. (2005) *The Penelopiad: The Myth of Penelope and Odysseus*. Toronto.

Austin, N. (1975) *Archery at the Dark of the Moon: Poetic Problems in Homer's* Odyssey. Berkeley.

Awkward, M. (1990) "'Unruly and let loose': myth, ideology and gender in *Song of Solomon*," *Callaloo* 13: 482–98.

Barrett, A. (1970) "The topography of the gnat's descent," *Classical Journal* 55: 255–7.

Barthes, R. (1977) *Image—Music—Text: Essays selected and translated by Stephen Heath*. London.

Barth, J. (1967) "The literature of exhaustion," *The Atlantic Monthly* 220: 29–34.

Barth, J. (1968) *Lost in the Funhouse*. New York.

Barth, J. (1980) "The literature of replenishment," *The Atlantic Monthly* 243: 65–71.

Baudrillard, J. (1994) *Simulacra and Simulation*. (trans. S.F. Glasser) Ann Arbor.

Bernabé, A. (2015) "What Is a *katábasis*? The descent into the netherworld in Greece and the Ancient Near East," *Les Études Classiques* 83: 15–34.

Betz, H.D. (1980) "Fragments from a catabasis ritual in a Greek Magical Papyrus," *History of Religions* 19: 287–95.

Bhabha, H. (1994) *The Location of Culture*. London and New York.

Bharucha, N. (2001) "Real and imagined worlds: Salman Rushdie as a writer of the Indian diaspora," in *Flight from Certainty: The Dilemma of Identity and Exile*, eds. A. Layat and F. Tolron. Amsterdam and New York: 51–62.

Bjork, P. (2009) "Song of Solomon: reality and mythos within the community," in *Toni Morrison's Song of Solomon*, ed. H. Bloom. Chicago: 35–56.

Blackford, H.V. (2012) *The Myth of Persephone in Girls' Fantasy Literature*. New York.

Bloom, A. (2007) *Away*. New York.

Bloom, H. (1973) *The Anxiety of Influence*. Oxford and New York.

Bloom, H. (1975) *A Map of Misreading*. Oxford and New York.

Bodewitz, H. (2002) "The dark and deep Underworld in the Veda," *Journal of the American Oriental Society* 122: 213–23.

Boelhower, W.Q. (1982) "The brave new world of immigrant autobiography," *MELUS* 9: 5–23.

Borsellino, M. (2007) "Blue and pink: gender in Neil Gaiman's work," in *The Neil Gaiman Reader*, ed. D. Schweitzer. Rockville, MA: 51–3.

Bouras, G. (2001) "Memories of living in between," in *Flight from Certainty: The Dilemma of Identity and Exile*, eds. A. Layat and F. Tolron. Amsterdam and New York: 17–25.

Bouson, J.B. (2009) "Quiet as it's kept: shame, trauma, and race in the novels of Toni Morrison," in *Toni Morrison's Song of Solomon: Bloom's Modern Critical Interpretations*, ed. H. Bloom. New York: 57–86.

Bowden, H. (2010) *Mystery Cults of the Ancient World*. Princeton.

Bowra, C.M. (1952) "Orpheus and Eurydice," *Classical Quarterly* 2: 113–26.

Brahen, M. (2007) "The thin line between," in *The Neil Gaiman Reader*, ed. D. Schweitzer. Rockville, MA: 140–8.

Braund, S. (1997) "Virgil and the cosmos: religious and philosophical ideas," in *The Cambridge Companion to Virgil*, ed. C. Martindale. Cambridge: 204–21.

Bremmer, J. (2014) *Initiation into the Mysteries of the Ancient World*. Berlin.

Brenner, G. (1987) "*Song of Solomon*: Morrison's rejection of Rank's monomyth and feminism," *The New England Quarterly* 15: 13–24.

Brown, C.G. (1991) "Empousa, Dionysus and the Mysteries: Aristophanes, *Frogs* 285ff.," *Classical Quarterly* 41: 41–50.

Bryant, C.G. (1999) "'Every goodbye ain't gone': the semiotics of death, mourning, and closural practice in Toni Morrison's *Song of Solomon*," *MELUS* 24: 97–110.

Bucknell, B. (2006) "Faith in the faithless: an Inter(re)view with Linda Hutcheon," *English Studies in Canada* 32: 157–71.

Bullaro, G.R. (2016) "The era of the 'economic miracle' and the force of context in Elena Ferrante's *My Brilliant Friend*," in *The Works of Elena Ferrante: Reconfiguring the Margins*, eds. G.R. Bullaro and S.V. Love. New York: 15–44.

Buller, J.L. (1995) "Looking backwards: Baroque Opera and the ending of the Orpheus myth," *International Journal of the Classical Tradition* 1: 57–79.

Burgess, J. (1999) "Odysseus and Gilgamesh in the Otherworld," *Classical Views/ Échos du monde classique* 18: 171–210.

Burgess, J. (2016) "Localization of the *Odyssey's* Underworld," *Les Études Classiques* 83: 15–37.

Burkam, A.L. (2002) Rev. of *Coraline*. *Horn Book* 78: 755–7.

Burkert, W. (1985) *Greek Religion*. Cambridge, MA.

Burkert, W. (1987) *Ancient Mystery Cults*. Cambridge, MA.

Burrow, C. (1997) "Virgils, from Dante to Milton," in *The Cambridge Companion to Virgil*, ed. C. Martindale. Cambridge: 79–90.

Butler, S. (2009) "The backward glance," *Arion* 17: 59–78.

Byatt, A.S. (1990) *Possession: A Romance*. New York.

Byatt, A.S. (1992) *Angels and Insects*. New York.

Byatt, A.S. (2001) "True stories and the facts in fiction," in *Essays on the Fiction of A.S. Byatt*, eds. A. Alfer and M.J. Noble. Westport, CT: 173–200.

Calvo-Martinez, J.L. (2000) "The *Katábasis* of the hero," in *Héros et héroïnes dans les mythes et les cultes grecs*, eds. V. Pirenne-Delforge and E. Suárez de la Torre. Liège: 67–78.

Campbell, J. (2004) *A.S. Byatt and the Heliotropic Imagination*. Waterloo, ON.

Carrier, D. (2000) *The Aesthetics of Comics*. Philadelphia.

Castaldo, A. (2004) "'No more yielding than a dream': the construction of Shakespeare in *The Sandman*," *College Literature* 31 (Shakespeare and Popular Culture): 94–110.

Cavanagh, J. (2016) "Indexicalities of language in Ferrante's Neapolitan novels: dialect and Italian as markers of social value and difference," in *The Works of Elena Ferrante: Reconfiguring the Margins*, eds. G.R. Bullaro and S.V. Love. New York: 45–70.

Chambers, I. (1994) *Migrancy, Culture, Identity*. London and New York.

Clark, R.J. (1978) *Catabasis: Vergil and the Wisdom Tradition*. Amsterdam.

Clark, R.J. (2009) "The Eleusinian Mysteries and Vergil's 'Appearance-of-a-Terrifying-Female-Apparition-in-the-Underworld' motif in *Aeneid* 6," in *The Cults of Magna Graecia*, eds. P.A. Johnston and G. Casadio. Austin: 190–203.

Clay, J.S. (2003) *Hesiod's Cosmos*. Cambridge.

Clauss, J.J. (1999) "Descent into Hell: mythic paradigms in *The Searchers*," *Journal of Popular Film and Television* 27: 2–17.

Coats, K. (2008) "Between horror, humour, and hope: Neil Gaiman and the psychic work of the Gothic," in *The Gothic in Children's Literature: Haunting the Borders*, ed. A Jackson, K. Coats, and R. McGillis. New York: 77–92.

Cole, S.G. (2007) "Finding Dionysus," in *A Companion to Greek Religion*, ed. D. Ogden. Malden, MA and Oxford: 327–41.

Conrad, J. (2012) *Heart of Darkness*. Introduction by A. Hochschild. New York.

Cooke, M. (1974) "The descent into the underworld and modern Black fiction," *The Iowa Review* 5: 72–90.

Cox, F. (2011) *Sibylline Sisters: Virgil's Presence in Contemporary Women's Writing*. Oxford.

Dascălu, C. (2007) *Imaginary Homelands of Writers in Exile: Salman Rushdie, Bharati Mukherjee and V.S. Naipaul*. Youngstown, NY.

de Jong, I. (2001) *A Narratological Commentary on the Odyssey*. Cambridge.

de Rogatis, T. (2016) "Metamorphosis and rebirth: Greek mythology and initiation rites in Elena Ferrante's *Troubling Love*," in *The Works of Elena Ferrante: Reconfiguring the Margins*, ed. G.R. Bullaro and S.V. Love. New York: 185–206.

Dick, B.F. (1975) "*The Waste Land* and the *Descensus ad infernos*." *Canadian Review of Comparative Literature* 2: 35–48.

Doherty, L. (1995) *Siren Songs: Gender, Audiences, and Narrators in the Odyssey*. Ann Arbor.

Dolansky, F. (2012) "Playing with gender: girls, dolls, and adult ideals in the Roman world," *Classical Antiquity* 31: 256–92.

Dova, S. (2012) *Greek Heroes in and out of Hades*. Lanham, MA.

Dover, K. (1994) *Aristophanes Frogs*. Oxford.

Duffy, C. (1999) *The World's Wife*. London and New York.

Edmonds, III, R.G. (2004) *Myths of the Underworld Journey. Plato, Aristophanes, and the "Orphic" Gold Tablets*. Cambridge.

Edmonds, III, R.G. (2011a) "Festivals in the afterlife: a new reading of the Petelia Tablet (OF 476.11)," in *Tracing Orpheus: Studies of Orphic Fragments*, eds. M. Herrero de Jáuregui, A.I. Jiménez San Cristóbal, E.R. Luján Martínez, R. Martín Hernández, M.A. Santamaría Álvarez, and S. Torallas Tovar. Berlin and Boston: 185–8.

Edmonds, III, R.G. (2011b) "Who are you? A brief history of the scholarship," in *The Orphic Gold Tablets and Greek Religion*, ed. R.G. Edmonds III. Cambridge: 3–14.

Edwards, B. (1985) "Deconstructing the artist and the art: Barth and Calvino at play in the funhouse of language," *Canadian Review of Comparative Literature* 12: 264–86.

Elderkin, K.M. (1930) "Jointed dolls in antiquity," *American Journal of Archaeology* 34: 455–79.

Eliade, M. and W. Trask (1972) "Zalmoxis," *History of Religions* 11: 257–302.

Ellison, R. (1952) *Invisible Man*. New York.

Falconer, R. (2005) *Hell in Contemporary Literature: Western Descent Narratives since 1945*. Edinburgh.

Farrell, J. (1991) *Vergil's Georgics and the Traditions of Ancient Epic: The Art of Allusion in Literary History*. New York and Oxford.

Farrell, J. (1997) "The Virgilian intertext," in *The Cambridge Companion to Virgil*, ed. C. Martindale. Cambridge: 222–38.

Feder, L. (1955) "Marlow's descent into Hell," *Nineteenth Century Fiction* 9: 280–92.

Feder, L. (1971) *Ancient Myth in Modern Poetry*. Princeton.

Felton, D. (2007) "The Dead," in *A Companion to Greek Religion*, ed. D. Ogden. Malden, MA and Oxford: 86–99.

Ferrante, E. (2008) *The Lost Daughter*. (trans. A. Goldstein) New York.

Ferrante, E. (2012) *My Brilliant Friend*. (trans. A. Goldstein) New York.

Ferrante, E. (2013) *The Story of a New Name*. (trans. A. Goldstein) New York.

Ferrante, E. (2014) *Those Who Leave and Those Who Stay*. (trans. A. Goldstein) New York.

Ferrante, E. (2015) *The Story of the Lost Child*. (trans. A. Goldstein) New York.

Ferrante, E. (2016a) *Frantumaglia: A Writer's Journey*. (trans. A. Goldstein) New York.

Ferrante, E. (2016b) *The Beach at Night*. (trans. A. Goldstein, ill. M. Cerri) New York.

Finkelpearl, E. (1990) "Psyche, Aeneas, and an ass, Apuleius *Metamorphoses* 6.10–6.21," *Transactions of the American Philological Association* 120: 333–47.

Fletcher, J. (1999) "*The Odyssey* rewoven: A.S. Byatt's *Angels and Insects*," *Classical and Modern Literature: A Quarterly* 19: 217–31.

Fletcher, J. (2002) "Lost in the underworld: John Barth reads the *Odyssey*," *Classical and Modern Literature: A Quarterly* 23: 65–76.

Fletcher, J. (2006) "Signifying Circe in Toni Morrison's *Song of Solomon*," *Classical World* 99: 405–18.

Fletcher, J. (2014) "The catabasis of Mattie Ross in the Coens' *True Grit*," *Classical World* 107: 237–54.

Foley, H. (ed.) (1993) *The Homeric Hymn to Demeter: Translation, Commentary and Interpretive Essays*. Princeton.

Franken, C. (2001) *A.S. Byatt: Art, Authorship, Creativity*. New York.

Freud, S. (1919) "Das Unheimliche," *Imago*, Bd. V: 297–324.

Frever, T.S. (2009) "'Oh! You beautiful doll!': Icon, image, and culture in works by Alvarez, Cisneros, and Morrison," *Tulsa Studies in Women's Literature* 28: 121–39.

Frye, N. (1976) *The Secular Scripture: A Study of the Structure of Romance*. Cambridge, MA.

Gaiman, N. (1988) *Preludes & Nocturnes*, Vol. 1. *The Sandman*. New York.

Gaiman, N. (1992) *Season of Mists*, Vol. 4. *The Sandman*. New York.

Gaiman, N. (1993) *Fables & Reflections*, Vol. 6. *The Sandman*. New York.

Gaiman, N. (1999) "Reflections on myth," *Columbia: A Journal of Literature and Art* 31: 75–84.

Gaiman, N. (2001) *American Gods: A Novel*, Ossining, NY.

Gaiman, N. (2012) *Coraline*. New York and London.

Gallippi, F. (2016) "Elena Ferrante's *My Brilliant Friend*: in search of Parthenope and the 'founding' of a new city," in *The Works of Elena Ferrante: Reconfiguring the Margins*, eds. G.R. Bullaro and S.V. Love. New York: 101–27.

Gazis, G.A. (2018) *Homer and the Poetics of Hades*. Oxford.

Genette, G. (1997) *Palimpsests: Literature in the Second Degree*. (trans. C. Newman, C. Doubinsky, and G. Prince) Lincoln, NE.

Gooding, R. (2008) "'Something Very Old and Very Slow': Coraline, uncanniness, and narrative form," *Children's Literature Association Quarterly* 33: 390–407.

Graf, F. (1987) "Orpheus: a poet among men," in *Interpretations of Greek Mythology*, ed. J. Bremmer. London: 80–106.

Graf, F. and S. Iles Johnston (2007) *Ritual Texts for the Afterlife: Orpheus and the Bacchic Gold Tablets*. London and New York.

Graziosi, B. (2002) *Inventing Homer: The Early Reception of Epic*. Cambridge.

Graziosi, B. and J. Haubold (2013) *Homer: The Resonance of Epic*. London.

Greenwood, E. (2009) "Shades of Rome in the poetry of Derek Walcott," in *Living Classics: Greece and Rome in Contemporary Poetry in English*, ed. S.J. Harrison. Oxford: 255–74.

Grinsell, L. (1957) "The ferryman and his fee: a study in ethnology, archaeology, and tradition," *Folklore* 68: 257–69.

Guthrie, W.K.C. (1935) *Orpheus and Greek Religion: A Study in the Orphic Movement*. London.

Hall, S. (1990) "Cultural identity and diaspora," in *Identity: Community, Culture, Difference*, ed. J. Rutherford. London: 222–37.

Hardie, P. (2010) "Spenser's Vergil: *The Faerie Queene* and the *Aeneid*," in *A Companion to Vergil's Aeneid and its Tradition*, eds. J. Farrell and M. Putnam. Malden and Oxford: 173–85.

Harris, A.L. (1980) "Myth as structure in Toni Morrison's *Song of Solomon*," *MELUS* 7: 69–76.

Harris, T. (2009) "*Song of Solomon*," in *Toni Morrison's Song of Solomon*, ed. H. Bloom. Chicago: 5–34.

Harrison, E.L. (1978) "Metempsychosis in *Aeneid* Six," *Classical Journal* 73: 193–7.

Hassan, I. (1971) *The Dismemberment of Orpheus: Toward a Postmodern Literature*. Oxford.

Heath, J. (1996) "The stupor of Orpheus: Ovid's *Metamorphoses* 10-64-71," *Classical Journal* 91: 353–70.

Heubeck, A. and A. Hoekstra (1989) *A Commentary on Homer's Odyssey: VII, Books IX–XVII*. Oxford.

Herrero de Jáuregui, M. (2011) "Priam's catabasis: traces of the epic journey to Hades in *Iliad* 24," *Transactions of the American Philological Association* 141: 137–68.

Herrero de Jáuregui, M. (2015) "Traditions of catabatic experience in *Aeneid* 6," *Les Études Classiques* 83: 329–49.

Hindon, M. (1973) "*Lost in the Funhouse*: Barth's use of the recent past," *Twentieth Century Literature*, 19: 107–18.

Holtsmark, E.B. (2001) "The *Katabasis* theme in modern cinema," in *Classical Myth and Culture in the Cinema*, ed. M. Winkler. Oxford: 23–50.

Hooks, B. (2002) "Postmodern Blackness," in *Postmodernism and the Contemporary Novel: A Reader*, ed. B. Nicol. Edinburgh: 421–8.

Horsfall, N. (2013) *Virgil, Aeneid 6. A Commentary*. 2 vols. Berlin.

Hurst, I. (2006) *Victorian Women Writers and the Classics: The Feminine of Homer*. Oxford.

Hurst, I. (2012) "'Love and blackmail': Demeter and Persephone," *Classical Receptions Journal*, 4: 176–89.

Hutcheon, L. (1984) *Narcissistic Narrative: The Metafictional Paradox*. London and New York.

Hutcheon, L. (1988) *A Poetics of Postmodernism: History, Theory, Fiction*. London and New York.

Hutcheon, L. (1989) *The Politics of Postmodernism*. London and New York.

Hutcheon, L. (2012) *A Theory of Adaptation*. London and New York.

Jahlmar, J. (2015) "'Give the devil his due': freedom, damnation, and Milton's *Paradise Lost* in Neil Gaiman's *The Sandman: Season of Mists*," *Partial Answers: Journal of Literature and the History of Ideas* 13: 267–86.

Jacoff, R. (2010) "Vergil in Dante," in *A Companion to Vergil's Aeneid and its Tradition*, ed. J. Farrell, M. and C.J. Putnam. Hoboken, NJ: 147–56.

Jameson, F. (1991) *Postmodernism, or, The Cultural Logic of Late Capitalism*. Durham, NC.

Jennings, L.V.D. (2008) *Toni Morrison and the Idea of Africa*. Cambridge.

Johnson, D. (1999) "Hesiod's descriptions of Tartarus (*Theogony* 721–819)," *Phoenix* 53: 8–28.

Johnson, W.R. (1976) *Darkness Visible: a Study of Vergil's Aeneid*. Chicago.

Johnston, S.I. (1995) "Defining the dreadful: remarks on the Greek child-killing demon," in *Ancient Magic and Ritual Power*, eds. M. Meyer, M. and P. Mirecki. Leiden: 361–87.

Johnston, S.I. (2017) "Many (un)happy returns: ancient Greek concepts of a return from death and their later counterparts," in *Coming Back to Life: The Permeability of Past and Present, Mortality and Immortality, Death and Life in the Ancient Mediterranean*, eds. F.S. Tappenden and C. Daniel-Hughes, with assistance of B.N. Rice. Montreal: 17–36.

Kardulias, D. (2001) "Odysseus in Ino's veil: feminine headdress and the hero in *Odyssey* 5," *Transactions of the American Philological Association* 131: 23–51.

Kennedy, S. (2018) *T.S Eliot and the Dynamic Imagination*. Cambridge.

Kenner, H. (1973) *The Pound Era*. Berkeley and Los Angeles.

Klimenkova, T. (1992) "Feminism and Postmodernism," *Philosophy East and West* 42: 277–85.

Konstan, D. and Nieto, P. (2011) "Orpheus reunited with Eurydice (on OF 1076–1077)" in *Tracing Orpheus: Studies of Orphic Fragments*, eds. M. Herrero de Jáuregui, A.I. Jiménez San Cristóbal, E.R. Luján Martínez, R. Martín Hernández, M.A. Santamaría Álvarez, and S. Torallas Tovar. Berlin and Boston: 345–50.

Kristeva, J. (1993) "Women's time," in *Feminisms: An Anthology of Literary Theory and Criticism*, eds. R.R. Warhol and D. Price Herndl. New Brunswick, NJ: 860–79.

Lackey, M. (2008) "A.S. Byatt's 'Morpho Eugenia': Prolegomena to any future theory," *College Literature* 35: 128–47.

Lada-Richards, I. (1999) *Initiating Dionysus: Ritual and Theatre in Aristophanes' Frogs*. Oxford.

Laneri, N. (2002) "The discovery of a funerary ritual: Inanna/Ishtar and her descent to the nether world in Titriş Höyük, Turkey," *East and West* 52: 9–51.

Langdell, C.C. (2004) *Adrienne Rich: The Moment of Change*. Westport, CT.

Lease, E.B. (1926) "A journey from this world to the next," *Classical Journal* 21: 599–606.

Lee, A. (2016) "Feminine identity and female friendships in the 'Neapolitan' novels of Elena Ferrante," *British Journal of Psychotherapy* 32: 491–501.

Lesser, W. (1987) *The Life Below the Ground: A Study of the Subterranean in Literature and History*. Boston and London.

Lincoln, B. (1980) "The ferryman of the dead," *Journal of Indo-European Studies* 8: 41–59.

Linguanti E. (2006) "Rushdie's *The Ground Beneath Her Feet*: different whatnesses," in *Salman Rushdie: Critical Essays* (v.2). eds. M. Ray and R. Kundu. New Delhi: 107–23.

Louden, B. (2011) *Homer's Odyssey and the Near East*. Cambridge.

Love, S. (2016) "'An educated identity': the school as a modernist chronotope in Ferrante's Neapolitan Novels," in *The Works of Elena Ferrante: Reconfiguring the Margins*, eds. G.R. Bullaro and S.V. Love. New York: 71–98.

Luck, G. (1959) *Latin Love Elegy*. London.

Lucy, N. (1997) *Postmodern Literary Theory: An Introduction*. London.

MacDonald, R.R. (1987) *The Burial-Places of Memory: Epic Underworlds in Vergil, Dante, and Milton*. Amherst, MA.

MacLachlan, B. (2004) "Women and nymphs at the Grotto Caruso," in *Mystic Cults in Magna Graecia*, eds. G. Casadio and P.A. Johnston. Austin: 204–16.

Marinatos, N. (1995) "Circe and liminality: ritual background and narrative structure," in *Homer's World: Fiction, Tradition and Reality*, eds. M. Dickie and O. Anderson. Bergen: 133–40.

Marshall, C.W. (2011) "The Furies, Wonder Woman, and Dream: Mythmaking in DC. Comics," in *Classics and Comics*, ed. C.W. Marshall and G. Kovacs. Oxford: 89–101.

Martindale, C. (1985) "Paradise metamorphosed: Ovid in Milton," *Comparative Literature* 37: 301–33.

McCaffery, L. (1991) "Introduction: the desert of the real," *Storming the Reality Studio: A Casebook of Cyberpunk and Postmodern Science Fiction*, ed. L. McCaffery. Durham and London: 1–16.

McClintock, A. (1984) "'Unspeakable secrets': The ideology of landscape in Conrad's *Heart of Darkness*," *Journal of the Midwest Modern Language Association* 17: 38–53.

McCloud, S. (1993) *Understanding Comics: The Invisible Art*. Northhampton, MA.

McConnell, J. (2013) *Black Odysseys: The Homeric Odyssey in the African Diaspora since 1939*. Oxford.

McHale, B. (1987) *Postmodernist Fiction*. London and New York.

McHale, B. (1992) *Constructing Postmodernism*. London and New York.

Merker, G. (2000) *The Sanctuary of Demeter and Persephone at Corinth*, v. 18, pt 4 (American School of Classical Studies) Athens.

Mobley, M.S. (1991) *Folk Roots and Mythic Wings in Sarah Orne Jewett and Toni Morrison*. Baton Rouge.

Mondal, A. (2007) "*The Ground Beneath Her Feet* and *Fury* and the re-invention of location," in *The Cambridge Companion to Salman Rushdie*, ed. A. Gurnah. Cambridge: 169–83.

Morris, M. (2002) "Feminism, Reading, Postmodernism," in *Postmodernism and the Contemporary Novel*, ed. B. Nicol. Oxford: 390–5.

Morrison, T. (1977) *Song of Solomon*. New York.

Murnaghan, S. (1987) *Disguise and Recognition in the Odyssey*. Princeton.

Murnaghan, S. (2011) "Classics for cool kids: popular and unpopular versions of antiquity for children," *Classical World* 104: 339–53.

Nesselrath, H.G. (2017) "Skeletons, shades and feasting heroes: the manifold underworlds of Lucian of Samosata," in *Reading the Way to the Netherworld: Education and the Representations of the Beyond in Later Antiquity*, eds. I. Tanaseanu-Döbler, A. Lefteratou, G. Ryser, and K. Stamatopoulos. Göttingen: 45–60.

Newton, R.M. (1984) "The rebirth of Odysseus," *Greek, Roman, and Byzantine Studies* 25: 5–20.

Nicol, B. (2009) *The Cambridge Introduction to Postmodern Fiction*. Cambridge.

Nixon, L. (1995) "The cults of Demeter and Kore," in *Women in Antiquity: New Assessments*, eds. R. Hawley and B. Levick. London and New York: 75–96.

Norden, E. (1903) *P. Vergilius Maro Aeneis Buch VI*. Leipzig.

Ogden, D. (2001) *Greek and Roman Necromancy*. Princeton.

Ogden, D. (2013) *Drakon: Dragon Myth and Serpent Cult in the Greek and Roman Worlds*. Oxford.

O'Higgins, L. (2003) *Women and Humor in Classical Greece*. Cambridge.

Olverson, T.D. (2010) *Women Writers and the Dark Side of Late-Victorian Hellenism*. London and New York.

Ostriker, A. (1982) "The thieves of language: women poets and revisionist mythmaking," *Signs* 8: 68–90.

Page, D. (1955) *The Homeric Odyssey*. Oxford.

Page, P. (1995) *Dangerous Freedom: Fusion and Fragmentation in Toni Morrison's Novels*. Mississippi.

Parkes, R. (2015) "Love or war? Erotic and martial poetics in Claudian's *de Raptu Proserpinae*," *Classical Journal* 110: 471–92.

Parsons, E., N. Sawers, and K. McInally (2008) "The Other Mother: Neil Gaiman's postfeminist fairytales," *Children's Literature Association Quarterly* 33: 371–89.

Patchett, A. (2011) *State of Wonder*. New York.

Peradotto, J. (1990) *Man in The Middle Voice: Name and Narration in the Odyssey*. Princeton.

Petridou, G. (2016) *Divine Epiphanies in Greek Literature and Culture*. Oxford.

Petit, T. (2016) "Sphinx et katábasis dans la peinture de vases," *Cahiers des études anciennes* 53: 113–50.

Pike, D.L. (1997) *Passage Through Hell: Modernist Descents, Medieval Underworlds*. Ithaca.

Pike, D.L. (2007) *Metropolis on the Styx: The Underworlds of Modern Urban Culture, 1800–2001*. Ithaca.

Platthaus, I. (2004) *Höllenfahrten: Die epische Katábasis und die Unterwelten der Moderne*. Munich.

Porter, A. (2013) "Neil Gaiman's Lucifer: Reconsidering Milton's Satan," *Journal of Religion and Popular Culture* 25: 175–85.

Power, H. (2010) "The *Aeneid* in the Age of Milton," in *A Companion to Vergil's Aeneid and Its Tradition*, eds. J. Farrell and M. Putnam. Malden and Oxford: 186–202.

Powell, B. (1991) *Homer and the Origin of the Greek Alphabet*. Cambridge.

Pustz, M. J. (1999) *Comic Book Culture: Fanboys and True Believers*. Jackson.

Radford, A. (2007) *The Lost Girls: Demeter-Persephone and the Literary Imagination, 1850–1930.* New York.

Reece, S. (2011) "Penelope's 'early recognition' of Odysseus from a Neoanalytic and Oral perspective," *College Literature* 38: 101–17.

Rehm, R. (1994) *Marriage to Death: The Conflation of Wedding and Funeral Rituals in Greek Tragedy*. Princeton.

Reider, N. (2013) "Tsuchigumo sōshi: The emergence of a shape-shifting killer female spider," *Asian Ethnology* 72: 55–83.

Reilly, C. (2000) "An Interview with John Barth, conducted by Charlie Reilly," *Contemporary Literature* 41: 589–617.

Reinhardt, K. (1996) in "The adventures in the *Odyssey*," in *Reading the Odyssey: Selective Interpretive Essays*, ed. S. Schein. Princeton: 63–132.

Rich, A. (1973) *Diving into the Wreck: Poems 1971–1972.* New York.

Rich, A. (1976) *Of Woman Born: Motherhood as Experience and Institution.* New York.

Richardson, N.J. (1974) *The Homeric Hymn to Demeter*. Oxford.

Ricks, C. ed. (1969) *The Poems of Tennyson*. Vol. 3 Essex.

Rigoglioso, M. (2005) "Persephone's sacred lake and the ancient female Mystery religion in the womb of Sicily," *Journal of Feminist Studies in Religion* 21: 5–29.

Robertson, N. (1980) "Heracles' 'catabasis'," *Hermes* 108: 274–300.

Ross, D. (1975) *Backgrounds to Augustan Poetry*. Cambridge.

Rudd, D. (2008) "An eye for an I: Neil Gaiman's *Coraline* and questions of identity," *Children's Literature in Education* 39: 159–68.

Rushdie, S. (1992) *Imaginary Homelands: Essays and Criticism 1981–1991.* London and New York.

Rushdie, S. (1999) *The Ground Beneath her Feet.* London and New York.

Roynon, T. (2013) *Toni Morrison and the Classical Tradition: Transforming American Culture.* Oxford.

Safran, W. (1991) "Diasporas in modern societies: myths of homeland and return," *Diaspora: A Journal of Transnational Studies* 1: 83–99.

Saïd, E. (1978) *Orientalism*. New York.

Sanders, S.l. (2009) "The first tour of Hell: From Neo-Assyrian propaganda to early Jewish revelation" *Journal of Ancient Near Eastern Religions* 9: 151–69.

Santamaría Álvarez, M.A. (2014) "El descenso de Dioniso al Hades en busca de su madre," in *Apocalipsi, Catàbasi I Mil.Lenarisme A Les Literatures Antigues I La Seua Recepció*, eds. J. Redondo and R. Torné. Amsterdam: 217–40.

Santamaría Álvarez, M.A. (2015) "The parody of the *katábasis*-motif in Aristophanes' *Frogs*," *Les Études Classiques* 83: 119–38.

Schulz, M. F. (1984) "The Thalian design of Barth's *Lost in the Funhouse*," *Contemporary Literature* 25: 397–410.

Schwab, A. (2016) "The reception of the Homeric Hymn to Demeter in Romantic Heidelberg: J.H. Voss and 'the Eleusinian Document'," in *The Reception of the Homeric Hymns*, eds. A. Faulkner, A. Vergados, and A. Schwab. Oxford: 343–66.

Scully, S. (1987) "Doubling in the tale of Odysseus," *Classical World* 80: 401–17.

Seelentag, S. (2012) *Der Pseudovergilische Culex: Hermes Einzelschriften* 105. Stuttgart.

Segal, C. (1989) *Orpheus: The Myth of the Poet*. Baltimore.

Segal, C. (2001) *Singers, Heroes and Gods in the Odyssey*. Ithaca.

Sharma, S. (2001) "Salman Rushdie: The ambivalence of migrancy," *Twentieth Century Literature* 47: 596–618.

Sheffer, J. (2010) "Recollecting, repeating, and walking through: Immigration, trauma, and space in Mary Antin's *The Promised Land*," *MELUS* 35: 141–66.

Shive, D. (1987) *Naming Achilles*. Oxford.

Shloss, C. and Tololyan, K. (1981) "The siren in the Funhouse: Barth's courting of the reader," *Journal of Narrative Technique* 11: 64–74.

Slater, N. (2003) "Looking for Proserpina: A.S. Byatt's notes on the *Aeneid*," *Literary Imagination* 5: 194–208.

Steveker, L. (2009) *Identity and Cultural Memory in the Fiction of A.S. Byatt*. London.

Stevens, B.E. (2015) "Virgil in Jules Verne's *Journey to the Center of the Earth*," in *Classical Traditions in Science Fiction*, eds. B.M. Rogers and B.E. Stevens. Oxford: 75–104.

Stevens, B.E. (2016a) "Ancient Underworlds in J.R.R. Tolkien's *The Hobbit*," in *Classical Traditions in Modern Fantasy*, eds. B.M. Rogers and B.E. Stevens, Oxford: 121–44.

Stevens, B.E. (2016b) "Virgilian Underworlds in A.S. Byatt's *The Children's Book*," *Classical Receptions Journal* 8: 529–53.

Smith-Josephy, S. (2011) *Lillian Alling: The Journey Home*. Halfmoon Bay, BC.

Soldedad Souza e Palma, L. (2006) "Imaginary places and fantastic narratives: Reading Borges through *The Sandman*," in *The Sandman Papers: An Exploration of The Sandman Mythology*, ed. J. Sanders. Seattle: 135–47.

Stroumsa, G.G. (1995). "Mystical descents," in *Death, Ecstasy, and Other Worldly Journeys*, eds. J.J. Collins and M. Fishbane. Albany: 137–54.

Suter, A. (2002) *The Narcissus and the Pomegranate. An Archaeology of the Homeric Hymn to Demeter*. Ann Arbor.

Tanaseanu-Döbler, I. (2017) "Introduction" in *Reading the Way to the Netherworld: Education and the Representations of the Beyond in Later Antiquity*, eds. I. Tanaseanu-Döbler, A. Lefteratou, G. Ryser, and K. Stamatopoulos. Göttingen: 12–27.

Taylor-Guthrie, D. (ed.) (1994) *Conversations with Toni Morrison*. Jackson, MS.

Thomas, R. (1999) *Reading Virgil and his Text: Studies in Intertextuality*. Ann Arbor.

Thurston M. (2009) *The Underworld in Twentieth-Century Poetry: From Pound and Eliot to Heaney*. New York.

Tiffin, J. (2006) "Ice, glass, snow: Fairy tale as art and metafiction in the writing of A.S. Byatt," *Marvels & Tales* 20: 47–66.

Todd, R. (1994) "The retrieval of unheard voices in British Postmodernist fiction: A.S. Byatt and Marina Warner," in *Liminal Postmodernisms: The Postmodern, the (Post-)Colonial, and the (Post-)Feminist*, eds. T. D'haen and H. Bertens. Amsterdam and Atlanta, GA: 99–114.

Toscano, M. (2010) "Love is Hell: Torment, sex and redemption in the Cupid and Psyche myth," in *Hell and its Afterlife: Historical and Contemporary Perspectives*. eds. M. Toscano and I. Moreira. Oxford and New York: 9–28.

Tsagarakis, O. (1999) *Studies in Odyssey 11*. Stuttgart.

Turner, V.W. (1967) *The Forest of Symbols: Aspects of Ndembu Ritual*. Ithaca.

Ulmer, G. (1985) "The object of Post-criticism," in *The Anti-Aesthetic: Essays in Postmodern Culture*, ed. H. Foster. Seattle: 83–110.

Ustinova, Y. (2009) *Caves and the Ancient Greek Mind: Descending Underground in the Search for Ultimate Truth*. Oxford.

Vaclavik, K. (2010) *Uncharted Depths: Descent Narratives in English & French Children's Literature*. Oxford.

Vasunia, P. (2013) *The Classics and Colonial India*. Oxford.

Wagner, H.C. Golden, and R.R. Bissette (2008) *Prince of Stories: The Many Worlds of Neil Gaiman*. New York.

Waheed, S. (2013) "Salman Rushdie, Edward Said, and moral courage," Asian American Writers Workshop, http://aaww.org/salman-rushdie-edward-said-and-moral-courage/. Accessed August 24, 2016.

Walcott, D. (1990) *Omeros*. New York.

Wallhead, C.M. (2007) *A.S. Byatt: Essays on the Short Fiction*. Berlin.

Walters, W. (1997) "'One of dese mornings, bright and fair,/Take my wings and cleave de air': The legend of the flying Africans and diasporic consciousness," *MELUS* 22: 3–31.

Warner, M. (1994) *From the Beast to the Blonde: On Fairy Tales and their Tellers*. New York.

Watkins, C. (1995) *How to Kill a Dragon: Aspects of Indo-European Poetics*. Oxford.

Waugh, P. (1984) *Metafiction: The Theory and Practice of Self-Conscious Fiction*. London.

Waugh, P. (1992) "Modernism, postmodernism, feminism: gender and autonomy theory," in *Postmodernism: A Reader*, ed. P. Waugh. New York: 189–204.

West, M.L. (1997) *The East Face of Helicon. West Asiatic Elements in Greek Poetry and Myth*. Oxford.

Whitman, C. (1958) *Homer and the Heroic Tradition*. Cambridge, MA.

Willcock, M.M. (1964) "Mythological paradeigmata in the *Iliad*," *Classical Quarterly* 14: 141–51.

Williams, F. (1971) "A theophany in Theocritus," *Classical Quarterly* 21: 137–45.

Williams, R.D. (1964) "The Sixth Book of the *Aeneid*," *Greece & Rome* 11: 48–63.

Wolkstein, D. and S.N. Kramer (1983) *Inanna, Queen of Heaven and Earth: Her Stories and Hymns from Sumer*. New York.

Worthington, M. (2001) "Done with mirrors: Restoring the authority lost in John Barth's Funhouse," *Twentieth Century Literature* 47: 114–36.

Yarnall, J. (1994) *Transformations of Circe: The History of an Enchantress*. Urbana and Chicago.

Zaleski, C. (1987) *Otherworld Journeys*. Oxford.

Zipes, J. (ed.) (1987) *Victorian Fairy Tales: The Revolt of the Fairies and Elves*. New York.

Index